THE BOOK OF GENESIS

The Book of Genesis

A Jewish Interpretation

Julian Morgenstern

SCHOCKEN BOOKS · NEW YORK

THE BOOK OF GENESIS, A JEWISH INTERPRETATION
was first published in 1919 by the Union of American Hebrew
Congregations.

Second Edition

Copyright © 1965 by Schocken Books, Inc.

*This edition is published
by arrangement with the Union of American Hebrew Congregations.*

Library of Congress Catalog Card No. 65–14826

Manufactured in the United States of America

CONTENTS

PREFACE

This book was written almost fifty years ago and was published by the Union of American Hebrew Congregations as the first volume of its series of Religious Education Text-books. It was designed primarily for use by Jewish religious school teachers. The first and only edition of the book was quickly exhausted, but, due largely to a reorganization of the Department of Religious Education of the Union, a second edition of the book was never issued.

However, for many years thereafter the demand for the book persisted and countless inquiries were received by the author as to where and how copies of the book might be obtained. These inquiries came not only from Jewish, but occasionally also from Christian sources. To all of them only a negative reply could be given.

No doubt in recent years, or even decades, the book has largely been forgotten. And yet it is felt that still today it can be of service, not only to a Jewish public, but also, in some manner and measure at least, to a Christian public as well. All material in the original edition which was directed immediately to Jewish religious school teachers, to guide them in their class instruction, has been omitted. In its present, revised form the book is designed in first degree for a Jewish reading public. But it should also have some value, so at least we believe, for a Christian public also, interested in Bible study and in the history and teachings of both Judaism and Christianity. It should have particular value for adult Bible study groups of both religions. It is with this thought in mind that it is now, after this very long interval, offered, in this second, slightly revised, edition, to the general public.

The book aims to be precisely what its title indicates, a Jewish interpretation of Genesis. We have had countless books on Genesis by Jewish authors. But, with rare exceptions, they have sought only to recount the stories of Genesis literally, without penetrating adequately to the fundamental Jewish spiritual truth beneath, and without consideration of the many significant discoveries and teachings of modern Biblical science with regard to Genesis. They have confounded Biblical myths, legends and traditions with what they have mistakenly called Biblical history. Thereby they have, on the one hand, only too frequently worked mischievous confusion and misunderstanding in the minds of those whom they sought to instruct, and, on the other hand, they have missed almost entirely the golden opportunity to impart the really basic truths of Judaism to the most receptive minds.

We have also had numerous scientific interpretations of Genesis, almost all by non-Jewish scholars. Their work has been almost entirely analytic in character. They have picked Genesis, and the entire Old Testament in fact, to pieces. They have resolved it into its component sources, and have determined with quite reliable accuracy when and under what conditions these were written. They have also determined when, how and by whom these originally independent sources were gradually combined, until at last our present Old Testament came into being.

But singularly enough, they have failed in considerable measure to determine the ends for which these sources were combined and the thoughts and aims which animated the editors. They have, apparently, tacitly assumed that this was an inevitable and largely incidental and purposeless process. Therefore they have failed to realize and to stress that the Old Testament, and particularly the Torah, the Five Books of Moses, is entirely a Jewish work, written by Jewish authors and edited by Jewish thinkers, the product of Jewish religious genius and a unit of Jewish religious thought and doctrine, and that it must be animated throughout by some deeply Jewish purpose, and can, in the final analysis, be correctly understood only when interpreted from a positive Jewish standpoint. Consequently, while science has taught us much about the Old Testament, new, unsuspected, and significant truths, it has failed almost entirely to catch its real Jewish purpose, spirit and flavor. For this reason the usual scientific, analytic interpretation of the Old Testament is inadequate and fails to achieve its ultimate and positive potentials.

The present work aims to be a popular scientific interpretation of Genesis, but an interpretation which is not merely analytic, and therefore largely negative and destructive, but which is also, and more pronouncedly, synthetic, constructive and Jewish. It accepts the established and irrefutable teachings of science with regard to Genesis, and seeks constantly to determine what is the fundamental Jewish thought and teaching of the various stories and groups of stories, for the sake of which their Jewish authors and editors cast them into their present form. It operates on the principle that the Old Testament is a Jewish work throughout, and that it can be understood correctly and authoritatively only when interpreted from the standpoint of its Jewish teachings. It proceeds with deep love and reverence for Judaism and its teachings and practices and for Jewish tradition and history. But it is animated by equal love and reverence for the future of Judaism and for the evolution and expansion which its beliefs and teachings must inevitably undergo in the constant and steady progress of human thought and knowledge and in the irresistible compulsion to adapt and apply these teachings and principles to the needs and standards of modern existence, in order that Judaism may continue to be, what it has always been, a true religion of life, by which men may not only die resignedly but, even more, may live nobly, bravely and usefully.

In this spirit and for this purpose and with this eager hope this book is offered once again, in this second edition, to the public, to a new, a larger and, religiously, a broader and more composite public. May this hope be richly fulfilled.

JULIAN MORGENSTERN

Macon, Georgia
August, 1964

INTRODUCTION

I

THE JEWISH RELIGION

Judaism is essentially a religion of this life and this world. Other religions may stress the thought that this world is merely the preparation for the world to come, that there lies the goal of all existence, and that we must live this life to the end and in such manner that we may attain to the life hereafter. But Judaism holds no such view. True, it affirms the doctrine of future life and of reward and punishment. But it has never magnified the other world at the expense of this. On the contrary, it teaches that this life is worth living for its own sake, that this world and all that it contains are good, that they were created by God for some purpose of good, and that man was put here by God to help realize by his own living this ultimate purpose of good. Judaism has, therefore, concerned itself chiefly with the tasks, duties and ideals of this life, assured that if this life be but well lived, the future, however it may be, will care for itself. Not salvation in the future world was its chief aim and concern, but faithful, conscientious performance of the daily, and often burdensome duties of this world. It has always cherished faith highly; but it was ever a true faith, which expressed itself in the lifelong conviction of the existence of one God, to know whom and to walk in whose way, daily and hourly, is man's supreme duty. Faith, in Judaism, could, and can, live and grow only with an ever-growing knowledge of God, and only so long as it could, and can, in turn, constantly transform itself into right living.

The Sources of the Jew's Knowledge of God

The Jew's knowledge of God has ever sprung from a twofold source. As the individual grew to manhood and wisdom, and his mind broadened, his experience deepened, his vision expanded, he could not but think more and more intensely about God and the universe and life. In consequence of an innate, psychological predisposition, the Jew has ever been a thinker about God and about the origin and purpose of life. Even his oldest myths and folklore, to a far greater extent, it would seem, than those of any other people, dealt with questions about God and creation, the meaning of life, and the origin of its fundamental social institutions and religious symbols. Much thinking could not but in time produce much knowledge. And, once gained, this knowledge was not lost; it was preserved in some form or other, and was transmitted from generation to generation as an integral part of Judaism.

From this developed the second source of the Jew's knowledge of God, far greater and more potent than the thinking and experiences of the individual. It was the combined and unified thinking of the many individuals who, through all the centuries, have made up the sum total of Israel's religious leaders and teachers. They pondered over not merely the questions and perplexities of individual experience, but also, and to a far greater degree, the problems and conditions of the whole people and of all mankind. They saw in Israel God's chosen people, first of all nations to know and worship Him, and whom He had therefore chosen as His messengers, witnesses of His truth unto mankind. Thus Israel believed itself to stand directly under God's dispensation. All fortunes and misfortunes it regarded as coming directly from God Himself to reveal His divine nature and His will and purpose with it and with the whole human race. In all the events of its history, as interpreted by its spiritual leaders, Israel ever saw God's hand working, and through the interpretation of its history aright it learned to know God and His true worship and life of service for all men. Israel's history has ever been the chief source of its knowledge of God.

Revelation

But in a certain sense there is still a third source, expressed in the one word, Revelation. This term implies that the Jew's knowledge of God is the result not only of his own expanding individual and communal religious consciousness and thought, but also, and perhaps even more, of God's actual and purposed revelation of Himself to Israel through divinely chosen and inspired men, whom we call prophets. Certainly the prophets so conceived of themselves, their message, and their work. They spoke and labored, not as mere human beings, but as impersonal agents through whom God Himself was irresistibly working. Volumes have been written to explain prophetic inspiration and revelation by natural law, and from a rationalistic and somewhat mechanical standpoint, and much light has been shed upon this very difficult problem. Yet we are constantly made to realize that only the human side of the prophet's nature and work can be thus analyzed and explained; the divine element, the manner of God's willing and working, remains ever above and beyond human analysis and comprehension. During a long period the prophets were the leaders in this wonderful unfolding of Israel's knowledge of God; through them eternal truths were revealed, which were indispensable for human knowledge and spiritual growth. We can scarcely believe that these prophets discovered these truths entirely through purely human processes. Surely God has willed that man should know more and ever more of Him and His way; the knowledge which these prophets, as sons of Israel, proclaimed, God must have allowed, and even caused, them to discover, as He allowed and caused no men and no people before them. Aye, this knowledge surely could not have been only discovered by these prophets; equally it must have been revealed to them by God. This is Revelation.

Actually, however, Revelation is hardly a third source of the Jew's knowledge of God, but merely the same two sources viewed from the reverse side, in their divine, rather than in their human, aspect. It says not only that the Jew's knowledge of God came through the religious experiences and discoveries of individuals, particularly certain peculiarly fitted individuals, and through the religious experiences and discoveries of the entire people in all the stages and through all the fortunes of its history, but also that God has willed that this knowledge come in this manner. Revelation, therefore, really affirms only that the two sources of the Jew's knowledge of God have a divine, as well as a human, origin and cause.

But in this sense Revelation means far more than as it is usually interpreted. True Revelation in Israel was through more than the prophets alone; or rather, they were merely the agents or mouthpieces of Revelation, and Revelation itself was greater and grander far than just these prophets themselves and their inspired words. The prophets were primarily the children of their own times, spurred to activity not only by the conviction that God had literally called them, but also by the realization of the moral and spiritual evils and needs of their own days. They, above all others, saw God's hand constantly present in Israel's history, and read His divine purpose and guidance in all the events thereof. They realized that God was revealing His will, not only through them to Israel, but also, and to a far greater degree, through Israel's history to Israel itself and to all mankind. Therefore their messages consisted in the main in interpreting to Israel of their own days the divine significance of its history. Israel's history was to them the chief source of God's revelation of Himself to His people; and whoever might interpret this history aright from the standpoint of God and of God's guidance of Israel and of all mankind, was a prophet, proclaiming, in accordance with God's will, the true knowledge of Him and His way unto all the world.

Therefore, for us today, whether we have new truths to proclaim, or only the old truths to reaffirm and teach, the essential requisite for an authoritative and inspiring knowledge of Judaism is a correct and constructive knowledge of Jewish history and of Jewish life and thought, that we, too, may see therein all the countless evidences of God's goodness, wisdom and love, and may learn, in turn, how He wills that we ourselves live as true Jews and true men and women.

What is Jewish History?

But what is Jewish history? History is more than mere chronicling of events, no matter how correctly. History is life. The history of any people is the full record of the life it has lived, the experiences it has endured, the trials it has undergone, the defeats it has suffered, the victories it has achieved, the thoughts it has conceived, the ideals it has striven for, the contributions to the welfare and progress of the human race which it has made. History is the correct and complete record of all causes and effects, of all forces at work, and of all results flowing therefrom, in the lives of individuals or nations. The history of any individual really begins long before birth, in the pre-natal conditions which must determine his physical, mental, and psychological makeup and much of his subsequent life. Nor does his history cease until his life has completely ended, and perhaps not even then; for the man lives on and his history continues in the forces and influences he has set in operation, and which go on working themselves out in the life of the human race until the end of time.

Similarly the history of a nation, of a people, or of a religion begins long before it actually steps forth upon the stage of existence. It begins in all the conditions, forces, and influences which work together to make that nation, people or religion what it is at the moment of real, concrete birth, and which largely determine its subsequent life and evolution. And its history does not end until it has utterly ceased to be, and the memory of it is completely lost, and the principles of national, social, or religious conduct, which it has evolved, are thoroughly uprooted, if that be possible, from the total life-experience and life-thought of mankind.

The history of Israel and of Judaism is, therefore, far more than the mere Biblical record of a few scattered events. It commenced far back in dim, pre-historic antiquity, when the first, primitive ancestor of the Jewish people began to move on earth. The Bible, unconsciously perhaps, voices a significant truth when it begins the history of Israel, not with Moses nor with Abraham, but with creation. And since Israel still exists today, unique among the peoples of the earth, and since Judaism still lives, and we proudly proclaim ourselves Jews, adherents of Judaism, endowed with a glorious mission unto mankind, it follows that Jewish history has not yet ended, and, so far as we can see and hope and pray, will never end. Jewish history is, therefore, the complete record of the life of the Jew, of his experiences, thoughts, beliefs, and practices, of his ever-growing knowledge of God and of life, as believed, proclaimed, and transformed into conduct, from the earliest, simplest, crudest, and most primitive beginnings down to our own present day; aye, even down to tomorrow, if we can but raise the curtain of the future but a little, and behold the stage set for tomorrow's act.

However, we are unable to trace our history in all its details back to its actual origin. The most we can do is to begin with the earliest period of our Bible narrative and follow the history of our people and our religion through successive generations and centuries, noting the fortunes which befell them, and through all these, whether good or ill, the ever-growing knowledge of God and of the meaning of life, and the constantly expanding consciousness of mission and message, down to our own day. We are, in a very real and positive sense, as important actors upon the stage of Jewish history as were the heroes and sages of old. We are the heirs of all our glorious past. To be true Jews we must know what Judaism is. And we can know what Judaism is only when we know its complete history, not merely in Bible times, but throughout all ages, and when, knowing Jewish history thus, we can reinterpret it in the light of present times, conditions, and needs, and can thereby make Judaism what it has always been in truth, not merely a religion of the past, but also a religion of the present and the future, a religion of God's true life on earth. It is a vast knowledge, and given only to the few to know with any degree of fulness. Yet upon every Jew rests the duty of learning all of Judaism that he can, that through it he may come to feel as a Jew, think as a Jew, and interpret life and duty as a Jew.

The Periods of Jewish History

It is a fallacy of a large public, sadly unfamiliar with Jewish tradition and literature, that the Bible is our only book, and that all our history is contained in the Biblical narrative. A moment's thought should show the incorrectness of this belief. Jewish history is more than the chronicle of a few events, all embraced in one short epoch, and all recorded in one book. It extends over several thousand years, during which its fortunes were most varied and complex.

Jewish history may be divided into seven periods, (I) the early Biblical period, to the Babylonian Exile (586 B. C.), (II) the late Biblical period, to the destruction of the Temple by the Romans (70 C. E.), (III) the Palestinian period, to the decadence of the Jewish schools in Palestine (about 375 C. E.), (IV) the Eastern period, when the center of Jewish life was in Babylon (until about 1000 C. E.), (V) the early European period, when the center of Jewish life had shifted, across Egypt and northern Africa, to southern and western Europe (until the expulsion from Spain, 1492 C. E.), (VI) the late European or Ghetto period, when the center of Jewish life had once more shifted, this time to central Europe, a period characterized largely by enforced Ghetto existence with its peculiar and far-reaching influences (approximately to the first quarter of the 19th century), and (VII) the modern period. In each of these vast periods Judaism was developing, expanding, adapting itself to new life and thought, contributing its share, and more than its share, to the spiritual progress of mankind.

To know Judaism aright we must know something of its history in each of these periods.

The Sources of Jewish History

Naturally the chief source for the history of the Biblical periods is the Bible itself. But the Bible is a large work, comprising, according to Jewish tradition, twenty-four books, the product of Jewish literary activity extending over approximately a thousand years. Actually the Bible is not so much a mere book, as it is a national literature, or at least the remains thereof. It can readily be seen that the various parts and books of the Bible, written at different times, under different conditions, and by different authors, are naturally of unequal value for the study of Jewish history. We can never, therefore, take the Bible in hand, read it off word for word, and feel confident that we have thus gathered the essential facts of Jewish history. We must learn to study carefully, think deeply, read between the lines, and get at the hidden truths beneath. We must ask ourselves constantly, who were the authors of these narratives, from what sources did they draw their material, for what purposes did they write, what was their conception of Jewish history and of Judaism, and how can we best put ourselves into their frame of mind, so that we may interpret their writings, not, as is so frequently done, haphazardly and fantastically, reading into them all manner of groundless conjectures and wild vagaries, but soberly, constructively, and Jewishly, as they meant them to be interpreted. Above all, we must never forget that history, true history, is primarily the record of the thoughts, ambitions, and ideals of a people finding concrete expression in its daily life. Therefore, to understand the history of even the early Biblical period we need to do more than to merely acquaint ourselves with the contents of the so-called Historical Books. The Prophets and the Holy Writings, which mirror so faithfully the thoughts, beliefs, and aspirations of the people, or at least of their religious leaders, must be studied and understood in equal measure.

With the later periods this task becomes more complex and difficult, yet not one whit less imperative. Israel's history after the close of the early Biblical period is far less the chronicle of a nation's achievements than the sad, yet inspiring, record of a people's sufferings, thoughts, aspirations, and beliefs, finding expression in a vast and diversified literature. It takes little account of deeds of warriors and heroes, but it has much to tell of rabbis, teachers, and thinkers, and of the thoughts they conceived, and the interpretation they gave to Judaism as the result of much thinking and deep and broad experience. The true key then to Israel's history in all the periods following the Babylonian Exile is rather the appreciation of what we might call the Jewish spirit, than a mere knowledge of passing events, the true Jewish spirit springing out of the life experience of the Jewish people in the face of all its trials and persecutions, and expressing itself in the literature, the stories, the dreams, and the visions of Jewish thinkers and teachers for almost two thousand years. If we can absorb something of this Jewish spirit, we shall be prepared to properly understand and interpret our Judaism of today. Perhaps the stories from the rabbis, contained in this book, may help in this worthy task. At least they will show how the moral and spiritual thoughts of the Biblical writers were interpreted, applied, and expanded by the teachers of Judaism of a later period, and will indicate how we, in turn, may interpret, apply, and even expand these teachings, and with them Judaism itself, in accordance with the beliefs, tendencies, and needs of our own time.

II

The Divisions of Genesis

The Book of Genesis is, in its present literary form and in its position as the first book of the Bible, a natural and effective introduction to the Pentateuch and, in a way, to the entire Bible. One central theme gives it distinct unity of thought and purpose. This central theme is God's selection of Israel to be the witness and messenger of His truth and His law unto all the peoples of the earth, and His testing and preparation of Israel for this arduous and sacred task. In its treatment in the book this central theme is resolved into four natural and logical concepts, (a) God and mankind, (b) God and Israel, (c) God's purification and preparation of Israel for His service, and (d) God's providence. The book itself may be divided correspondingly into four groups or cycles of stories, (a) chapters I-XI, stories about mankind in general, (b) chapters XII-XXV, 18, the story of Abraham, (c) chapters XXV, 19–XXXVI, the story of Jacob, and (d) chapters XXXVII-L, the story of Joseph. Detailed consideration of these groups of stories establishes the relation and contribution of each to the central theme of the book.

The first group of stories, chapters I-XI, contains a very interesting collection of ancient Israelite myths and folk-tales. They give the answers to some of the primitive questions of life, as conceived by the vivid and naive imaginations of our early ancestors. Genesis I and II, for example, answer that most fundamental question of all, how did the world come into existence and life actually begin? Genesis II and III form a collection of folk-tales, carefully worked together, which answer in primitive manner such questions of existence as why the serpent, unlike all other animals, crawls upon his belly, why man must labor painfully for his livelihood, why, unlike the animals, man wears clothes, and why there comes into man's life a love for another being, not related by blood or birth, surpassing his love for father and mother. Chapter IV tells, in the form of a charming folk-tale, how men began to worship God and how death came into the world. Chapters VI-IX relate the great flood myth. Chapter XI contains the folk-tale of the origin of the different languages and nations.

Manifestly these first stories of Genesis are not history at all. They are without exception myths and folk-tales, similar in many details to the myths and folk-tales of other primitive peoples. In fact, they contain, particularly in the

creation and flood stories, much that was borrowed directly
from non-Israelite sources. Yet in one vital respect these
myths and folk-tales do differ radically from those of all
other peoples. They breathe through and through the spirit
of the one, living God, the Creator of the universe and of
life, who looks out upon all that He has made, alone and
unaided, and finds it very good. This is the thought and
spirit of Judaism in them. And this Jewish thought and
spirit distinguish these myths and folk-tales from all others,
and make them the priceless, eternal heritage of the Jew,
and only through him of the world at large.

These stories tell of the creation by God, not of Israel
alone, but of all mankind. God is the Creator and Father
of all men, and all men are equally His children. He has
commanded them to walk with Him and live nobly and usefully. When they turn from Him and tread forbidden paths,
He punishes them necessarily and justly, but also sorrowfully and reluctantly. But with the next generation He
makes a covenant of love, never to bring another flood to
destroy mankind. Instead, should mankind sin again, He
will raise up one little people, which shall stand close to Him
and keep His law, and walk faithfully in His way, and serve
Him as His messenger and the witness of His truth unto
all mankind. And through this people mankind shall come
at last to know God and to walk with Him, even as He had
intended at creation. This little people, God's firstborn, as
it were, was to be Israel.

The problem of these first eleven chapters, and, in a way,
of the entire Book of Genesis, is threefold, (a) the relation
of all the peoples of the earth to God, the Creator of all,
(b) the particular relation of Israel to God, and (c) the
particular relation of Israel to the other nations. Both problem and solution are decidedly universalistic in conception
and character. God is not merely the national deity of
Israel, as conceived in the earlier period of Israel's religious
evolution, nor is Israel a nation living only by and for itself.

Israel is a nation among the other nations of the earth, and its fortunes are inseparably bound up with theirs. And Israel's God is not its God alone, but the Creator of the entire universe and the loving Father of all men. To Him alone their worship is due. His law they should keep, and in His way they should walk. All this they must eventually learn through Israel.

A universalism so all-embracing and positive, can have developed in Israel and found such systematic and definite expression only after Israel had begun to outgrow its early, restricted nationalism and nationalistic conception of God and religion, through having come into close and protracted contact with other nations and other religions and cultures. Then only did it commence to concern itself with the vital question of the relation of itself, a little and weak nation, to the mighty empires which surrounded it, and the role which it was destined to play in the history of mankind according to the all-wise plan of the Creator of the universe. Biblical science has proved that these first stories in their present, connected, literary form are, in the main, the product of the period beginning in the first half of the seventh century B. C., when Judah became tributary to Assyria and was dominated by Assyrian culture and thought, and continuing for almost two centuries, into the Babylonian Exile, when, torn from the land of its birth and settled in a foreign country and in a strange environment, Israel nevertheless continued to exist as a unique, religious people. What more natural than that in such times and under such conditions, Israel's spiritual leaders should evolve a positive, universalistic conception of God and of mankind and of Israel's own destined role in the great, eternal, human drama? Similar universalistic thoughts and concepts are discernible in the prophetic writings of this same period; witness such passages as Jeremiah XVIII, 7ff.; XXV, 15ff.; XXVII, 2ff.; XXIX, 4ff., and above all the writings of the great, unknown prophet of the Babylonian Exile, commonly known as Deutero-Isaiah, Isaiah XL.-LV.

The procedure of the authors of these first eleven chapters of Genesis is readily comprehended. They took a number of ancient legends and folk-tales, which had been current in Israel for many generations. They also borrowed from Babylonian literature, with which the dominant Babylonian culture had acquainted them, such myths as those of creation (Genesis I) and of the flood. And they reinterpreted these stories from the standpoint of Judaism, as they had come to understand it, and wove them together and wrote them down in their present, connected, literary form. Thus they led up, naturally and logically, to the story of Abraham in chapters XII-XXV, 18, with its central thought of God's selection of Israel.

Here the interest of the authors narrowed. Abraham is the main figure; only incidentally do we hear of other persons. Abraham was really represented by these authors as the prototype of the people of Israel. The life of Abraham, his virtues and faults, his trials and discipline, his relation to God and his consciousness of divine selection and mission, were recounted only to mirror these same conditions in Israel's life. Not impossibly the man, Abraham, may have lived, and may have been the actual progenitor of Israel, or of a part of Israel. But in the main, these stories about Abraham, too, were legends which sprang up in ancient Israel at different times and for varying purposes. They were handed down orally for many generations, until at last, during the eighth, seventh and sixth centuries B. C. they were gradually woven together and written down in the form in which we have them now.

A careful study and interpretation of these stories in the light of the times and conditions which produced them, bring out clearly the Jewish truth inherent in them. For example, the story of the sacrifice of Isaac (XXII) is a legend which took form in prophetic circles of the northern kingdom at some time between 850 and 750 B. C. During this period the horrible practice of child-sacrifice flourished. The people believed that God demanded the sacrifice of children as the most precious gift mortals could bring. This belief the prophets combated in every way possible. Thus they conceived and developed this legend that Abraham, the traditional ancestor of Israel, also had thought that God demanded such a sacrifice, and so he prepared to offer up his own son. But before the sacrifice could be completed, God Himself intervened and provided for the sacrifice of a ram in place of the child. Thereby He signified that animal sacrifice alone was acceptable to Him, and that human sacrifice must never be offered. Such was the original form and purpose of this legend. But later writers, in turn, revised and enlarged upon it. They now told that God had actually commanded Abraham to sacrifice Isaac, not, however, with the intention of really allowing this sacrifice to be offered, but merely to test Abraham's faith by his willingness to give up at the divine behest that which was dearest to him in life. Thus this legend, the origin of which can be so clearly determined, became in the hands of these later writers an effective means of presenting concretely that fundamental Jewish doctrine and Jewish virtue of absolute faith in God.

In this way these writers of the eighth, seventh and sixth centuries B. C. made use of many of the ancient Abraham legends and traditions. They wove them together into one great cycle of stories, united by one common theme. This was the thought that God tried Abraham repeatedly. For, as has been said, Abraham was to them less a single, historical person, than the prototype of all Israel. In the first group of stories, in chapters I-XI, they had told how, after mankind had again departed from God, God had determined to provide for their ultimate regeneration by selecting one people to receive His law and become the messenger of His truth unto all men. This people was Israel. The words of XII, 1-2, spoken by God to Abraham, but really meant by these authors to apply to all Israel, "Get thee out of thy country and from thy kindred and from thy father's house, unto the land that I will show thee . . . and be thou a blessing . . . and in thee shall all the families of the earth be blessed", are the connecting link between these two groups of stories. They tell, simply and clearly, of God's selection of Abraham and Israel for this glorious mission. The blessing they were to bring to all the families of the earth was the knowledge of God and His law. But selection alone was not enough. God's service is never easy. His chosen servant must possess many virtues, faith, obedience, willingness to serve, self-restraint, readiness to sacrifice self for others, all-embracing love for fellowmen. Before they could become truly God's servant and go forth into the world to fulfill their divine mission, these Biblical writers sought to teach, Abraham and Israel had to be repeatedly tried by God, and their possession of these indispensable qualities and virtues had to be tested and proved. This thought of God's trial of Abraham and of Israel to prove their fitness for their great, eternal, universal mission. is the central theme of the Abraham cycle of stories, which makes them both a unit in themselves, and a unit with the first cycle of stories in I-XI and with the Jacob and Joseph cycles which follow.

For to a certain, though less marked degree, not only Abraham, but also Jacob and Joseph are prototypes of Israel; or rather God's relation with these two patriarchs typifies God's relation with all Israel. That Israel might faithfully discharge its mission, it must not only be tested and proved, but if it do possess faults and vices, and do lack any of the requisite virtues, the former must first be eradicated and the latter developed, before it can be ready for God's service. Above all else the vices of selfishness, covetousness and deceit, if such exist at all in Israel, must give way to unselfishness, capacity for self-sacrifice, and perfect righteousness. He alone who, in his eagerness to serve God and fellowmen truly, can forget self and personal advantage entirely, is worthy of the divine call. God works only with perfect tools. For His service He selects the best tools available. But if these best tools be still imperfect, they must be corrected and made right, that they may be fit for God's use. Israel was the best tool for God's service, the story tells us, and these Biblical writers would have us believe, better than Ishmael or Edom, the other traditional descendants of Abraham. But even so Israel was not perfect. It had first to be purified and ennobled, that it might become ready to carry on the work committed to Abraham, and which had descended to it as a precious birthright, of bringing blessing to all the families of the earth. But such purification is never easy. It demands years of trial and suffering and bitter struggle, until at last all evil inclination is purged from the soul. Then only is the tool ready and fit for God's use.

Such is the central theme of the third portion of Genesis, chapters XXV, 19–XXXVI. Here, too, a number of ancient legends were employed by the authors in order to give concrete and forceful expression to their main thought. Here, too, there is only a modicum of actual history. Jacob, too, may have been a historical person and a progenitor of Israel, or of a part of Israel. Nevertheless, the real truth of the Jacob story is spiritual rather than historical. The entire Jacob story is a unit. It pictures the complete moral regeneration of a singular, yet perfectly natural man, craven, selfish and deceitful at the outset, yet in the end sublimely purified and ennobled; it is the impressive drama of a repentant soul. The doctrine of repentance which it presents is that which Judaism has formulated and given to the world. Jacob is the prototype of all Israel, and Jacob's repentance and purification, the authors this story imply, and the prophets from Hosea on have taught, are the repentance and purification which all Israel must undergo. And the perfection to which Jacob at last attains, is the perfection for which every Jew and all Israel should strive, that they may become worthy of and fit for the sacred privilege and mission of service to fellowmen for which God has called them.[1]

The fourth division of Genesis, chapters XXXVII-L, contains an altogether different kind of narrative. A few of the incidents of the Joseph story, as, for example, the Potiphar's-wife episode and the figure of a Semite as chief counsellor of Pharaoh and the second in the kingdom are probably borrowed from Egyptian legend and history.[1] The name Joseph, too, is identical with an ancient Israelite place or tribe name, found upon an early Egyptian monument. But beyond this there is probably not a single historical fact in the entire Joseph story. Or if there be such facts, they are only a substratum for what is at best a historical romance pure and simple, perfectly constructed and forcibly presented. It begins with the account of Joseph's boyhood and unpleasant relations with his brothers, and their jealousy because of their father's undue love for him and also because of his dreams, and their revenge for his having borne tales to their father. In consequence he is sold into Egypt and comes into the house of Potiphar. Because of Potiphar's wife he is cast into prison. Here he meets the royal butler, and through him comes before Pharaoh. He interprets the king's dream, and as a reward is raised to an exalted position. Eventually his brothers come before him to buy corn, but do not recognize him. He deals with them as the ruler, sending them home with the desired grain, but retaining one in prison in order to test them. They return, bringing the youngest brother in accordance with Joseph's command, and by their conduct prove the regeneration of their former evil natures. At last, the crisis of the story, when it seems that not only they, but also their old father, must perish, Joseph discloses his identity and a happy family reunion follows.

It can be readily seen that this is a complete romance.

---

[1] A more full and analytic introduction to the Jacob cycle of stories is given below, pp. 222-281.

[1] Cf. C. F. Kent, *Heroes and Crises of Early Hebrew History*, 148f.

One event leads up to another naturally and dramatically until the crisis is reached; the interest never lags; the dreams contribute artistically to the development of the story; the portrayal of character is faithful and effective, the pathos real and touching; and the moral and spiritual lesson which runs through the entire story is sincere and convincing.

The central thought of the story, for the sake of which the romance was written, is expressed concretely and forcibly in the words of Joseph to his brothers (L, 20), "Ye meant evil against me; but God meant it for good, to bring to pass, as it is this day, to save much people alive". This thought rounds out the teachings of the earlier portions of Genesis, and makes of the book a single unit of Jewish thought and doctrine. Not only has God created the universe for good, but He constantly controls and guides it toward its destined goal of good. His work was not finished with the single act of creation, but it goes on day by day, manifest in the wonders of nature and in the still more wonderful evolution of human history. Lovingly and wisely God has endowed man with free-will, as the story of Eden teaches, and it rests with man to choose between good and evil. But even if man does choose wrongly, and evil results from his sinful misuse of God's gifts, this is not the end. For somehow, in ways which the little mind of man can not comprehend, but the indubitable effects and proofs of which he can see in all history, even though man may mean evil, God means it nevertheless for good; and in His own time out of all man's evil God somehow brings greater good for all mankind. God has called Israel and revealed to it His law and sent it forth to bring this law unto all the world. But Israel does not work alone, unsupported by God who sent it. God, too, works in His own way, and His providence watches over men and nations. And if Israel but holds fast to its faith in God and in its mission, and labors truly and loyally as one people, as "brethren, the sons of one man in the land of Canaan" (XLII, 13), though danger threaten and the future seem black, it need not fear. God is still with it, and the goal of its labors will surely be attained.

Such, in brief, is the complete thought of the Book of Genesis.

The Authors of Genesis

The preceding discussion has made it clear that the stories of Genesis were not written down accidentally nor merely for the sake of the narratives they recount. Their writers selected these stories deliberately out of a great mass of ancient Israelite myth, legend, and tradition, and couched them in their present form for a definite purpose. Nor was their aim to present the actual facts of history. They must have realized that in the literal sense much of their material, at least in the form in which they developed it, was unhis-·torical. And even if they did believe that they were writing history, they doubtless understood that their presentation was by no means complete and consecutive, and likewise, that their interest was only secondarily historical.

We have seen that the stories of Genesis fall naturally into four main groups, that in general each single story or incident seems to voice some profound, Jewish, ethical and religious thought, that these various single stories are in turn closely correlated, so that each group gives concrete expression to some larger and more significant and distinctive principle of Judaism, and that, finally, the Book of Genesis itself is a unit, centering about the doctrine of God's selection and preparation of Israel to be His people, His witness and the bearer of His law of life, redemption, and blessing unto all the peoples of the earth. The Book of Genesis was not all written at one time, nor by one man, nor even by one single group of men. It is the product of literary activity in both the northern and southern kingdoms, extending over approximately four hundred years, from the beginning of the ninth to the end of the sixth century B.

C., or probably even a little later. This long and eventful period witnessed the most momentous events in Israel's history, the rise and decay of prophecy, the downfall of both northern and southern kingdoms, the exile of Judah, the nation, to Babylon, and the eventual return of a fragment thereof as a religious community. During this eventful period religious and ethical ideas, beliefs, and principles naturally experienced a far-reaching evolution. The thoughts and outlook of the later writers of Genesis were necessarily far broader, higher, and more inclusive than those of their predecessors. It was these very latest writers who gave the book its present form, and added to, recast, and worked into it their own universalistic conception of God and of mankind and of the life and destiny of Israel.

A moment's thought shows that the religious and ethical teachings of Genesis, and the evident, underlying purpose of the entire book accord completely with the teachings of the great prophets of Israel. The conceptions of God as the sole Creator, and of the absolute goodness of His creation, of human free-will and responsibility, of sin and repentance, of the divine selection and preparation of Israel, of the purifying and ennobling effects of God's trial of His children, of the manifestation of God's power, providence, and love in human history, these and all the other teachings of Genesis find repeated and detailed expression in the sublime utterances of Israel's prophets. Or, rather, the teachings of Israel's prophets are concretely illustrated and enforced by these stories of Genesis. For the most part the prophets presented their thoughts and teachings in abstract form. They could hardly have done otherwise. But the uneducated and untrained masses could only dimly comprehend the full significance and application to their own lives of the prophets' words. Still today the human mind finds it easier and more natural to visualize ideas and to think concretely rather than abstractly. Could the teachings of the prophets be expressed concretely, and their application to the lives of individuals and to the collective life of Israel be positively illustrated, they would certainly be much better understood, and in all likelihood much more widely accepted and applied by the people.

Just this was the underlying and conscious purpose of most of these writers of Genesis; and not merely of the writers of Genesis, but of the authors of the greater part of the Pentateuch and of a considerable portion of the entire Bible. Hosea proclaimed the doctrine of repentance and divine love and forgiveness, but the stories of the flood, of Sodom and Gomorrah, and of Jacob showed concretely what true repentance is, and how divine forgiveness may be attained. Isaiah spoke of faith, but the story of Abraham told what absolute faith in God really means. All the prophets insisted, more or less consciously, upon the conception of God as the controller and guide of all history, and particularly of Israel's history. But the story of Joseph illustrates concretely and convincingly the wondrous way in which God's providence constantly works through history. Deutero-Isaiah gave clear and positive expression to the doctrine of Israel's selection by God and its mission to all the peoples of the earth, but the entire Book of Genesis, as cast into its present form by its latest writers and revisers, tells concretely why and how God chose Israel, and gradually disciplined and prepared it for its sublime task.

Thus the thought of almost the entire Book of Genesis is prophetic, and its purpose is clearly to enforce and apply the teachings of the prophets by means of concrete illustrations based upon Israel's ancient traditions and legends. It may therefore be inferred that in the main these authors of Genesis were followers of the great prophets, filled with conviction and enthusiasm for the prophetic conception of Israel's history and religion. They sought to support the prophetic movement by concretizing the fundamental prophetic teachings and principles in narrative form, so that they might be more fully understood and applied by the people. In particular they sought to enforce the basic prophetic doctrine, that God has been and will be ever present in Israel's history, manifesting His divine power and love and purpose with Israel, and that the people can always assure themselves of His protection and favor by walking with Him truly and living in accordance with His law, which, in His love, He had revealed to them, and by discharging faithfully the mission for which He had chosen them. These writers, though frequently manifesting literary powers of the highest merit, were not the great prophets themselves, and on the whole there is little originality of prophetic thought in their writings. They were rather ardent followers and supporters of the prophets who sought to win for their masters a larger and more comprehending audience. /

The Religious and Spiritual Significance of the Stories of Genesis

Just because the prophetic idea and movement were fundamentally ethical and moral, these stories of Genesis sound a positive ethical and moral note. But they teach, not abstract ethics and morals, but ethics and morals as an integral part of Israel's religion, as conceived and evolved through Israel's religious history, and from the standpoint of Israel's God and the standard of life established by Him. The patriarchs are each models of Jewish life and teaching. Abraham's hospitality, his faith in God, his readiness to make even the supreme sacrifice of his only, beloved child, typify the Jewish ideal of hospitality, of faith, sacrifice and obedience. Not Abraham's faith alone is pictured, but also and even more, the Jew's eternal faith in the God of his fathers. Abraham is far less a historical character than the type of all Jewish life, faith and devotion.

Similarly Jacob, at first deceitful, covetous and unscrupulous, yet in the end purified, noble and magnanimous, is less a historical person than the exemplar of the great, eternal truth, first fully enunciated by Hosea, of the power of true repentance, repentance which comes not quickly nor easily, but as the result of long and bitter trial and purgation, when through the dark and terrifying night we wrestle with the evil spirit of our own lower selves and base inclinations, and at last, when the dawn of the new day breaks, we step forth triumphant, purified and regenerate, to live a new life, the life which God has ever called upon the Jew to live.

Joseph, too, hero of a beautiful romance, is the inspiring pattern of the characteristically Jewish virtues of self-control, resistance to temptation, high idealism, loyalty to kindred, people, and religion. Above all, he is the exponent of the profound faith in God's goodness, wisdom, and providence, which constitutes the fundamental conception of God that Judaism has evolved and ever upheld.

All in all, therefore, Genesis contains, not literal history, but an illustrated record of many of the fundamental spiritual truths which Israel has, through long and often bitter and grievous experience, discovered, and proclaimed to the world. Therefore a true knowledge of Genesis presupposes a full appreciation of the prophetic origin and spiritual significance of the book. Such real appreciation must bring with it clear understanding of, and firm belief in, these principles of Judaism.

BIBLIOGRAPHY

Montefiore, Claude G., *The Bible for Home Reading*, vol. I, pp. 1–59; 554–589.

Kent, Charles Foster, *The Heroes and Crises of Early Hebrew History* (*The Historical Bible Series*).

Kent, Charles Foster, *The Beginnings of Hebrew History* (*The Students' Old Testament Series*).

Ginzberg, Louis, *The Legends of the Jews*, 4 vols. (Jewish Publication Society).

Polano, H., *Selections from the Talmud*.

Isaacs, Abram S., *Stories from the Rabbis*.

Rappaport, Samuel, *Tales and Maxims from the Midrash*.

Rappaport, Samuel, *Tales and Maxims from the Talmud*.

Weis, L., *Talmudic and Other Legends*.

Jewish Encyclopedia, selected articles, such as *Abraham, Adam, Creation, Flood, Folk-Lore, Genesis*, etc.

Hastings' *Dictionary of the Bible*, selected articles.

Pfeiffer, Robert H., *Introduction to the Old Testament*.

Gunkel, Hermann, *The Legends of Genesis*.

Mercer, Samuel A. B., *Extra-Biblical Sources for Hebrew and Jewish History*.

The Westminster Historical Atlas to the Bible, edited by G. Ernest Wright and Floyd V. Filson.

I

THE STORY OF CREATION

(Genesis I - II, 4)

And God saw everything that He had made, and, behold, it was very good. (Genesis I, 31.)

The heavens declare the glory of God,
And the firmament showeth His handiwork. (Psalm XIX, 2.)

Read Psalm VIII, with particular emphasis on vv. 3-6.

The Book of Genesis opens most naturally with an account of the creation of the universe. This account has been generally accepted as historically correct. A careful analysis of the narrative, however, as well as the discoveries of modern science, prove that this can not be actual history, but, as has already been indicated in the Introduction, is a myth pure and simple, many of the details of which have been borrowed from a much older Babylonian myth.

Be that as it may, it does not lessen in the least the spiritual value of this creation story for Judaism. For even though many of the details be borrowed from the Babylonian, the whole story has been rewritten and recast and reanimated by the Jewish spirit, until it has become virtually new. In its present form it gives expression, more forceful and sublime, perhaps, than any other passage of the Bible, or, for that matter, of any other book, to the fundamental Jewish conception of God, majestic, transcendental, and spiritual, who, Himself, in His real being, is unknowable by man, who can be comprehended only through consideration of the grandeur, beauty, wisdom, and goodness of His works. As the Psalmist has said,

The heavens declare the glory of God,
And the firmament showeth His handiwork.

One fact should be realized at the outset, that this story was hardly meant to be primarily an objective account of the way in which creation was thought to have actually happened. The author has merely taken the older myth, systematized its details, and adapted it to his purposes. One of these purposes was to show that the Sabbath of Judaism was, so he believed, the oldest religious institution of mankind, established by God at the very moment of creation. In other words, not the details of the story are essential, or were essential, even in the author's mind, but rather the fact of the institution of the Sabbath as the day of rest and worship of God, and the fitting climax to the six days of useful labor, first proclaimed by Israel, and learned from Israel by civilized mankind.

Not only this, but the story reflects through and through the unique Jewish outlook upon the universe and upon life. The concluding words of the account of each day's creation, "And God saw that it was good", and the concluding words of the entire story, "And God saw everything that He had made, and, behold, it was very good", express the fundamental Jewish belief in the goodness and wisdom of God, and in the goodness and wise purpose of this earth and of human life thereon. Judaism has always taught that this world is good, and that life here is worth living for its own sake, that God has created everything in wisdom and love, and has placed man here for a good and wise purpose, to live usefully and nobly in accordance with the divine will, as it is given him to know this.

In contrast with many other religions, ancient and modern, Judaism has never taught the absolute existence of evil alongside of good. On the contrary, Judaism has always insisted that since God is a God of good, everything which He has created must be for good, and that the normal order of things is only good. Only through man's misuse of God's gifts or defiance of God's will and disregard of His purpose in life does evil come. The following parable, told by the wise rabbis of old in commenting upon this story of creation, expresses this principle most forcibly. When God first created the trees they rejoiced to be alive, for existence seemed so good. But when, the next day, He created the iron, the trees all trembled with fear and said, "This iron will chop us down". But God reassured them, "No, not until you trees yourselves furnish the handle to the axe, will the iron have power to harm you". So it is in the life of all men; from God comes good alone, and all His gifts are for some purpose of good; but when men misuse these gifts, or fail to apply them to their appointed purpose, evil results. That is the only real evil in the world. Thus Judaism has ever believed, and has proclaimed the truth, voiced throughout this story of creation, that life itself and the universe and everything connected therewith are good, that God has created all in wisdom, goodness and love, and has placed man at the head, has fashioned him in His own image, and endowed him with all high qualities, in order that he may rule this universe wisely, in the way and for the purpose which He has ordained. Again in the words of the Psalmist,

Thou hast made him but little lower than the angels,
And hast crowned him with glory and honor.
Thou hast made him to have dominion over the works of Thy hands;
Thou hast put all things under his feet.

Understanding this Jewish conception of the nature of the universe, and of the position of man, and of the exalted purpose of his existence, the divine command to observe the Sabbath acquires new significance. Life has its purpose of good appointed by God. But this purpose of good does not realize itself nor come of its own accord. It can be attained only by man's earnest and conscientious labor. God has ordained that man should be colaborer with Him in the world's work. Thereby He has exalted man above all other creatures. In this labor man finds his chief pleasure, and life comes to have value, and to seem sweet and beautiful and worth living. The life of that person who finds no real work to do, must seem indeed dull and sad, useless and misspent. In other words, Judaism teaches that man's work is one of the good things, in fact, the crowning blessing of life, ordained by God.

Yet all labor and toil, day in and day out, must take the zest out of life, and make existence dreary and cheerless. God has created man to be the lord of the universe, and not its slave or drudge. For just this reason God has instituted the Sabbath, and has bidden man rest on this day from labor and toil, that he may rejoice in the consideration of the goodness and the beauty of the universe and of life, and in the knowledge of the dignity and the opportunity of his exalted position, and that he may thank God reverently and joyfully for all His bounty and love. It is the precious Sabbath which enables men to rightly appreciate and enjoy the sacred privilege of life. And, as our prayer-book says, so nobly and so truly, "He alone, who has labored well during the week, and, according to his strength, has contributed to the greater work of humanity, will enjoy the sweetness of the Sabbath. To him who, obedient to Thy law, has performed what was given him to do, the Sabbath is a fountain of joy, of hope and strength". Therefore God has instituted the Sabbath for Israel and for all mankind, and has made it the sign of His everlasting covenant with Israel (Exodus XXXI, 16f.). And through His prophet He has spoken unto Israel:

If thou turn away. thy foot because of the Sabbath,
From pursuing thy business on My holy day;
And call the Sabbath a delight,
And the holy of the Lord honorable;

And shalt honor it, not doing thy wonted ways,
Nor pursuing thy business, nor speaking thereof;
Then shalt thou delight thyself in the Lord,
And I will make thee to ride upon the high places of the earth,
And I will feed thee with the heritage of Jacob thy father;
For the mouth of the Lord hath spoken it.   (Isaiah LVIII, 13f.)

NOTES

The name of this book, Genesis, comes from the Greek. It means "beginning" or "creation". The first translation of the Hebrew Bible was made into Greek during the third and second centuries B. C. It was made for the benefit of the Greek-speaking Jewish community of Alexandria, and was called the Septuagint. Most of the subsequent translations of the Bible into European languages were made from this Greek, rather than from the original Hebrew version. In consequence many of the books of the Bible are commonly cited by their Greek names. In Hebrew Genesis is called *Bereshith*, from the first word of the Hebrew text, which means "in the beginning". Similarly the other books of the Pentateuch are called in Hebrew by their first significant words.

V. 3. Creation is here and throughout this chapter represented as having come about merely at God's command. God uttered His divine word and the thing commanded immediately came into being. This is the significance of the words, "And it was so", occurring after each separate act of creation; cf. Psalm XXXIII, 6-9.

V. 5. The giving of the names here and elsewhere is in accordance with the ancient belief that the name of a thing is an essential part of its being. Not until a thing had received its name was it considered really complete and existent. Hence the giving of the name here is the very last step of each act of creation (cf. Gen. II, 19 and 23).

That evening is here mentioned before morning is due to the fact that our ancestors reckoned the day from sunset to sunset, and therefore in their reckoning evening preceded morning.

V. 6ff. The conception of the universe which underlies this chapter is very interesting. Naturally it is not at all scientific, and from a modern standpoint it may seem rather crude. It can be best explained by an illustration. Imagine a large bowl filled with water, upon the surface of which, and in the center, floats a round piece of bread. At a little distance above the lower bowl is another bowl, also filled with water. In the bottom of the upper bowl are little openings, which may be either opened or closed. The two bowls of water above and below, represent two great oceans or reservoirs of water. The piece of bread is the earth, which floats upon the surface of the lower ocean. The pores in the bread represent the holes in the earth, through which the water from below bubbles up to the surface in the form of springs and wells (cf. the expression, "The water under the earth", Exodus XX, 4). The ocean above is the source of the rain, which falls to the earth beneath through the little openings or windows in the bottom of the bowl (cf. Gen. VII, 11 and VIII, 2). The bottom of the upper bowl is the heaven or firmament, which God spread out in the midst of the waters, to divide the waters above the earth from those below. In this heaven the sun, moon and stars are 'fixed. This is the conception of the universe which lies at the bottom, not only of this chapter, but of many other parts of the Bible. The rabbis later expanded this conception considerably and spoke of seven heavens, one above the other, and also seven earths one below the other.

V. 9. "The waters under the heaven," i. e. the lower of the two bodies of water now existing.

V. 11. Here God does not directly create the grass, but merely speaks the word which endows the earth with power to cause the grass and plants to spring forth. In other words God's word endows the earth with the power of plant propagation.

V. 14. The question is often asked, and is generally found troublesome, "If the sun, moon and stars were created only on the fourth day, how could light have existed on the very first day of creation, and also how could plant life, for which sunlight is indispensable, have begun on the third day?" The ancient rabbis tried to answer the first question with the tradition that the light of the first day was different from, and superior to, the light of the sun. This original light at first filled the whole universe. But when Adam sinned, this light was taken away, to be restored to man, however, when the Messiah shall come at the end of time. Meanwhile mankind must content itself with the light of the sun, moon and stars, created on the fourth day. Other traditions told that God himself was clothed with light, and that this light emanated from Him and filled the universe before the creation of the sun (cf. Psalm CIV, 1-2). However, it is clear that these are only unsuccessful, though pious and reverential, attempts to account for what is obviously an anachronism on the part of the author. Inasmuch as he measures creation from the very beginning by days and evenings and mornings, it is clear that he had in mind the orderly succession of day and night, of light and darkness caused by the presence or absence of the light of the sun. Similarly, the simple and natural answer to the second question, how could plant life have begun on the third day, if the sun was not created until the fourth day, is that the author of this story apparently had no knowledge of the connection between the light and heat of the sun and plant life and growth. However, since, as we have seen, the framework of the story is of far less import than the Jewish thought which the story illustrates so well, anachronisms like these can be readily overlooked.

V. 22. God's blessing upon the animals is not to be regarded as a mere, pious wish that they be fruitful and multiply, but, just as in v. 28, it bestows upon them the power of self-propagation. In fact, throughout the Bible, God's blessing is never a mere wish, but always contains the means of self-fulfilment if only properly applied.

V. 26. The words, "Let *us* make man in *our* image", are probably a survival of the older version of this myth, which spoke, not of one God, but of many gods (cf. III, 22). The present monotheistic form of the story is the result of the adaptation of the original Babylonian myth to the standpoint of the Jewish religion.

In this connection it may be remarked that frequently Jewish Biblical students are startled, and even shocked, when the thought is first presented to them that this creation-story, and also the flood-story and a number of other Biblical traditions and thoughts were borrowed from Babylonian mythology and literature. A moment's consideration, however, suffices to show that there is nothing unnatural or shocking in this fact, and that the admission of its correctness detracts not one whit from the credit and glory of Judaism. Nations, like individuals, must live alongside of each other and exchange cultural products of intellect and spirit, even as they exchange material products of field and factory. It would be a sorry people, just as it would be a sorry individual, which had to discover and learn everything for itself through its own, ofttimes bitter, experience, and could not learn from contact with other peoples and acquaintance with their history and thought. Israel is no exception to this rule. Throughout its history it has always been able to exchange the best of its knowledge and culture for the best of the knowledge and culture of its neighbors, the Babylonians among others. But Israel has never been a parasite upon the world; it has always given in exchange value received, and on the whole the balance of credit is in its favor.

Nor is this all. Not even Shakespeare created the plots of all his immortal plays. The great majority he borrowed from one source or another. But in their original sources these plots would have had little or no permanent interest for the world, and would in time have been lost or forgotten. It was Shakespeare's genius that made these plots live and become the literary treasures of the world. Somewhat similarly, though to a degree far more exalted, as the genius of a God-inspired people surpasses infinitely the genius of an individual, even a Shakespeare, Israel borrowed this creation-story and the flood-story. In their original form these stories would, at the most, have had only a passing interest for the student of archaeology or history. It was Israel's religious genius which breathed into them a spiritual truth and universal message which made them live, and live not for Israel alone, but for all men and all ages. Israel borrowed, yes, but it borrowed something that was almost worthless; it touched this with the magic wand of its spirit, and thereby transformed it into something of eternal, priceless value. In voicing this spirit of Judaism, the old myths have become new and living stories, in which the spiritual element contributed by Judaism is greater and of vaster significance than the framework and the few details borrowed from the Babylonian. The old Babylonian myth was lost and forgotten two thousand years ago. It is the Jewish story which has lived, because of the Jewish spirit and the Jewish truth contained in it, and has become a part of the great spiritual heritage of the Jew, and a part of his priceless gift to mankind.

V. 27. According to this story God created man and woman at the same time, and as the final act of creation, just as He had previously created the male and female of every other species of animals.

V. 29. This verse implies that originally God had intended that man and the animals eat only herbs. Later, after the flood, permission was given to eat flesh (Gen. IX, 2ff.). It was the ancient belief that in the Messianic age the original condition will be re-established, when once more the cow and the bear shall feed together and the lion eat straw like the ox (Isaiah XI, 7).

II

THE GARDEN OF EDEN

(Genesis II, 4—III, 24)

Then the Lord God formed man of the dust of the ground, and breathed into his nostrils the breath of life. (Genesis II, 7.)

I call heaven and earth to witness against you this day, that I have set before thee life and death, the blessing and the curse; therefore choose life, that thou mayest live. (Deuteronomy XXX, 19.)

Read Psalm XXIV, 1-6.

The story of the Garden of Eden is one of the most beautiful, not only in the Bible, but in all literature, and has deservedly come to be regarded as one of the world's immortal classics. Its story is told simply and directly. The several incidents are clearly and concisely pictured. The climax is dramatic, when the guilty pair, conscious of their sin, must come forth from their hiding-place at God's call, and by excusing themselves with a half lie, incriminate themselves irrefutably.

Despite its simplicity and brevity, the portrayal of character is delicate and effective. The serpent, cunning and evil-minded, purposely overstates God's command and asks, "Hath God said: Ye shall not eat of any tree in the garden?" And the woman, guileless and unsuspecting, falls into the trap, and even enlarges upon God's actual words, "Of the fruit of the trees of the garden we may eat; but of the fruit of the tree which is in the midst of the garden, God hath said: Ye shall not eat of it, neither shall ye touch it, lest ye die". And when she has, so naturally and humanly, let herself be enticed by the alluring beauty of the tree and the seeming benefits which it might confer, and has eaten, her first thought is of her husband; "and she gave also unto her husband with her, and he did eat". And finally, when directly charged by God with their sin, each seeks to shift the responsibility; the man puts the blame partly upon the woman and partly upon God Himself, for having made her, and the woman in turn shifts the blame to the serpent. Touches so delicate reveal the master's hand.

The story shows remarkable power of condensation and suggestion. The one sentence, "And they were both naked, the man and his wife, and were not ashamed", pictures their state of pristine innocence far more effectively than any detailed explanation. Similarly, after both have eaten of the forbidden fruit, and both they and the reader of the story are anxiously awaiting the results, the few words, "And the eyes of them both were opened, and they knew" . . . what did they know; what was this strange and wonderful knowledge which came from eating the forbidden fruit? . . . "they knew that they were naked", are powerfully suggestive. Not a single one of the blessings which they had so eagerly anticipated, had come to them, but only the recognition of their nakedness. With this comes first the sense of shame, and they hasten to hide from their Maker in the gloom of the trees. And there come also the full consciousness of sin, and the realization that the serpent had in fact deceived them. They had expected so much; and although the serpent's words were literally true, and they had not died, yet after all they had gained so little, and at so great a price.

However, although the author of this story was a supreme artist, the story is by no means entirely the product of his own fertile imagination. He has taken a number of ancient folk-tales, the product of the childhood period of Israel's cultural evolution, and with delicate art has woven them together around a single, central theme. This told of the first man and woman, placed by God, and living care-free and at ease in a beautiful, well-watered garden of trees. Of all the trees they might eat, except the one just in the center of the garden. But one day they disobeyed and ate of the forbidden tree. Immediately they were driven from the garden, and were forced thereafter to gain their livelihood by tilling the hard and often unresponsive soil.

The origin of this story is easily determined. The background of the unwatered, barren earth and its oasis-like garden of trees growing about the single, life-giving spring of water, is unmistakable. Even more indicative is the theme that the supreme good is to live in a beautiful, well-watered garden of trees and eat without toil of their fruit, and that the supreme evil is to be compelled to till the soil and, in sweat of brow, eat of its produce. To a people even only slightly advanced in civilization, tilling the soil for a livelihood does not seem an evil or a curse, but the normal state of existence and the divinely appointed destiny of man. But the nomad of the Arabian Desert looks out upon life through different eyes. His food supply is monotonous and scanty indeed, but this is more than compensated for by the perfect freedom of the desert which he enjoys. He works only when he pleases and as little as he pleases, and only at the, to him, noble occupation of caring for his sheep and camels. He is here today and gone where he will tomorrow. He is his own lord and master, and the absolute equal of every man. And he looks down with undisguised contempt upon the farmer, for all time bound to one spot, compelled to bend his back in servile toil, only too often to reap but thorns and thistles, and doomed to cringe and tremble before a despotic government, and humbly and unresistingly give of his hard-won gain for taxes at the unwarranted bidding of others. Clearly this story must have originated in those remote, prehistoric days, long before the time of Moses, when our ancestors still roamed the great Arabian

Desert as nomads, and found their easiest living in the
occasional oases with their springs of water and their
bounteous trees, and from their heights of unrestrained freedom to live and wander at will, looked down upon the poor
tiller of the soil as an accursed being. Or, if it did not
originate then, it must have been very soon thereafter, before
our ancestors had passed over completely and willingly to
the settled, agricultural life, and before their conception of
existence had been transformed from the nomadic to the
agricultural.

Into this central story the author has ingeniously and
artistically worked a number of other folk-tales, many no
doubt of equal antiquity. They are all typical folk-tales,
such as our ancestors must have once possessed in great
number. In nature they differ very little from the folk-
tales of other primitive peoples. But in subject matter they
do show immeasurable superiority. For most folk-tales turn
about such incidental and superficial questions as "Why the
sea is salt", or "How the rabbit got his long ears", or "Why
there is a man in the moon". Certainly our ancestors, too,
had many simple tales like these, as the stories here of
"How the animals got their names", and "Why the serpent
crawls upon his belly", show. But in addition, they treated
of problems which other primitive peoples seldom, if ever,
divined, such basic problems òf life as "Why a man leaves
his parents for his wife", "Why childbirth is so painful",
"Why woman is inferior to, and dependent upon, man",
"Why man must labor so ceaselessly and bitterly", and the
like.

These are problems which touch upon the elemental and
eternal mysteries of existence, and with the solution of which
the world is still, in a certain sense, wrestling. That our
ancestors should have conceived of these deep, basic, philosophic problems almost at the very beginning of their intellectual and cultural evolution, may well indicate that, in

contrast to the minds of other peoples, the Jewish mind is by nature meditative, philosophic, introspective, with a certain intuitive apperception of the fundamental truths and problems of life.

And comparison of these ancient Israelite folk-tales with those of other primitive peoples reveals something of far deeper import. Not only do the folk-tales of other peoples for the most part ask such superficial questions as "Why the sea is salt", but they answer them in purely mechanical manner, in the form of a story in which the actors are mere human beings and animals, or, at the most, fairies and genii. Thus the well-known Scandinavian folk-tale tells that the wicked brother stole the good brother's magic mill and bade it grind salt. But when the ship was full, he had forgotten the magic word, which alone could stop the mill, and so the ship sank. And the mill lies on the bottom of the sea, still grinding salt; and that is why the sea is salt. In significant contrast, these Biblical folk-tales answer all their questions from the standpoint of God, the Creator. Manifestly from the very beginning, God, or probably in the very earliest form of the stories, a divine being, was the chief actor, and all things came to be as they are in accordance with His will. Man leaves his parents for his wife because God fashioned her out of the bone and flesh of her husband, and thus they are truly one. The serpent crawls upon his belly because God so punished him. And mankind is divided into different nations, speaking different languages because God so ordained.

The Bible affirms, and we believe, that Israel was chosen by God to receive His law, and to proclaim it and the knowledge of Him and His true worship to the world. However, it is frequently objected that this can not be true, for a just God could not choose one people in preference to another. But a wise and loving father carefully studies his sons to learn their different natures and aptitudes. And of one he makes a physician, of another a merchant, and of still another a farmer. To have condemned them all to be farmers, or merchants, or physicians, would have been unjust and cruel. So God calls each of His children to the task for which it is best fitted. The Greeks He bade bring to the world the sense of order, symmetry and beauty, and these became, in one line of evolution, art, and in another line, orderly, proportionate thinking, logic, and philosophy. The Romans He bade bring to the world organization, law, government, administration. And unto Israel He revealed Himself, and bade Israel bring this knowledge of Him to the world, because, of all peoples, Israel was best fitted to receive this knowledge and to discharge this mission. Israel was best fitted because its mind and soul were attuned to God and, of all peoples, it could best absorb the knowledge of God, which He sought to reveal to all His children; because, as these folk-tales show, from the very dawn of its history Israel thought about God and pondered over the mysteries of life from the standpoint of God. Much thinking must in time beget much knowledge. So Israel came to know about God sooner than any other people. Therefore the task of proclaiming this knowledge devolved upon Israel, and Israel was chosen by God for its glorious mission. And since, as we believe, and as the world has come to believe with us, the knowledge of God and His worship and the life He has intended that men shall live, is the supreme knowledge, therefore Israel is, above all others, God's chosen people, chosen not for special favors at God's hands, but because, of all peoples, it was best fitted for this sublimest mission of all. This vital and inspiring truth of Israel's innate and eternal religious genius, and of God's choice of Israel therefore as His messenger and the witness of His truth unto mankind, the full appreciation of these ancient folk-tales of our fathers brings home most convincingly and appealingly.

In time, as is but natural, a number of these ancient folk-tales gradually grew together, and at last a connected and virtually new story evolved, our present story of the Garden of Eden. Through this new story there runs one thought, but dimly apparent in the old folk-tales, a thought which has become a basic principle of Judaism, and which distinguishes Judaism from other religions more sharply almost than any other doctrine. It is the thought that God has placed man here on this beautiful earth to live a life of purity and usefulness, to eat the good fruit which is permitted, but to refrain from the forbidden fruit, no matter how beautiful and alluring. God has created man for a purpose of good, and bidden him strive to fulfil this purpose. He has given man intellect and conscience that he may perceive the good and be warned of the evil. And He holds out to man the promise of reward for right living and of punishment for wrong. But with all this God has endowed man with free-will, with power to choose between good and evil, between obedience and disobedience.

As the story says, "Then the Lord God formed man of the dust of the ground, and breathed into his nostrils the breath of life". In expounding this chapter the rabbis of old laid great stress upon this thought that God had formed man of dust, yet had Himself breathed into him the breath of life, a part of His spirit. Thus, they taught, unlike the animals, man is the child of two worlds, the earthly, lower world of dust, and the heavenly world of God's spirit. In some qualities he resembles the animals of earth, and in others the angels of heaven. Had God made man only like the angels, he would have lived forever; had he been entirely like the creatures of earth, he would have died speedily. So God gave him a double nature; if he is righteous, he attains eternal life, but if he sins, he perishes. If he lets his earthly nature prevail, he sinks inevitably to the level of the beast. But if he follows the inclination of God's spirit within him, he rises higher and ever higher, until he becomes, in the Psalmist's words, "but little lower than the angels, and crowned with glory and honor". And the goal of all human living and striving is to become even like unto God Himself. "Ye shall be holy; for I the Lord your God am holy" (Leviticus XIX, 2), is the divinely appointed standard of human righteousness.

But holiness and righteousness are not mere passive conditions of existence. They must be striven for, and can be attained only by constant struggle, which at last conquers the earthly, animal cravings of the body of dust, and leaves the divine, spiritual element triumphant. And only in the struggle and the victory lie the merit of goodness and the justification of divine reward for right living. Had man no choice but to be good or to be evil, in accordance with divine predestination, there could be no reason for, nor justice in, reward or punishment. Therefore, in His wisdom God has so fashioned man, that it rests with him alone to choose the right or the wrong, the blessing or the curse, life or death. The words of Moses unto all Israel just before his death, ' I call Heaven and earth to witness against you this day, that I have set before thee life and death, the blessing and the curse; therefore choose life, that thou mayest live", express most clearly this principle of Judaism. It is given to man to make his own life, good or evil, to determine whether he will walk in purity with God, or must hide in guilt and shame, in darkness and shadow. We become just what we make ourselves, angels or beasts as we choose.

All this is clearly implied in the story of the Garden of Eden. It tells that man's life on earth began with a command from God. A command implies the necessity of choosing between obedience and disobedience. It matters not that the reason for the command is not given, that God did not explain to the man His purpose in forbidding the fruit of the tree. Very often we can not understand the purpose of

God's ways, nor read aright all the mysteries of His wisdom, goodness and love. Neither can the little child always comprehend the wise and loving motives which prompt a parent's command. But even as the little child obeys its parents' commands unquestioningly, because of its implicit faith in them and in their wisdom and love, which it has experienced in so many ways, so must we obey God's commands unquestioningly, with perfect faith in them and in His wisdom, goodness and love, which we, too, know so well from boundless experience. Actually the serpent had told the truth, when it said, "Ye shall not surely die", and God's word had not been fulfilled. Yet the truth of the serpent's word was only literal and superficial, and it brought only misfortune and sorrow. And although on the surface God's word had seemed false, at the bottom there lay the great, eternal, unquestionable truth, that God's commands, however strange and unreasonable they may seem to shortsighted man, are always meant for good and not for evil. And he alone, who walks in God's ways and keeps His commandments at all times, is assured of perfect happiness and blessing. The consequence of disobedience and sin is expulsion from the garden of God into the bleak and cheerless world without, where life loses all beauty and joy, and becomes burdensome and ugly. To us God's commands come constantly, though ofttimes we can not understand the reason why. At times it may even seem that God's bidding is wrong, or unjust, or cruel. But always there is that deep, eternal foundation of truth and justice beneath, and we must obey promptly and unquestioningly and with complete trust, knowing full well that God's purpose is sure, and that His goodness and love fill all the universe, knowing also that only thereby can we continue to live and walk with God in the beauty of purity and innocence.

And the story tells even more. So long as the man and the woman obeyed God's command, even though they did not understand it, they were privileged to live with God in His garden of delight, and they were happy. With sin came shame and the impulse to hide, and sorrow and punishment. They were driven from the beautiful garden forever, and forced to till the soil and gain their livelihood by bitter toil. Yet even in this God's love and mercy were manifest. For only by work, true, useful work, which makes the world better and happier, can we gain true happiness and feel that we are fulfilling the purpose for which God has placed us here on earth. But always the consequences of disobedience and sin are shame, unhappiness, and punishment. No longer can we look our loved ones in the face. We hang our heads and seek to hide from their accusing glance. Friends and companions and the world at large put faith in us no more, for they can not tell what we may do and wherein we may disobey next. And so we are driven from the beautiful garden of happiness and association with trusting loved ones and friends, and we hide ourselves, solitary and alone, from all the world.

But even this is not the end of disobedience and its punishment, our story tells. From men we may perhaps hide, but from God's all-seeing vision, never. Soon He will call unto us, too, "Man, where art thou?", and we, too, will come, trembling and ashamed, from our dark hiding-place, and stand before our Maker for judgment. This, our religion teaches, we can not escape, for in the end we must all be judged. And the judgment, Judaism holds, is sure and absolutely just, whether for punishment, as in the story, or for reward. Yet God's love rules supreme, and He has held out to man the beautiful, inspiring hope of repentance and eventual pardon. The rabbis told that when God made man, He took dust from each of the four corners of the earth, in order that no one spot might boast, "Man was made from me alone", but that man might be, as it were, the child of the entire earth, and possess the qualities of the whole universe. But as a last thought, He took one handful of dust from the spot where the altar of Solomon's temple was later to stand, in. order that man might ever be inclined to seek after God, and repent and make atonement for his sins. But the Jewish doctrine of repentance and atonement demands more explanation than this, and must be deferred for later consideration.

For the present it suffices to realize that this beautiful story of the Garden of Eden presents concretely and convincingly the Jewish conceptions of man and of life, man possessed of the knowledge of right and wrong, and able to choose between them, able, through choosing rightly, through choosing life and living in accordance with God's commands, to realize the divine in his nature and to rise to the heights of the angels, or failing in this, to sink to the level, or below the level, of the beasts. It is for man to choose life, to choose blessing. This is God's purpose with him. This is the life God has meant for him to live, and this alone is pleasing to God. In the Psalmist's words:

> Who shall ascend into the mountain of the Lord?
> And who shall stand in His holy place?
> He that hath clean hands and a pure heart;
> Who hath not taken My name in vain,
> And hath not sworn deceitfully.
> He shall receive a blessing from the Lord,
> And righteousness from the God of his salvation.

NOTES

A little consideration will show that actually this story gives an account of creation different from, and totally independent of that in Genesis I. Here man is created first, and after him the trees. Then, that man be not alone, God creates the animals, one after the other, to be helpmates to him. But not one proves suitable for this purpose. Finally God creates woman from man's rib, and now, "bone of his bone and flesh of his flesh", she proves the desired helpmate.

The conception of God here also differs radically from that in

Genesis I. There God is transcendental and spiritual; He merely speaks His divine word and the various acts of creation ensue. Clearly this conception is the product of an age of philosophy and theology, which refused to think of God as possessing human attributes or discharging such peculiarly human functions as coming in contact with mortals or working with His hands. In Genesis II and III, on the other hand, God is conceived in purely human mould, the only way in which the mind of early Israel could picture Him. He fashions man from the dust with His hands, and breathes of His own breath into the man's nostrils. He is the lord of the garden, and takes His daily walk therein in the cool of the day, and converses familiarly with His creatures. This conception of the Deity is far more crude and primitive, even while more simple and poetic, than that of Genesis I. This is not only because, as has been said, these folk-tales are the product of the earliest period of Israel's cultural and religious evolution, but also because even their present literary form is the work of a period earlier than that of the composition of Genesis I, when the conception of the Deity had not yet been completely spiritualized.

Formerly the attempt was frequently made to determine the exact location of the garden of Eden. The arguments were based chiefly upon the accounts of the four rivers in vv. 10-14. Of these four rivers, only two, the Euphrates and the Tigris, can be positively identified. Various hypotheses have been advanced to identify the other two. In general the garden of Eden has been located in the upper Mesopotamian valley, or in the highlands of Asia Minor or Armenia, where both the Euphrates and Tigris have their sources. However, all these attempts are entirely fanciful and valueless. Biblical science has established, on the one hand, that vv. 10-14 are not a part of the original story, but were inserted long after the story proper was written, and on the other hand, that the original author or authors had no clearly defined conception of the location of Eden. Now they seem to put it in the extreme east, and again in the extreme west. It is obvious that it was a purely mythical conception. Therefore all attempts to localize it with precision rest upon an entire misunderstanding of the origin and true nature of the story.

V. 6. The Hebrew word, *ed*, which is usually translated "mist", occurs in only one other, and a rather obscure, passage of the Bible, Job XXXVI, 27. The real connotation of the word has always been uncertain. The majority of the oldest translations of the Bible rendered it "spring". Other translators interpreted it as "cloud". The customary translation "mist", although traditional, seems to have little justification. Evidence newly come to light indicates that the earliest translation, "spring", was probably correct. Certainly the picture of this spring rising from out the earth, and the trees growing around it, and the stream flowing forth therefrom to water the garden, and four great rivers issuing from this, accords better with the entire story than if we translate *ed* "mist". Likewise the spring in the desert with the garden of trees growing around it, in other words an oasis, is in full harmony with the desert origin and background of this story which we posited above.

V. 7. The Hebrew word for "man" here is *adam*, while the word for "ground" is *adamah*. The implication is that man received this name, *adam*, because he was made from the ground, *adamah*.

V. 8. *Eden* really means "pleasure". Probably the original story spoke only of a *gan eden*, a "pleasure garden". In time, however, the original meaning was forgotten, and *eden* came to be regarded as a proper name designating a certain country. A moment's consideration will show that the original story must have represented Eden as the pleasure garden not of the man and the woman, but of the Deity who dwelt therein (Cf. XIII, 10; Ezekiel XXVIII, 13; XXXI, 3-9). This same conception exists in the mythologies of other primitive peoples.

V. 9. The reference here to the tree of life occasions some difficulty. Not only does this tree play no role at all in the subsequent story proper, but II, 17; III, 3, 11 and 17 clearly imply that God had forbidden but one tree alone. The rabbis of old solved this problem by saying that God needed to prohibit only the tree of knowledge, for it surrounded the tree of life on all sides like a hedge, and whoever would penetrate to the latter must first hew for himself a path through the tree of knowledge. It is a suggestive thought that only through the attainment of true knowledge can we win at last to true life.

However, from a purely scientific standpoint it is clear that the original story spoke of only one tree in the center of the garden, the fruit of which God had forbidden to the man and his wife. The references to the tree of life were inserted by a later writer, at some time after the original story was first written down. It is noteworthy that vv. 23 and 24 tell twice, and with differing motives, of the expulsion of the man from the garden. Manifestly v. 23 is the conclusion of the original story, and tells that in accordance with the terms of the curse, man was driven from the garden to till the soil.

Vv. 22 and 24, and also the reference in II, 9 to the tree of life, are the insertions of the later writer. II, 15 was likewise inserted by him. For on the one hand, it repeats unnecessarily the thought already stated in v. 8, that God had placed the man in the garden, and it adds the statement that man was to dress the garden and keep it. But since tilling the soil and bitter toil are, in the story proper, the punishment for his sin, and the implication is therefore, that previously man did not have to work, but merely plucked his food of fruit from the trees without trouble, this statement that man had to dress the garden is clearly out of place. The story is complete, harmonious, and most effective if it is omitted.

Probably, too, the original story spoke only of "the tree which is in the midst of the garden", and did not at first indicate its nature by calling it "the tree of the knowledge of good and evil". This was partially revealed by the serpent. But unfortunately the serpent knew nothing of the real consequences of eating of the tree. Thus its true nature was learned only through bitter experience. All this is implied in the language of III, 3, 11 and 17, which speak only of "the tree which is in the midst of the garden". Certainly the dramatic impression is heightened, if the tree be designated only as "the tree which is in the midst of the garden", and it be left for its true nature to be discovered only when its fruit is first tasted

Vv. 10-15 are not an integral part of the narrative, but were inserted by some late writer. They disturb the continuity of the story, while v. 15 repeats unnecessarily what was previously sufficiently stated in v. 8. Many attempts have been made to identify the Pishon and the Gihon rivers, but all in vain.

V. 16. According to this story man was at first to eat only of the fruit of the trees. Only as the result of the curse does he come to eat bread and the produce of the soil. In this respect, too, this creation-story differs essentially from that in Genesis I. There the herbs of the field were from the very first given to man for food.

Vv. 18-20 tell most naively that God created the various kinds of animals one after the other, intending that each, in turn, should be the proper helpmate for the man. But He failed in each attempt. Therefore He determined at last upon a different plan. He took a part of the man's own body, and from this fashioned his helpmate; this attempt succeeded. It is clear that this ancient folktale really seeks to account for the origin of animals. The naive conception that man and the animals occupy the same plane of existence, and that therefore animals might possibly be suitable mates for men, is a common motive in primitive folk-lore. Likewise the thought that God failed repeatedly in what He attempted, evidences the primitive character of this tale, particularly when contrasted with the impressive picture of God's transcendent omnipotence in Genesis I.

V. 20. For the significance of giving names to the animals, cf. note to I, 5.

V. 23. Another Hebrew word for "man" is *ish*. The corresponding word for "woman" is *ishah*. The implication here is that since woman was made from a part of man, she received the name *ishah*, apparently, though not actually, derived from *ish*, "man".

Chapter III, v. 1. The story seems to imply that the serpent originally walked erect, and only through the curse came to crawl on his belly. This, too, is the explanation of the ancient rabbis. Christianity sees in the serpent the devil, the power of evil. Judaism, however, knows nothing of the devil. Such a conception of a power of evil, independent of and opposed to God, would contradict Judaism's fundamental teaching of the absolute oneness and omnipotence of God.

V. 15. The basis of this folk-tale is, of course, the natural human horror of serpents.

V. 16. This verse voices the common Oriental conception of woman's inferiority to man.

V. 17. *Adam* is here, as also in II, 20 and III, 21, seemingly used as a proper name.

V. 20. The name Eve (*chavvah*) is here represented as being etymologically akin to the word *chay*, "a living being".

V. 21. Skins of animals are here said to have been the first regular human garments. The fig leaf girdle of V. 7 was, of course, only a temporary covering of nakedness.

V. 22. This verse not only implies that eternal life was thought to be an attribute of the gods, but, as the language clearly indicates, it also pictures the ancient belief in the existence of more than one god. Cf. note to I, 26. We need no longer feel shocked at the thought that our ancestors passed through the polytheistic stage of religious belief before they finally arrived at the idea of monotheism, and that a few vestiges of the ancient belief still survive in the oldest passages of the Bible.

V. 24. Eden apparently is here located at the extreme western end of the earth, since the only entrance is from the east. In II, 8 it is located in the extreme east.

The cherubim are usually conceived of as a class of angels or subordinate divine beings, represented generally with a human face and head, the body of one kind of animal, the legs and feet of another, and the wings of a bird. The conception is probably of Babylonian origin. Psalm XVIII, 11 represents God as riding upon a cherub.

It is not certain just what "the flaming sword which turned every way" was. It was probably based upon some peculiar, mythological conception.

III

CAIN AND ABEL

(Genesis IV, 1-16)

Am I my brother's keeper?   (Genesis IV, 9.)

Behold how good and how pleasant it is
For brethren to dwell together in unity!   (Psalm CXXXIII, 1.)

Read the whole of Psalm CXXXIII.

The story of Cain and Abel, too, is in origin a folk-tale, answering the almost universal questions, How did men begin to worship God? and How did death come into the world? It, too, probably had its birth in the nomad period of Israel's history. This is to be inferred from the conception of sacrifice which the story pictures. Not Cain's sacrifice of the produce of his fields is acceptable to God, but Abel's sacrifice of the firstlings of his sheep. Not only was this always the normal sacrifice in ancient Israel, but it also had its origin in the old, desert life, when field products were almost entirely unknown, and the only true sacrifice consisted of the best of the sheep. From this standpoint field products constituted an insufficient and unworthy sacrifice. For this reason the story, written entirely from the nomad point of view, condemns the sacrifice of Cain and approves that of Abel.

But although a folk-tale in origin, there runs through this story, as through the folk-tales already considered, the dominant, religious spirit of Judaism. In its present form the story deals primarily with the problem of brotherhood. Its thought is summed up in Cain's question, "Am I my brother's keeper?" He had expected a negative reply. But to his utter surprise and consternation the answer came back, if not expressed directly in words, yet fully implied in God's dealing with him, "You are your brother's keeper, and are responsible for his life and welfare and happiness". This is Judaism's unvarying answer to this eternal, universal question, and this answer makes this story for us more than a mere folk-tale, as it was at first; it makes it pulsate with Jewish life, thought, and belief.

To a certain extent even primitive peoples have answered this question in much this same way, that man is his brother's keeper, provided, however, that that brother be actually of one's own flesh and blood. Brotherhood was originally limited to members of the clan or tribe. And even in this twentieth century the conception of brotherhood has seemingly developed but little beyond national and denominational lines. Men are still held far apart by racial, national, or religious differences. Competition is an approved principle in modern economic life. And often, for little or no cause, ties of flesh and blood are severed at a stroke. In the social life of many peoples, and in our own social life today, brotherhood is often held in light esteem

In significant contrast, Judaism has advanced a positive conception of brotherhood and brotherly guardianship. It holds that we are our brother's keeper in the most literal sense; that we are responsible, not only for his life, but likewise for his welfare, happiness, and opportunity for development. In the first place, it has affirmed this idea in relation to the real family life. The family and the home in Israel have always been institutions whose sanctity paralleled in every respect that of the Temple itself. In the Jewish home parents and children, brothers and sisters, have been bound together by the closest and most indissoluble ties, until the Jewish home and Jewish family life have become proverbial. Our history is rich in stories of brotherly devotion.

Brotherhood has always meant more to the Jew than to all other peoples, mutual love and tenderness, responsibility and guardianship, opportunity and cooperation.

A well-known story of the rabbis strikingly illustrates this Jewish conception of brotherly love. There were once two brothers, who possessed adjoining fields, which they had inherited from their father. One year the crops were bad, and famine and starvation threatened. One night, as he lay upon his bed, the older brother thought to himself, "My brother is younger than I, and needs his strength more". So he rose and went to his field, and took of his sheaves and put them in his brother's field. That same night the younger brother, lying upon his bed, thought to himself, "My brother is older than I, and married, and his needs are greater than mine". So he, too, arose and took of his sheaves, and put them in his brother's field. In the morning each found to his surprise, that in some mysterious way the sheaves, which he had put in the other's field, had returned whence they came. The next night the incident was repeated, and again on the third night. But on this night it happened that the two brothers went out to their fields at the same time. When they saw what each was doing, they kissed each other and wept for joy. And the act was so pleasing to God, that later the field, sanctified by the love of the two brothers, was deemed worthy to become the site of the great and beautiful Temple of Solomon.

In the second place, Judaism has applied its conception of brotherly love to all Israel. When the sons of Jacob went down to Egypt to buy corn and stood before their brother Joseph, whom they had wronged, they did not recognize him, although he knew them. Nevertheless, when, in order to test them, he pretended to believe that they were spies, and roughly asked them who they were, they unwittingly gave an answer which expresses an eternal truth. "We thy servants are twelve brethren", they said, "the sons of one man in the land of Canaan" (XLI, 13). Ever since, the truest name and proudest title by which the Jewish people has been called, and has delighted to call itself, is *b'nai yisrael*, "Children of Israel". All Israel are brothers, the rabbis taught, bound together by the closest ties of common ancestry, fellowship, and love. Upon each Israelite rests the obligation of caring for his Jewish brother, and of promoting his happiness and opportunity for full and right living. After the destruction of the Temple at Jerusalem by the Romans in 70 C. E., the victorious general Titus carried away as captives hundreds of thousands of Jewish youths and maidens, and sold them as slaves in all the great markets of the world. So many there were that the market was glutted, and the price of slaves fell to a fraction of what it had been before. Sad indeed was the fate in store for them. But at least wherever fellow-Jews dwelt, these miserable slaves were at once bought up by their devoted coreligionists and given their freedom.[1] That was true Jewish brotherhood.

Similarly, through all the centuries, when persecution and oppression, the like of which the world has never known, have been Israel's lot, Jews have stood close together in the firm conviction that they were all truly brothers, upon each of whom rested responsibility for the protection, welfare, and happiness of those brothers, less fortunate or more oppressed than they. Even today we Jews have the reputation of caring for our weak and unfortunate and needy far more systematically, thoroughly, and generously than any other people. Nor do we call it "charity", for the Hebrew language and the Jewish religion have no term which quite expresses the thought of this word. We call it *tsedakah*, "justice", and we voice thereby the significant Jewish thought that our brethren have an inalienable and just claim upon

---

[1] Graetz, *History of the Jews* (English translation), II, 311f.

us for help and support in distress. The conviction that we are our brother's keeper has become deeply ingrained in the Jewish consciousness and the Jewish character, and is a guiding principle in much of our Jewish life today.

And in the third place, in the course of its historic and religious unfolding, Judaism has come to realize and proclaim an even broader and grander conception of brotherhood. It was born in the thought first expressed by the prophet Malachi,

> Have we not all one father?
> Hath not one God created us? (Malachi II, 10.)

Judaism has expanded this thought far beyond what even the prophet himself conceived, for it has declared that if all men have one Father, then, be they who they may, all men must truly be brothers. The conception of universal brotherhood, which is today beginning to enter somewhat into the social, economic and political life of nations and of mankind, is one of Judaism's priceless gifts to the world. Persecuted by almost all peoples among whom he came to dwell, driven from place to place, from city to city, and from nation to nation, often denied where to lay his head even for a night, the Jew has nevertheless persisted in his conviction of the universal Fatherhood of God and the universal Brotherhood of Man. And he has boldly declared through all the ages, that despite racial, social, or religious separation, despite warfare, bloodshed, and oppression, all men are created in the image of the one, universal God, and are therefore bound together by ties too strong to be broken even by warfare, enmity, and hatred. This message of universal brotherhood, peace, and love, first realized by the Jew, and proclaimed by him to all the world, must become the saving principle, which will eventually cause the disarmament of nations, and bring all men to feel that they have more to bind them together than to separate them, and that they can realize the true ideal of life, the true purpose of existence, only when they come to believe, and to live their belief, that we are all our brother's keeper. The Psalmist has truly said,

> Behold how good and how pleasant it is
> For brethren to dwell together in unity!
> For there the Lord commanded the blessing,
> Even life forever.

Another significant thought is suggested by v. 7 and by the outcome of the story. The verse itself is difficult of exact translation. The words, "shall it not be lifted up?" are a pure guess at the possible meaning of a Hebrew word in the sentence, which, as it stands, is corrupt and absolutely untranslatable. It is probably as good a guess as any other. However, the general meaning of the verse and its context seems clear. God chides Cain for his unwarranted jealousy of his brother, and says to him, "If thou doest what is right, shalt thou not receive reward from the Lord? And if thou dost not do what is right, then sin lieth in wait for thee, and its desire is for thee to overcome thee. Nevertheless thou mayest gain the mastery over it". It is the thought of the story of the Garden of Eden in a somewhat new dress. Man is endowed by God with the power to choose between good and evil. And not only has he this power, but sooner or later he is forced in some way or other to make this choice. Already as little children there comes to us the compulsion to choose between good and evil, between obedience and disobedience, between righteousness and sin. Some choose the right, and ever thereafter choosing the right becomes a little easier. And at last, if only they train themselves carefully and steadfastly to choose only the right and to shun all wrong, doing the right becomes a part of their nature. They have gained the mastery over the inclination to sin, and reward from God is sure to be their portion.

Others, alas, choose the wrong. And in time, as we have learned the earthly nature within them prevails completely, and they sink to the level of the beasts of the earth. As the verse says, sin lies in wait for them, crouching at their very door, as it were, and its desire is constantly for them to overcome them. At last it gains its end. If we persistently choose the evil, and yield to the allurement of sin without a struggle, as some do, we lose at last all power to choose the good, and become completely creatures of evil and sin. Rabbi Akiba, one of the wisest of Israel's ancient teachers, used to say, "At first sin is like a thread, which can be snapped with but the least effort. But in the end it becomes like a cable, which can never be broken". And another teacher, Rabbi Isaac, used to say, "Sin is at first only the guest; in the end, however, it becomes the host".

The truth of these adages is well exemplified by the story of Cain. He began by choosing the wrong, and envying and hating his brother, just because Abel's sacrifice had proved more acceptable to God. And he ended by killing his brother, the most awful crime known to man. Sin had triumphed over him, and he was completely in its power. He had hearkened to the call of the earthly nature within him; he had acted as the beasts themselves act when they prey upon one another, and he had sunk therefore to the very level of the beasts. In consequence he was driven out from the habitations of men, and lost all human companionship. The hand of every man was against him, as against a feared and hated beast. By his own act he was doomed to wander ceaselessly, a fugitive and an outcast, up and down the earth, never safe, never at rest, never daring to pause for even a moment, with the mark of the sinner and the beast upon him, and fearing for his life before every man. Such is the fate of the sinner ever, and sooner or later his sins are sure to be visited upon him by God.

And some there are, and most of us are of this class, who hesitate and vacillate, who choose now the good and now the evil. Sometimes the voice of God within leads them to choose the right; and sometimes they hearken to the call of their earthly natures and choose the wrong. How is it with them? This life may be likened to a beautiful park, in which God has established two roads. The road on the left seems at first to lead straight ahead, and to be broad and firm and easy to travel. And the other road on the right, seems narrow and insecure under foot and forbidding, and it is impossible to look far down it and determine whither it leads. Between the two roads, high up where all may read, is the warning sign, "Turn to the right". But the road on the left seems much the better and pleasanter and more inviting, and most people disregard this sign, if they see it at all, and take the broad and easy path. Soon, however, they realize that the path is not straight, that it curves away to the left, farther and farther from the narrow road. And it becomes ever harder under foot, and those who tread it grow foot-sore and weary. It becomes narrow, too, and overgrown, and brambles and briars on the wayside snatch at the tired wanderers, and pierce and tear and wound. Very soon the wise and clearsighted begin to think of the other road on the right. Luckily for them, every now and then paths appear on the right side, each with the sign, "Turn to the right". And one by one the wise turn aside into these paths, and at last regain the narrow and straight road. Only the blind and the weak, and those who are too lazy or too stiff-necked, refuse to turn aside. And with each step their road becomes darker and narrower and more painful, and it ends at last in destruction and punishment for all who persist in it.

The paths which lead to the right are the only hope for those who, despite the first warning sign, enter upon the wrong road. At first there are many such paths, and even though a false start has been made, it is still no very difficult thing to "turn to the right". Gradually, however, the paths become fewer and farther apart, and longer and harder to travel, as the broad road bends ever farther to the left away from the true and straight road. At last they cease altogether, and those who still continue in the crooked way are hopelessly lost. Yet up to the very last path it is possible to depart from the evil way and "turn to the right". It means hard and bitter struggle and much time lost for having strayed from the true course, but at last we can win to the straight road and to true happiness, and can attain the goal of usefulness and blessing which God has appointed for all existence, if only we persist in our struggle and steadfastly choose the right. Sin will overcome us at last, if we yield weakly to it. But so long as we struggle, we may still gain the mastery. The paths are repentance, acknowledgment of sin, self-abasement, atonement and divine forgiveness. All these lead back to the right road, the way God has meant that mankind should tread. The rabbis said, "He who acknowledges his sin and humbles himself in this world, will not be put to shame in the world to come". Truly, if we choose the right and do well, we shall receive reward from the Lord; but if we do not do well, then sin croucheth at the door, and for us is its desire, and it must at last overcome us. Then we will be like Cain, and his fate will be ours.

But even this by no means exhausts the teaching of Judaism in regard to sin and punishment, and repentance and forgiveness.

NOTES

The above outline presents two distinct and independent teachings of Judaism, that of human brotherhood, and that of the possibility of mastery over the inclination to sin.

V. 3. Each brings a sacrifice of his own calling, Cain of the produce of his fields, and Abel of the firstlings of his sheep. That Abel's sacrifice is accepted and Cain's is not, is, of course, due to the nomad standpoint from which the story was written, that the life of the shepherd is more natural, better and more pleasing to God than that of the farmer, and consequently the shepherd's sacrifice is better than the farmer's.

Various answers have been given to the question, why was Abel's sacrifice pleasing to God and Cain's not? They are, of course, all the product of fancy. The customary answer is that Abel offered his sacrifice gladly, while Cain's was given grudgingly, or that Cain gave promiscuously, while Abel gave his best. There is, of course, absolutely no basis in the Biblical story itself for any such justification.

V. 7. As every one knows, printing is a comparatively modern invention. Before it all books were copied by hand. In consequence not only were books, or rather manuscripts, rare and precious, but they were also quite likely to contain many errors, due to inexact copying or other causes. Even today in copying we frequently omit a letter or misread a word or overlook an entire sentence, and thus mistakes creep into our copy, which can be corrected only by careful and minute comparison with the original. In ancient Israel similar conditions obtained. In copying manuscripts scribes were only too liable to err. Nor did they always exercise sufficient care in copying and correcting. Mistakes once made, were necessarily perpetuated in copies made from the defective manuscript. In consequence more or less numerous mistakes exist in the Hebrew text of all the books of the Bible. Those books, which for one reason or another were regarded as least sacred, and were accordingly copied least frequently and with least care, as for example the Books of Samuel and Ezekiel, contain the most mistakes, or, as it is generally stated, their Hebrew text is most corrupt. On the other hand, the books which were considered most sacred, the Torah for example, were not only copied most frequently, but also with the most scrupulous care; in consequence they were subject to the least liability of error and to the greatest possibility of correcting errors by comparison with other manuscripts. Therefore, while here and there some mistakes do occur in their text, they are nevertheless the least corrupt of all the books of the Bible. Not infrequently the nature of the mistake can be readily discerned from the context or in other ways, and it can be corrected. Quite often, too, with the help of parallel passages in the Bible, or by retranslating the very oldest translations of the Bible back into Hebrew, the original text can be recovered. Occasionally, however, all these established, scientific methods fail. And while, for one reason or another, ungrammatical Hebrew for example, or lack of proper context, we can not fail to recognize that the Hebrew text is corrupt, we are totally unable to amend the text, or even to guess with any degree of certainty what the original reading and meaning may have been. This explanation will apply to a small number of such hopelessly corrupt and untranslatable passages, with which we shall be compelled to deal. V. 7 is such a passage.

V. 9. Notice the cleverness of both question and answer. It indicates the true artist's hand.

V. 10. At the bottom of this verse lies the conception of blood revenge. In the desert the law of blood revenge is the fundamental principle of social life. If a member of one family or clan or tribe has been killed, some member of the family, clan, or tribe of the murderer must be killed in his stead. Otherwise, it was thought, if no blood were shed or no vengeance taken, the soul of the murdered person could not rest, but must torment the surviving relatives until the proper blood revenge was exacted. This is the thought underlying the words, "The voice of thy brother's blood crieth out to Me from the ground". This is additional evidence of the nomad origin and basis of the story.

This practice of blood revenge our ancestors brought with them out of the desert into their settled life in Palestine. But as the years passed and their civilization developed they gradually outgrew the original, cruel practice. The custom arose of imposing a fine upon the murderer or his family, and also of distinguishing very carefully between intentional and unintentional murder. Where the killing was clearly unintentional, provision was made for the slayer to flee to a city of refuge, and thus go unpunished (Numbers XXXV, 11-34; Deuteronomy XIX, 1-13). But where it could be proved through competent witnesses that the killing had been premeditated, the murderer was executed, under the supervision of the proper authorities, by the relatives of the murdered man.

It can readily be seen from this what a grave and often malicious misrepresentation it is, to say that Judaism has always insisted upon the principle of eye for eye and tooth for tooth. This was merely a natural and necessary stage of moral and social evolution through which Israel, like all other peoples, once passed. Judaism, as we all know, has advanced far beyond this original principle of retribution. Certainly every Jew should know how to refute this ignorant and unjust charge, whenever made.

V. 11. In consequence of the curse the soil becomes immediately unproductive and ceases to respond to Cain's tillage. This is, of course, comparable to the effect of a blessing (cf. note to I, 20).

V. 14. The Hebrew word for soil, *adamah,* means "tilled ground" as contrasted with the desert or the wilderness.

The question is often asked, if Cain and Abel were the first children of the first man and woman, why need God have placed the sign upon Cain's forehead to warn anyone against killing him? This is merely a beautiful story, and may well therefore be unclear, or even self-contradictory, in some of its details, The same answer may also be given to the very common and troublesome question, who were the wives of Cain and Abel? The rabbis had the tradition that each had married his twin sister, and that this was one of the causes of Cain's jealousy of his brother. But there is no Biblical basis at all for this tradition.

Vv. 16-24 contain ancient material, for the most part genealogical in character, which has absolutely no connection with the Cain and Abel story. The picture of Cain, living with his wife and begetting children, and even building the first city, and consequently dwelling among men, accords but ill with the preceding picture of Cain, the child of the first pair of mortals, and the murderer of his brother, who was driven out by God from association with other men. It is patent that these verses come from some different source. They have a decided cultural interest in that they seek to account, in true folkloristic manner, for the origin of three of the most primitive occupations or modes of life, viz. the nomad graziers, musicians, and blacksmiths.

The mention of just these three occupations, and the silence of the passage as to all other occupations, are interesting and significant. Clearly the traditions recorded in these verses sprang from a social environment in which these were the chief modes of life, and other occupations were either unknown, or of altogether minor importance. Unquestionably this was the desert, nomad environment, from which, we have learned, the folk-tales of the garden of Eden and Cain and Abel stories also sprang. Among the Beduins of the Arabian Desert, still today as in ancient times, herding of camels, sheep, and goats is the chief source of livelihood. Furthermore they frequently have clan or tribe bards or rhapsodists, who, on every suitable occasion, sing or chant the heroic deeds of the tribe. And at frequent intervals there come to them itinerant blacksmiths or tinkers, members of outcast tribes of ill repute, who mend their kettles or other metal utensils, or even make new ones, in return for food or other similar compensation.

V. 16. Since, according to this verse, the land of Nod is to the east of Eden, it follows that here also Eden is located in the extreme west; cf. note to III, 24.

Vv. 23f. These verses contain a fragment of a very ancient poem, sometimes known as "The Song of the Sword". The meaning of the verses is very obscure. Many interpretations have been suggested, but all purely hypothetical and fanciful, and without the slightest basis of fact. The verses probably refer to some old tribal myth or legend which has otherwise been lost entirely.

V. 26. "Then men began to call upon the name of the Lord"; these words imply that with the first generation after creation the true worship of the God of Israel under His own proper name actually began. Other and contradictory accounts of the time and manner of the beginning of the worship of the God of Israel are found in other parts of the Bible.

IV

THE FLOOD

(Genesis VI-IX)

Noah was in his generations a man righteous and wholehearted; Noah walked with God.   (Genesis VI, 9.)

Have I any pleasure at all that the wicked should die? saith the Lord God; and not rather that he should return from his ways, and live?   (Ezekiel XVIII, 23.)

Read Isaiah LV, 6-9.

It has been said by eminent scholars that the thought of a great flood which once swept over the entire earth, and from which only one human pair escaped, to become the progenitors of a new human race, is one of the most common and universal motives of mythology. A great German scholar has shown in a well-known book,[1] that almost all primitive peoples had a flood-myth in some form or other. Our ancestors were no exceptions to this rule. The story of the flood is for many reasons one of the most interesting in the entire Bible.

A number of apparent difficulties exist in the Biblical narrative. One verse (VI, 19; cf., also VII, 15), tells that two of every kind of animal were brought into the ark, while a verse somewhat later (VII, 3), puts the number at seven pairs of every clean, and one pair of every unclean animal. Now the flood is represented as lasting forty days and forty nights (VII, 12, 17; VIII, 6), and again as continuing for exactly one year. Other, though not quite so

[1] Hermann Usener, *Die Sintflutsage.*

obvious, contradictions are also present. From this it may
be inferred that in ancient Israel more than one version of
this flood story existed, just as was the case with other
Biblical stories. The present narrative really contains details
taken from more than one of these ancient versions, and not
perfectly harmonized.

More significant is the fact that this story, like the creation story in Genesis I, has a striking parallel in Babylonian
literature. The Babylonian story told that one of the great
gods, En-lil, enraged at the inhabitants of a certain city, determined to destroy them with a flood. But another god,
Ea, revealed the impending doom to Ut-Napishtim, and bade
him, in preparation for the flood, build a ship, the exact
dimensions of which he disclosed unto him. Just before the
flood began, Ut-Napishtim led into the ship all the members
of his family, sailors to work the ship, and animals of every
kind. Ea himself closed up the ship after all had entered.
The storm raged for six days, so frightfully that all living
creatures perished, and even the gods were terrified at the
destruction they had caused, and which they were powerless
to end. But on the seventh day all was still; the ship floated
alone upon the face of the water. After twenty-four hours
a little island appeared. The ship grounded fast upon the
top of a high mountain. After seven days a dove was sent
forth, but soon returned. Later a swallow was sent forth,
but it, too, returned. At last a raven was sent forth, and
did not return. Thereupon Ut-Napishtim led forth all the
occupants of the ship. A sacrifice was offered, about which
the gods swarmed greedily like flies. En-lil was pacified by
the other gods, and finally bestowed upon Ut-Napishtim and
his wife the blessing of eternal life.

The similarity between this Babylonian myth and our
Biblical story is striking. Clearly one is borrowed from the
other. And since the Babylonian story is the older, it must

be that our Biblical story is borrowed from the Babylonian original.

Actually, however, the points of similarity between the original Babylonian version of the flood-story and the Biblical version are of less significance than the numerous points of difference. Since the Biblical story is borrowed from the Babylonian, these points of difference were more probably purposed than accidental. They must have been introduced into the Biblical story deliberately, in order that it might voice certain vital and fundamental Jewish truths.

The first essential difference is in the conception of the Deity. The Babylonian gods are many; they are depicted in gross and anthropomorphic manner; they are subject to outbursts of anger, are powerless to control the storm which they have caused, and are even terrified by it; too late they regret the evil consequences of their ill-considered act; and they swarm like flies greedily about the sacrifice. In direct and significant contrast, the God of the Bible is only one, supreme, all-wise and all-powerful, sublime and spiritual. In the Babylonian story the ship is manned by sailors and helmsman. But in the Biblical story the ark floats along, cared for only by God, and in no danger of foundering, guided by His providence, that at last His wise and loving purpose might be fulfilled.

But one difference is significant above all others. The flood is brought by the Babylonian gods and all mankind is destroyed merely because one god has been personally angered by the people of a single city. Only through the favor of another god do one man and those with him escape. In marked contrast, the Biblical story depicts the increasing sinfulness of mankind, despite God's purpose of good. Only after waiting patiently for ten long generations in the hope that mankind would repent of its evil, and only when, at last, convinced of the total and hopeless corruption of the human race, does God, in sorrow, determine upon their destruction. But the one man who does not merit the common fate, him alone with his family God saves.

"Noah was in his generation a man righteous and wholehearted; Noah walked with God." Thus the Bible characterizes the hero of the flood-story, and at the same time contrasts him with the rest of his generation. "Noah walked with God". In this simple phrase the entire Jewish scheme of life is summed up. God has placed us here on earth, we have learned, for a definite purpose. He has endowed us with rich gifts and powers, and has bidden us use these to fulfil the purpose of existence. If we obey, then we live as God has meant that we should live, and mankind is blessed by our living. Such living the Bible calls walking with God, treading the path of life which He has ordained.

To turn away from God and to cease to walk with Him and in His path is rebellion against God and defiance of His law of life. The Hebrew verb for to turn away is *sur.* The noun derived from this verb-stem, *sarah,* means rebellion, iniquity, sin. But this is not the end. Though we may have departed far from God and His way, and be sunk deeply in sin, still we are not hopelessly lost. We can still return to God, and once more tread His path and walk with Him. The Hebrew verb for to return is *shuv,* and the derivative noun, *t'shuvah,* means returning or repentance. And that, Judaism teaches, is all that repentance is, a returning to God, seeking Him out in deep contrition, and beginning once more to walk with Him, with the firm resolve in our hearts never again to turn away from His path. No matter how far we may have strayed, we can still return to Him if we will. Ever His pardoning love reaches out to us, for He is a God of justice, yes, but a God whose justice is tempered by love and mercy and the desire, not to punish, but to forgive. As the prophet Ezekiel said, "Have I any pleasure at all that the wicked should die? saith the Lord;

and not rather that he should return from his ways, and live?"

Such is our Jewish teaching of life and sin and repentance and divine forgiveness, based upon our knowledge of God's goodness and love, His all-wise purpose for men, and His absolute justice in dealing with men. This is the fundamental Jewish truth which the Biblical flood-story was made to convey, and which shows its vast spiritual superiority over its Babylonian original.

Beautifully illustrating God's love and His desire for the repentance, rather than the death, of His sinning children, the rabbis amplified the Biblical story by relating that God had announced the flood to Noah one hundred and twenty years before it began. So Noah, at God's bidding, planted a forest, from which in time he might build the ark. When the people gathered round and asked what he was doing, Noah told of the impending flood and urged them to repent and live righteous lives, that God might forgive them, and perhaps not bring the flood; for God is truly, as the Bible says, "merciful and gracious, long-suffering, and abundant in goodness and truth." (Exodus XXXIV, 6.) But they only laughed at Noah and his words. Years passed and the trees grew big and strong. Noah continued to urge the people to repent, but still they laughed and mocked and persisted in their evil ways. At last Noah began to cut down the trees and build the ark. With only his three sons to help he labored on, believing firmly in God's word, while the people scoffed more loudly than ever. Soon the ark was completed and Noah and his family and the animals entered. Seven more days God allowed, as the final opportunity for the people to repent. Though the clouds were dark and lightning flashed, they refused to believe or to cease from their sinful conduct. But when the flood began and the water rose higher and higher, they crowded about the ark, and in fear and anguish declared that now they believed and repented

and were sorry for their past, and begged to be taken in.
Thus sinners do always when the consequences of their sin
at last come upon them. But all in vain; God Himself had
closed up the ark, and it was not to be opened until the flood
had ceased. As the waters rose higher and higher, the
people in despair ascended the mountains. Soon, however,
the highest summits were covered and all living creatures
without the ark perished, and the race of sinners came to
an end.

But the one righteous man in that generation, the one man
who walked with God and lived the life He intended that
man should live, and who tried by word and example to
lead others to righteousness, him and his family God kept
alive to become the parents of a new and better and more
righteous race. With him He established His covenant, and
sealed the covenant with His bow, the rainbow which shines
so beautifully in the sky, when the bright sun breaks through
and scatters the dark clouds, whose ends seem to rest upon
the earth, but whose arch spans God's heaven. Thus the
rainbow, which bridges heaven and earth, tells us that although we live on earth, we may still, through righteousness,
walk with God. It bids us hope and rejoice, for God's covenant is with us, too, if only, like Noah, we strive to be
righteous and wholehearted in our generation.

The fundamental Jewish principles expressed in the story are
accordingly, God's justice and love, the life which He has ordained
that man should live, the sin in departing therefrom, the evil and
sorrowful consequences of sin, and the possibility of repentance,
which God, in His love, ever holds out to man.

NOTES

V. This chapter records the tradition that ten generations elapsed
from creation to the flood. This tradition, too, was borrowed from
an ancient Babylonian myth, which told of ten successive kings,
the first men, who reigned in unbroken succession from creation to
the flood. The tenth and last of these kings was the hero of the

Babylonian flood story, just as Noah, the tenth in the Biblical list, was the hero of the Biblical flood story. The names of several of these mythical Babylonian kings seem to be identical with some of the names in the Biblical list; this is additional proof of the relationship of these two traditions. The Babylonian myth, furthermore, represents these kings as ruling for inordinately long periods, just as the Biblical tradition ascribes exceeding length of days to each of these pre-diluvian patriarchs. For further consideration of these legendary ages, cf. note to VI, 3 and VII, 6. The names of the majority of these patriarchs here are practically identical with those given in IV, 17-23. Undoubtedly these two passages record varying versions of one and the same tradition, at one time current in ancient Israel.

Vv. 21-23 contain a fragment of an ancient Israelite myth, of which Enoch was the hero. The three hundred and sixty-five years of his life suggest the three hundred and sixty-five days of a solar year. In all likelihood Enoch was a solar hero, and the Enoch story was a solar myth, similar in many respects to the solar myths of other ancient peoples. Later Jewish tradition speculated quite freely about this figure of Enoch and his translation to heaven. Eventually it made Enoch the hero of one of the earliest, best known and most important Jewish apocalyptic works, the Book of Enoch (cf. *Jewish Encyclopedia* V, 178ff.). This book represents Enoch as being taught by the angels, after he had been carried to heaven, all the mysteries of heaven and earth, of time and eternity.

VI, 1-4. These verses, in their present form and position, are intended to depict the increasing depravity of mankind. Actually they constitute the remains of an ancient myth, which must have been current in Israel, at a very early period. This myth must have told of marriages of the sons of the gods with human maidens, and of gigantic offspring therefrom. As v. 4 implies, these giants must have been famous for mighty deeds. Of these the ancient myth undoubtedly told in detail. The references remind forcibly of the Greek myth of the Titans. The ancient Israelite myth may well have been similar to that in many respects. The ancient myth, it is clear, told of many gods and their offspring. But since this conception was so diametrically opposed to the fundamental principles of later Jewish monotheism, the ancient myth was allowed to gradually disappear from Jewish tradition. We regret its loss, for naturally we wish to know as much as possible of the beliefs, mythology and folklore of our earliest ancestors. But at least we are grateful for these few references, which enable us to vaguely reconstruct one of the myths in which our fathers must have once delighted.

V. 3. Possibly there lurks in this verse some mythological idea comparable to the Greek legend of the four ages, gold, silver, brass and iron, and the reduction in each of the span of human life. Similarly the Bible tells that before the flood the ages of men ranged from the seven hundred and seventy-seven years of Lemech to the nine hundred and sixty-nine of Methuselah (V). From the flood to Abraham the ages were reduced from the six hundred years of Shem to the one hundred and forty-eight of Nahor (XI, 10-32). Abraham lived one hundred and seventy-five years (XXV, 7), Ishmael one hundred and thirty-seven years (XXV, 17), Isaac, one hundred and eighty years (XXXV, 28), Jacob, one hundred and forty-seven years (XLVII, 28), Joseph, one hundred and ten years (L, 26), Moses, one hundred and twenty years (Deuteronomy XXXIV, 7), and Joshua, one hundred and ten years (Joshua XXIV, 29). By the time of David, according to Jewish tradition, based upon Psalm XC, 10, the limit of human life had been fixed by God at seventy, or at the most eighty, years. The implication of the tradition is that each reduction of the span of life was due to the increasing sinfulness of man.

V. 4. *Nephilim* means etymologically, the fallen ones, or those who were cast down. Chiefly upon the basis of this etymology and this legend, the tradition of the fallen angels who were banished from heaven developed in Jewish lore, and passed thence into the beliefs and literatures of many peoples and creeds. This tradition inspired Milton's *Paradise Lost* in part.

V. 14. The Hebrew word *tebah,* generally translated ark, really means a kind of box. The same word is used for the little basket or box in which the babe Moses was placed (Exodus II, 2). The use of the word here shows how altogether deficient was our ancestors' knowledge of seafaring. The ark is here represented as a rectangular shaped box, divided into three stories, which floated with exactly half its volume in the water and half above. Cf. note to VII, 20.

Gopher was apparently a kind of wood used for building. The pitch was used to calk the seams.

V. 15. The cubit was apparently slightly less than two feet in length. Cf. *Jewish Encyclopedia*, XII, 483.

V. 21. By "food that might be eaten," is meant only herbs. According to I, 29, permission was at first given to men and animals to eat only herbs. Not until after the flood was permission given to eat flesh, with the restriction however that no blood might be eaten (IX, 3).

VII, 6. The great age here ascribed to Noah, and in V, to the other antediluvian patriarchs, is altogether mythical and theological, and without the slightest historical basis (cf. note to VI, 3).

V. 11. According to this verse and v. 24 and VIII, 4, 13, 14, the flood lasted just 365 days, i. e. one solar year. A lunar year consisted of approximately 354½ days, i. e. 12 x 29½+ days, the duration of one cycle of the four phases of the moon. The flood is said to have lasted altogether 365 days, from the 17th of the second month of one year, to the 27th of the same month of the next year. The Jewish calendar is reckoned according to the lunar year. But since there is a difference of 10, or more approximately, 10½ days between a solar and a lunar year, the Jewish calendar observes a leap year, consisting of one extra month of twenty-nine days, seven times in every cycle of nineteen years. This makes possible a very close harmonization.

The explanation of the reference to the "springs of the great deep and the windows of heaven" will be found in the note to I, 6. The implication is that the original state of chaos, before the land had appeared, as described in Genesis I, was for the moment reestablished.

V. 20. The tops of the mountains are covered fifteen cubits deep, i. e. just half the entire depth of the ark (cf. VI, 14-15, and note). The author means to say that the waters were just deep enough for the ark, submerged to exactly half its depth, to float over the tops of the highest mountains. Therefore at the very moment when the waters begin to sink, the ark rests fast upon the summit of the highest mountain.

V. 24. The waters increase for one hundred and fifty days, then run off for one hundred and fifty days, and sixty-five days are allowed for the earth to dry.

VIII, 1. The winds blow down upon the waters, and keep them from rising higher.

V. 3. Don't ask where the waters went to. Probably back into the subterranean ocean, whence they were said to have come. If children ask, tell them that our ancestors probably imagined that the waters ran off into the ocean, about which, not being experienced sailors or travelers, they had very vague and peculiar notions.

V. 4. Ararat is really a very high mountain in Armenia. Probably it was the highest mountain known to the ancient Semites. Probably, too, our ancestors had no definite idea of its location. Many travelers have ascended Ararat in search of the remains of the ark. Some, misled by vivid, orthodox imaginations, claim to have found remains, or traces. But the majority admit that there is nothing there.

V. 7. The statement that the raven was sent forth first and did not return, is probably not an integral part of the story proper, but must have come from some other version of the myth. For if the raven did not return, Noah would presumably have at once inferred that the waters had already abated, just as he did later when the dove did not return.

V. 11. The freshly plucked olive leaf showed that the waters had abated sufficiently for the olive trees, which do not reach a great height, and do not flourish in high altitudes, to be above water, and to be fresh and green once more.

In expounding the incident of the dove bringing back the olive leaf, the rabbis told that this olive leaf came from out the garden of Eden. For in God's mercy the gates of Paradise had been opened to the dove, and she had been free to pluck whatever she wished. And the wise rabbis asked, "If that were so, why then, did she not pluck something sweet and fragrant and precious, rather than the bitter, worthless olive leaf?" But questions like this they asked only to answer them themselves in their wisdom. And so they said, "She plucked the bitter olive leaf and brought it to Noah, to show him that better far is the bitter which cometh from God than the sweet and fragrant which come only from man".

V. 12. That the dove did not return, showed that she could feed and care for herself, and consequently that the waters had completely run off.

V. 22. The blessing implied in this verse is that the orderly course of nature and of life shall never be interrupted again in order to punish mankind for whatever sins it might commit in the future.

IX, 1-2. First God renews for Noah and his posterity the original blessing of fruitfulness, spoken over mankind at creation; cf. I, 28.

V. 3. Cf. note to VI, 21.

V. 4. The ancient conception was that the soul, and hence the life, dwelt in the blood (cf. IV, 10). Therefore the blood might not be eaten, for that would be equivalent to eating the actual life and soul of the animal. This is the basis of the old Jewish custom of slaughtering animals by cutting their throats, in order that all the blood might flow forth from the veins and arteries, and of carefully salting meat before it is cooked, in order to draw out all the remaining blood. In this way the command, not to eat the blood, is kept most punctiliously.

V. 6. This verse seems to justify capital punishment for murder.

V. 9. The fulfillment of the promise of the covenant in VI, 18.

V. 13. The rainbow is called God's bow. Probably this implied that the lightning was conceived of as His arrows shot from His bow. A vague, mythological conception seems to underlie all this.

The rainbow has played an important role in mythology, as is shown by the Greek legend of Iris, and the Scandinavian conception of the rainbow as the bridge to Walhalla, the abode of the gods.

Vv. 20-27. These verses have no connection at all with the flood story. Instead, much after the manner of IV, 17-26, they tell that Noah was the first man to plant a vineyard and to discover, through shameful experience the nature and evil qualities of wine. It is, of course, a typical folk-lore motive. On the basis of this Biblical tradition the rabbis conceived of the following interesting and suggestive story. They told that when Adam was driven forth from Eden, he carried with him a shoot of the vine which grew in the garden. Noah found this and determined to plant it. He was assisted in this task by none other than Satan himself. But before actually beginning the work, Satan first slaughtered in succession a lamb, a lion, a pig and a monkey and let their blood flow over the vine. When Noah asked what was the significance of this, Satan answered that each of these four animals symbolized the qualities of the vine. Before man drinks of its fruit he is innocent as a lamb. If he drinks of it in moderation he becomes strong and bold, like a lion. If he drinks too much, however, he becomes like a pig in thought and act. And if he drinks to excess and becomes intoxicated, he acts like a monkey, not knowing what he does, but behaving in silly and foolish manner, making himself the object of the raillery and contempt of all, and bringing shame upon himself, even as Noah did.

Vv. 25-27 are poetic in character. They attempt to describe the political and economic relations of the three different groups of peoples known to ancient Israel. They also account for the condition of subordination and practical servitude of the remnant of the original Canaanite inhabitants of Palestine after the Israelite conquest; cf. Joshua IX.

X. Upon the basis of this chapter the Caucasian race has been divided by scholars into three ethnic groups, named after the three traditional sons of Noah, the Semitic, the Hamitic and the Japhitic or Indo-Germanic, as it is more commonly called. This classification is more convenient than exact and scientific. We know that the Sabaeans (Sheba) and the Ethiopians (Cush), which vv. 6-7 include among the Hamites, really belonged to the Semitic group. On the other hand, the Elamites and Lydians were not Semites, despite the statement of v. 22. Israel is, of course, a Semitic people.

V

THE TOWER OF BABEL

(Genesis XI, 1-9)

Let us make a name. (Genesis XI, 4.)

A good name is rather to be chosen than great riches. (Proverbs XXII, 1.)

Read Micah IV, 1-4.

If the entire human race were descended from one man, as the Bible tells, and as many people still believe, how did it come to be divided into separate peoples and nations, and how did these come to speak different languages? These are interesting questions, which science is still asking today. This little story of the Tower of Babel contains what our ancestors conceived to be a satisfactory answer to these questions. The answer is, of course, in the form of a charming folk-tale. For, naturally, our ancestors knew nothing of science and could not study these problems scientifically nor give a scientific answer. But we are more thankful for this beautiful folk-tale, with its wealth of inspiring thought and spiritual truth, than we would have been for the most scientific and correct answer to these questions that might ever be given. In studying our Bible, we seek not natural science, but thoughts and knowledge of God and of the life He has meant that mankind should live. Of these this story is full.

The rabbis of old taught that for a long time after the flood, mankind lived happily together, in peace and harmony and love. Then they were only one people and spoke only one language. This language, the first language ever spoken, the language which even God and the angels used, so our fathers told, was Hebrew. Because of this, and also because our Bible was written in it, they called this language reverently the *l'shon hakkodesh,* "the holy language", or "the language of God". Many people today, who are not even Jews, are happy to study and to know Hebrew. And surely we Jews ourselves should be eager to know as much as possible of this beautiful and holy language of our fathers.

In time, as mankind increased in numbers, a false ambition to make a name for themselves, seized them. They began to build a great city and a tower so high that it would reach up to heaven, for they thought that thus they might get up to God. They labored on ceaselessly, and at last the city was finished, and the tower was rising higher and higher. But the higher the tower rose, so the wise rabbis told, the more the old spirit of love, harmony and peace disappeared. They were so eager to finish their task and win their great name, that they ceased to care for each other. If a man fell from the tower and was killed, no one grieved, for there were plenty more men, and they could not take time to stop. But if, perchance, a brick fell to the ground, then they grieved exceedingly, for some one must climb down to pick up the brick, since it was needed in building, and thus much valuable time was lost. Because of their selfish ambition and desire a brick now seemed to them more precious than a human life. Thus they came to put a false value upon things, and to misunderstand the purpose of life. Small wonder, therefore, that God was displeased, and determined to put an end to this state of things. So mankind was scattered over the whole earth, and came to form separate peoples and to speak different languages.

But at this very same moment, so the Bible implies, and so the rabbis also taught, God determined to create one people as His very own, who should stand nearer to Him than any other, and should speak His own holy language,

Hebrew. This people was Israel. But Israel was not to be God's chosen people, merely that God might love it better than all other peoples, and bestow upon it a larger share of favor and blessing. Israel was to be God's servant and messenger unto mankind, charged with the task of teaching all the world about God, and His life of peace and brotherly love and true worship. For this reason God taught Israel first the knowledge of Himself, and revealed to it His law. And if Israel, in turn, teaches this knowledge truly to mankind, and exemplifies by its life, by the life of every single Jew, the way in which God wants all mankind to live, then at last mankind will learn this knowledge, and come to live in accordance with God's will. Then once more, through Israel, peace and happiness and love will reign throughout the world. In accordance with His promise, instead of bringing another flood to destroy mankind when they became wicked, God now prepared to create Israel, to teach men the true way to live, and to bring mankind back to the right path, and thus save them from the evil consequences of their sin. And in time, through Israel the true unity of the human race will be once more restored, the unity which will rest upon a stronger and more enduring basis than considerations of mere common language and dwelling together, the unity of God's spirit in all men, which binds them together as one family, brothers, God's children, created in His image, and fills them with the sincere desire to walk in His way and to do His will.

Another beautiful thought, too, is contained in this story. The people imagined that by building a high tower they could actually get up to God, and thus make for themselves a name which would never perish. But they failed. Many people still have ambitions like this. They say to themselves, "I will make myself famous, so that my name shall be on every tongue, and people will call me 'Great' ". Others say,

"I will live a good life, free from all sin, in order that at last I may get up to God". Perhaps, in order that they may not sin, they go off and live by themselves, away from everybody else. But they always fail. Why? Have you ever, upon some beautiful, starry night, looked at the constellation known as the Great Bear, or the Dipper? Six stars you can see very plainly. But one star, the one which joins the handle to the cup, is not easily seen. You know it is there; but when you look at it directly you can not see it. But turn your gaze slightly, and look at one of the other stars nearby, and then, indirectly, you see the star you have been seeking, shining out as brightly and beautifully as the rest.

Just so it is with consciously trying to be great and to be good and to make a name for ourselves. With only this one purpose and this one ambition we can never succeed. We can never become great just by working to be great, for this is a selfish end, and no one can become great by being selfish. No one ever deserved to be called great merely because of what he did for himself. Only those men and women have been considered truly great by the world, who have found some great and good work to do, some work entirely unselfish, whose only purpose is to help others and to make them better and happier. And they have done this work, thinking only of the good and happiness they are bringing to others, and never of themselves or that they may be called great. Thus these noble men and women do much good and bring much happiness and blessing, until at last the world begins to call them "Great", or even better, "Good". Thus, and thus alone, do they make a name for themselves. But such a name is the finest reward which one can get, for it will never die; it lives on and on, even after we are no more, and mankind honors and loves our memory long, long after we have passed away. Therefore the Bible says truly,

The memory of the righteous shall be for a blessing (Proverbs X, 7).

and again,

A good name is rather to be chosen than great riches.

And in the same spirit the rabbis taught that the great man needs no tombstone to cause his name to be remembered. His wise words and his deeds of loving-kindness are his lasting monument. And they also said, "There are three crowns, the crown of the Torah, the crown of the priesthood, and the crown of royalty; but the crown of a good name surpasses them all".

And this story says even more, that we can not get up to God merely by trying to get there, by saying, "I will do nothing but think of God and pray to him day and night". For this would mean thinking only of self and one's own desires, and not of others. It would be just like the people who did not care if a man fell from the tower and was killed, but grieved if a brick fell down. Even the desire to get up to God becomes selfish and wicked, when we think only of self. Surely God did not intend that we should live in this way. Of course we must think of God a great deal, and pray to him for help and strength to do right, and thank Him for all the happiness and blessing He bestows upon us every day. But we must also do the work which He has intended us to do, and particularly the work which He has chosen Israel to do. By our words, and even more, by our lives, we must teach the world all that God's life on earth means, and thus help all men to live better and nobler. We can get up to God ourselves only by helping others, too, to get there. God does not want that only a few, but that all His children, whom He loves equally, should come close to Him. We can not be truly good just by going off by ourselves and never doing wrong Such lives are altogether useless and wasted, and miss entirely the purpose for which God has created them. Man is a social being, Judaism teaches, and must live in the world, among his brothers and for his brothers, to realize the purpose of existence. Being good means not only doing no wrong, but also, and even more, doing much that is right. We can do this right only by helping others, and never thinking of ourselves and the reward we may get. We work not for the reward, but for the good we can do and the happiness we can bring. As one of the wise teachers of old used to say, "Be not as servants who serve the Master in order to receive reward, but be as servants who serve the Master not in order to receive reward; and let the fear of God be upon you."

With this story of the Tower of Babel the first group of stories of Genesis comes to an end. As was stated in the Introduction, they are decidedly universalistic in character. They deal primarily with the question of the relation of all peoples whom God has created to Him, the one, universal God of all mankind. A logical and systematic unfolding of this general theme can be readily perceived. From the fundamental concept of the creation of the universe by God for a definite purpose of good, and the institution by Him of the two complimentary and proportionate phases of human life, work and rest, the theme advances to a more detailed consideration of the specific purpose of the creation and existence of man, and of the peculiar nature of man as fashioned by God. The Paradise story teaches that man is possessed of a divine as well as of an earthly nature; that right living means harkening to the call of the divine within, and by choosing the good and using the gifts which God has bestowed upon us rightly and for their destined end, to become co-laborers with God in the exalted task of realizing the purpose of good for which this universe was created. But why should man labor thus, ofttimes painfully and with great sacrifice? The answer, suggested by the Cain and Abel story, is because we are our brothers' keepers, because

man is a social being, has been created by God not to seek
his own selfish ends, but to live with his fellowmen, his
brothers, and share with them the general responsibility, and
labor with them for the common good. But, since man is
endowed with the power to choose between right and wrong,
what happens if man chooses the wrong, and not only refuses
to apply his powers and gifts to their appointed uses, but
even applies them deliberately to base uses? The flood story
answers that man is responsible to God for the good or evil
of his life, and that God punishes the evil even as He
rewards the good, for He is primarily a God of justice; but
His justice is tempered by mercy; therefore He punishes
only reluctantly and late, and constantly holds out to man
the possibility of repentance and forgiveness and renewed
right living.

Thus far these have been universal questions and problems. They deal with the relation of all mankind to God.
God has created all men for the same purpose of good, and
demands from all men certain positive standards of life and
conduct. There is a universal, ethical law for all men, and
even, in a way, also a certain universal ritual law, summed
up in the proper observance of the Sabbath and in the pro-
hibition of eating blood. All men must conform to these
laws.

But what if mankind forgets these laws, or does not
understand how to evaluate them correctly? The Tower of
Babel story hints that God has in His wisdom and love provided for even this contingency. He will not destroy sinning
mankind; instead He will raise up one little people, His
chosen people, whom He will train and discipline and prepare to receive a full and concrete statement of His law of
life, that this people may first live in accordance with this
law and come to understand it thoroughly, and may then
undertake its appointed task of bringing the knowledge of
this law to the rest of mankind. Thereby all men will come

to live the life which God has intended, and the purpose of creation and existence will be at last fulfilled. This little people is Israel; and through Israel, these stories of Genesis, and in fact the entire Bible, imply, that golden age shall at last be realized, so gloriously pictured by the inspired prophet:

In the end of days it shall come to pass
That the mountain of the Lord's house shall be established as the
      top of the mountains,
And it shall be exalted above the hills;
And peoples shall flow unto it.
And many nations shall go and say:
'Come ye, and let us go up to the mountain of the Lord,
And to the house of the God of Jacob;
And He will teach us of His ways,
And we will walk in His paths':
For out of Zion shall go forth the law,
And the word of the Lord from Jerusalem.
And He shall judge between many peoples,
And shall decide concerning mighty nations afar off;
And they shall beat their swords into plowshares,
And their spears into pruning-hooks;
Nation shall not lift up sword against nation,
Neither shall they learn war any more.
But they shall sit every man under his vine and under his fig-tree,
And none shall make them afraid;
For the mouth of the Lord of hosts hath spoken.

The next thought in the logical unfolding of the general theme is, of course, the election and training and disciplining of Israel for its great mission. As was stated in the Introduction, this is the thought of the Abraham cycle of stories. The Tower of Babel story, therefore, is not only the conclusion of the first group of the stories of Genesis, but it is also the connecting link between this first group of stories and the Abraham cycle. With this introduction we are prepared to consider the Abraham stories in detail.

NOTES

V. 2. "From the east", is a very obscure expression, the exact meaning of which can not be determined. It seems to imply that the starting-point of the migration was not Ararat, but rather Eden, which, according to II, 8, was situated in the extreme east. Cf. the note to III, 24.

Shinar, an ancient name for the Mesopotamian valley.

V. 3. In this valley stone suitable for building purposes is very scarce. In consequence bricks, made of clay, and usually burned, have always been used, even in the construction of the most magnificent structures of the ancient Babylonian empire. Asphalt or bitumen, which is very plentiful in that region, was quite commonly used for mortar in such construction. This is what is meant by "slime."

V. 4. It is frequently claimed that the reason for building the tower was that the people might have a place to which to flee, should God ever bring another flood. Actually there is no such implication in the Biblical story. There the purpose is clearly stated to have been to enable the people to make a name for themselves, and also to prevent their being scattered over the earth. Just how the latter purpose would be served is not stated.

V. 4. The idea of a tower with its top in heaven was probably based upon acquaintance with ancient Babylonian temples. These were generally built in the form of immense pyramid or step towers. They must have frequently reached a height of from two to three hundred feet. To the nomad of the Arabian Desert, accustomed only to tents, or to the lowest and meanest of hovels, these Babylonian temple towers must have seemed indeed to reach up to heaven. From this it may perhaps be inferred that this legend of the Tower of Babel had its origin in the days when Israel still roamed the Arabian Desert as nomads, and either itself beheld, or heard other nomads tell of these lofty Babylonian towers.

V. 5. According to this verse God dwells in heaven, but must come down to earth to see what is going on here. It is clear that at the time of the composition of this story, the conception of the Deity had not yet reached the full height of its eventual spiritual development in Israel.

V. 9. The etymology of the name, Babel, here is altogether incorrect. The name Babel is the same as that of the city, Babylon. This name was of course much older than the Hebrew language, and naturally can be explained correctly only from the Babylonian language. In Babylonian the name probably means "gate of the god", or perhaps better, "gate of heaven". The explanation of the name here is, of course, only a Hebrew folk-etymology, and entirely without historical basis.

Vv. 10-32. The purpose of this genealogy, and of that in V and IX, 28 and X, 1, is to trace the descent of Abraham, the traditional ancestor of Israel, from Adam, and particularly to show that Abraham, and therefore Israel also, were descended from the very first man in the direct line of the eldest son, and were, therefore, the very elite of mankind. This was a naive national conceit of ancient Israel.

For the ages of these patriarchs cf. note to VI, 3.

V. 28. Ur was a very ancient city in the extreme south of the Mesopotamian valley. It was the seat of one of the oldest Babylonian kingdoms and cultures. Numerous interesting and valuable Babylonian inscriptions have been unearthed there.

For the rabbinical tradition accounting for the death of Haran cf. p. 107.

V. 31. Haran was an important city in northwestern Mesopotamia, situated on the great highroad of antiquity which led from 'Egypt and the Mediterranean coast to Assyria and Babylon.

VI

THE CALL OF ABRAHAM

(Genesis XII, 1-9)

Be thou a blessing. (Genesis XII, 2.)

Ye are My witnesses, saith the Lord,
And My servant whom I have chosen. (Isaiah XLIII, 10.)

Read Psalm CV, 1-10.

With chapter XII begins the second portion of the Book of Genesis, which deals primarily with the questions of God's relation with Israel, and Israel's relation with the rest of mankind. What has been said in the Introduction in regard to this section of the Book (II, p. 19ff), need not be repeated. The reader is urged to review that portion of the Introduction carefully, and to keep the thoughts presented there constantly in mind, while studying the Abraham cycle of stories.

In the last lesson we learned that the rabbis of old told that when, after the flood, mankind once more became corrupt, instead of causing another flood, God determined to bring into the world one people, who should be, or become, wholly righteous, and to whom, therefore, He might reveal His law. This people He would take as His own, His servant, charged to teach to all the world the real meaning of His law and His life, and thus bring mankind to righteousness. Now we hear of God's call to Abraham, the progenitor of this people, to leave land and birthplace and father's house, and, accompanied only by his faithful wife, Sarah, and his nephew, Lot, to set out upon a long and weary pilgrimage. But while he did not know his journey's goal, nor the hardships in store for him, still he did know full well the reason for the journey and the purpose for which God had called him. It was that he might be a blessing. As we learned in the last lesson, being a blessing means not caring only for self, but serving others and forgetting self entirely. God even told him who these others would be. "In thee shall all the families of the earth be blessed". Unto all mankind he was to bring blessing.

Abraham was not the only man whom God called. We have already learned that He called Noah. We shall hear later that He called Moses, Samuel, Isaiah, Jeremiah, and many others. But this much we can see already, that when God calls anyone, it is always for something very important and very good, always that the person whom He calls may be a blessing unto others.

Many people imagine that God called people only long ago, in Bible times, but no longer calls people today. But surely they are mistaken. God calls people still today to be a blessing, though perhaps not in exactly the same way as of yore. He must have called Washington and Lincoln, and many other noble men and women, and they must have understood and obeyed, just as Abraham did.

In fact, we may be sure that He calls everybody in some way, and commands them to be a blessing. Only not everybody hearkens to His call. The Bible tells of one man, Jonah, whom God called to do a certain task, which was very hard, but which would have brought much good and happiness to many people. But Jonah thought only of himself and his own comfort, and of how difficult the work was, and what it would cost him. So he tried to run away to a distant country. But God brought him back and made him do the work anyway. But it could hardly have been done as well as if Jonah had done it willingly, in the same spirit as Abraham.

It is always best to do the work gladly, to hearken to
God's call at once, and to answer, as we shall learn later
that Abraham answered, "Here am I", that is, "Here am I,
ready to do Thy work". There is so much good to be done,
and men have so many needs to serve, that God really calls
to every one. He calls when we are little children, and He
continues to call throughout our lives, to do His work, whatever good we can, and thus be blessings to mankind. And
everyone can be like Abraham, if only he wills to be, and is
not too lazy and selfish.

But God's call was not to Abraham alone. It was not
just Abraham, the one man, through whom all mankind was
to learn about God, and was thus to be blessed, but the
whole people, Israel, Abraham's descendants. Abraham is,
as was said in the Introduction, the model and type of all
Israel. The words, "Be thou a blessing", were spoken quite
as much to all Israel, and therefore to every single Jew.
God has called all Jews at all times to be a blessing, to live
pure, noble and holy lives, and to teach the world, more by
example and influence than by actual words, what it means
to serve Him truly, and to live as He has meant that all
mankind should live.

> Ye are My witnesses, saith the Lord,
> And My servant whom I have chosen.

These words were spoken by God to all Israel through one
of His inspired prophets. They express fully and convincingly the truth of God's choice of Israel and the service
He has called Israel to do.

Israel's history, too, has been like that of Abraham in
many respects. We may be sure that it was no easy journey
upon which Abraham had to go, until he at last found rest
and peace in Canaan. It meant the sacrifice at God's command of all that he then held dear, native land and birthplace and father's house, all the loved ones at home, all the

companions of youth, all the ties of affection and loyalty, which are among the most precious things in life. It meant, also, journeying out at God's command, for no apparent reason other than that God had commanded, into an unknown and strange and, not improbably, hostile world, with no intimation of how long the journey would last, what obstacles would have to be overcome, and when, if ever, and where it would end. It was a sore test of Abraham's faith in God, and of his fitness for the mission of blessing for which God had called him. And Abraham stood the test.

To Israel, too, God's command came, almost two thousand years ago, to leave country and birthplace in Palestine, and wander out over the whole earth, not knowing whither it was going, knowing only that God had ordained this, in order that Israel might better be a blessing, and that through it all the peoples, among whom it came to dwell, might learn better the knowledge of God. Israel, too, has had to endure much upon this journey. It has suffered cruel persecution and misery, more almost than any other people that has ever existed. But like Abraham, it has never allowed its sufferings to turn it from its path. Israel, too, was strong in its perfect faith in God; it knew always that God was watching over it and leading it on, and that everything which befell it was in accordance with God's will and purpose for it. So Israel has been faithful throughout the centuries, and still today it is doing God's work. And we Jews should be proud and happy that God has called us as His servants, to bring blessing unto all mankind. Even though it is never easy to be a blessing, even though it must cost us dear, as it did Abraham and Moses and Jonah, and everyone else whom God has ever called and who has harkened to the call, still we should be proud and happy that we are Jews.

The knights of the middle ages had a significant watchword, *noblesse oblige*, "nobility obligates". It meant that they must conform to a loftier standard of conduct and morality than the average person. Things which the ordinary man might permit himself to do, were forbidden to them. Anything which was the least questionable, or had the slightest taint of immorality or impropriety, was beneath them. Whoever violated any of these principles, forfeited his knighthood, at least in theory, because he had, by his act already forfeited his claim to nobility.

So, too, with us Jews, "nobility obligates". In a very positive sense we are the spiritual nobility of the world, and ours is a proud heritage of honor. When the ancestors of the present great nations of Europe were still roaming their native woods as half-clad barbarians, unlearned in aught save the chase and war, our fathers had long since accepted God's law, had called the Bible into being, and had entered upon their glorious mission of justice, brotherhood, and peace, which is destined in time to redeem the world from the consequences of savage lust for war, bloodshed, and power. With us, even more than with the knights of old, "nobility obligates". We Jews may not do many things which others still allow themselves. Thanks to our three thousand years of spiritual training, and to the consequent deeper insight and knowledge which have come to us, we Jews should have, and do have, a higher standard and ideal of righteous and moral conduct than other peoples. This alone constitutes our all-sufficient title to the spiritual leadership of the world. But what we are not willing to live, we can not hope to teach. For this reason with us, too, "nobility obligates", or, much better and truer, "knowledge obligates". And he who will not live as a Jew should live, and thereby do his part in the great work of being a blessing, for which God has called all Israel, has truly forfeited his right to the name and privilege of being a Jew. But if only every Jew will live as Jews ought to live, in accordance with the sublime, spiritual teachings of Judaism, then surely the world must be greatly blessed through us, and must come in turn to honor the

Jewish people, and to bless the name of Father Abraham, through whom God's call first came to Israel.

Because Abraham was such a great and good man, very many well-known stories were told about him by the rabbis, in addition to those recorded in the Bible.

There is a charming story, which tells how Abraham came to worship one God. In those days people thought that there were many gods. They even made images, or idols, of wood, stone or metal, and foolishly believed that these were gods, who had made the universe, and had even made them. One evening Abraham was walking about just as the stars came out, one by one. He was struck by their beauty, and thought, "Surely these are the gods". But soon the moon rose, full and bright, and her radiance obscured the stars. Then Abraham thought, "No, this must be god". But at last the dawn came and the moon paled, and Abraham said, "Surely the moon can not be god, for its light has become dim and weak". Then the sun rose, majestic and glorious, and Abraham thought, "At last this is the real god". But at evening the sun sank, and once more the stars appeared. Then Abraham thought long and hard; and finally the truth dawned upon him, that none of these, beautiful though they were, could be god; that there must be some power of good and love behind all these, whose servants they were and whose law they obeyed, and this must be God. So he bowed down and worshipped the one God of all the universe. Then it was that God first called to him to be a blessing unto all mankind.

Thereupon Abraham began to teach the knowledge of the one, true God. At first he sought to teach his own fellow-townsmen. But this was a difficult task. His own father, Terah, was a maker and trafficker of idols. One day he left Abraham in charge of the shop, while he went out. A man came in to buy an idol. Abraham asked him, "How old art thou?" "Sixty years old", was the answer. "Alas", replied Abraham, "for the man sixty years old, who would worship an image made only yesterday". Realizing his folly, the man left the shop.

Soon a woman entered with a vessel of fine flour, which she gave to Abraham and bade him offer it as a sacrifice to those gods. Instead Abraham took a stick and broke into pieces all the idols except the largest. Into its hands he put the stick, and set the vessel of fine flour before it. Soon Terah returned. When he saw the damage, he stood aghast for a moment, and then asked in angry voice, "Who did this?" Abraham answered, "While you were out a woman brought this vessel of fine flour as a sacrifice to all these gods. But that big, greedy god there wanted it all for himself, so he took this stick and beat the others and broke them in pieces". At this Terah became furious. "What is this nonsense? Don't you know that these are only idols of wood and stone, and can not move?" Then Abraham calmly replied, "Let your ears harken to what your lips have said. If these are only idols of wood and stone, which can not even move, then what folly to think them gods and worship them!"

Thus Abraham taught, and gradually many began to understand. At last the news of Abraham's teaching came to the ears of Nimrod, the powerful and cruel king. He sent for Abraham and said, "If thou wilt not worship the gods which thy father makes, then worship the fire as I do". But Abraham answered, "Why not rather worship the water, which can quench the fire?" "Very well", replied Nimrod, "worship the water". But Abraham continued, "And why not then the clouds which contain the water; and why not then the wind which drives the clouds before it? No, I can worship neither fire, nor water, nor clouds, nor wind. I can worship only the one God, the Creator and Master of all these". At this the king became furious, and commanded that Abraham be cast into a great, fiery furnace, and that his brother, Haran, also be cast into the furnace with him. For Haran had been half persuaded of the truth of Abraham's words, and this was known to the king. Yet Haran did not yet trust in God completely. When Nimrod had commanded that Abraham be cast into the furnace, Haran had said to himself, "I will wait and see how this turns out. If Abraham's God saves him, then I will believe in Him and worship Him. But if not, then I will continue to worship the gods of my father".

So both were cast into the terrible furnace. But the fire could not harm Abraham. The ropes which bound him were burned away, but his flesh was not even scorched, and he walked about safe and unharmed in the midst of the fire. After three days the furnace was opened. To the surprise of all, Abraham came forth uninjured. He had been saved by God, because he trusted in Him. But Haran, who had not trusted, and was not ready to do God's will at all costs, him the fire had consumed completely. But even this did not open the eyes of the wicked king. He still sought Abraham's life, and the people, in terror of the king, dared not harken to Abraham's words. At last God commanded Abraham to journey forth unto the place which He would show him, and there begin anew his task of being a blessing to all the families of the earth.

NOTES

In this and the subsequent stories the name Abraham is used in preference to Abram, and Sarah to Sarai. The incident of the change of the names of Abram and Sarai, recounted in XVII, while interesting, has for us, on the whole, no deep religious significance. In ancient Israel, as among other primitive peoples, the name was regarded as an essential and inseparable part of a person or thing. Until it had received its proper name it did not fully exist (cf. note to I, 5). The change of Abram's name implies a radical change in his nature and personality, which makes him virtually a new being with a larger and more important role in life and new duties and obligations. He is no longer the simple Abram, but the great

Abraham, "the father of a multitude of nations" (XVII, 5). Likewise, in virtue of her correspondingly exalted position Sarai's name
is changed to Sarah, "princess" (XVII, 15). Similarly, in recognition of the great change which had come over him, by reason of
which he had become in truth a being altogether different from what
he had been before, Jacob's name was changed from Jacob, "the
deceiver", to Israel, "the champion of God" (XXXII, 29).

There is reason to think that this incident of the change of name
was not a part of the original Abraham story. It is not at all
essential to the main narrative. For this reason we use the name
Abraham throughout.

V. 1. The language here seems to imply that Haran was regarded by the author of this story as the birthplace of Abraham.
This, of course contradicts the statement of XI, 28-31 that Abraham
was born in Ur of the Chaldeans. However, we have had similar
contradictions in the Biblical narrative before, and need not be
disconcerted by this. Manifestly these two contradictory statements
are the work of two different writers.

V. 5. The words, "to go to the land of Canaan", or rather the
Hebrew of which they are the translation, were not a part of the
original story, but were inserted by some late writer. It is easy to
see that they spoil the point of the story. The story, in its original
form, told that Abraham obeyed God's command without knowing
whither he was going. He was led only by implicit faith in God.
As v. 7 clearly states, not until he had actually come to Canaan, to
the vicinity of Shechem, did God reveal to him that this was the goal
of his journey. This fact was perceived and admitted by the rabbis
of old, even despite the explicit statement of v. 5 that Abraham knew
from the outset that Canaan would be the end of his journey.

V. 6. In Palestine trees are not very common. In consequence
trees of unusual size and appearance have always been singled out
as landmarks. This tree near Shechem was particularly famous.
It is referred to again in Deuteronomy XI, 30. The name, *Moreh,*
means "teacher" or "oracle". The ancient Canaanites, who gave
this tree its name, must have thought that a god dwelt in it, and frequently communicated his will to mortals from there. Such a belief
was common among the Canaanites and also in ancient Israel; cf.
the story in II Samuel, V, 24.

V. 7. According to the ancient conception, an altar was indispensable for worship. V. 8 speaks of another altar which Abraham
built between Bethel and Ai, and XIII, 18 tells of a third altar

erected by Abraham in the grove of Mamre, where he finally took up his permanent abode. The Bible seems to imply that at every stage of his journey Abraham erected an altar unto God, in order to worship Him properly and to thank Him for His protection and blessing.

V. 8. "To call upon the name of the Lord," i. e. "to worship God," cf. XIII, 4.

V. 9. "Toward the South", literally, "toward the Negeb". The extreme southern portion of Palestine, which borders upon the desert, was known as the Negeb. It was in this district, in the vicinity of Beer-sheba, that the Bible represents both Abraham and Isaac as usually sojourning.

These verses tell that Abraham journeyed through the entire land of Palestine, from north to south, implying that thereby he established his claim to possess it, in accordance with God's promise.

Vv. 10-20 record an ancient tradition, parallel versions of which are found in XX and XXVI, 1-11. It is not absolutely essential to the Abraham story.

VII

ABRAHAM AND LOT

(Genesis XIII-XIV)

Let there be no strife between me and thee.   (Genesis XIII, 8.)

A soft answer turneth away wrath.   (Proverbs, XV, 1.)

Read Psalm XXXIV, 12-15.

We said in the last lesson that Abraham was a great man. He must have been very great to have heard the call of·God so plainly, and to have obeyed so promptly and so completely.   And the outcome of his hearing and obeying, the existence of the Jewish people and of our Jewish religion today, is conclusive proof of his greatness.

But this is not the only proof.   True greatness does not consist only in doing great things.   Opportunities to do great things come only occasionally, even to great people.   But the little things which must be done, and done right, come constantly to both great and small.   If a man should do a few big things well, but should fail in all the little things, we could hardly consider him truly great.   Perhaps the true test of greatness is the way a man does the little things.   If he finds them hard, or if they take too long, or if he hesitates too much, or does them in slip-shod manner, we may be sure that he will never be able to do great things.   But if he does the little things right and promptly, without doubt and hesitation, if he shows himself the master in little things, then we may believe that he will be equal to the big things when they come.

Thus we see that the great man must be always ready to

do the right thing in the right way. In childhood he must train himself, possibly with the help of loving and wise parents and teachers, to be always ready to do little things aright, until gradually it becomes a habit. Just as the pianist must first learn the position of the keys, but in time, through constant practice, his fingers unconsciously always strike the right key, so the person who has in him the making of a truly great person and a true gentleman, comes in time to always do the right thing in the right way, immediately, unhesitatingly, and almost without having to stop and think. It has become a part of his character. Perhaps just these many little things, rather than the few big things, furnish the best test of true greatness.

Just such a test, applied to Abraham, we read of in this lesson. And the way in which he stood the test shows how truly great he was. When his shepherds and those of Lot quarreled, he might have become angry. And when the time came to separate, he might have said, "I am the older, and you owe me very much already, for all the kindness I have shown you. Therefore I am entitled to the first choice". It would have been perfectly true, and Lot could not have objected. But it would probably have caused jealousy, hatred, and unhappiness between them. Abraham showed his true greatness in wishing to avoid this at all costs. Therefore he said, "Let there be no strife between me and thee". And knowing Lot as he did, he allowed him the first choice. Lot made a selfish choice, for he took the land which seemed the more fertile and desirable, and left to Abraham what he thought the poorer land. We shall see later that after all he had made a bad choice, and that Abraham's land turned out to be better.

Thus Abraham did the right thing and spoke the right word at just the right time. Thereby all strife and trouble were avoided, and he and Lot parted, not in anger, but in love. The story goes on to show how Abraham's love for

Lot continued thereafter, despite the latter's selfish choice. When Lot was taken prisoner, it was Abraham who rescued him. All this reveals the true greatness of Abraham. And it proves the truth of the wise proverb from the Bible,

A soft answer turneth away wrath.

Turning away wrath and working for peace are always characteristic of the truly great man. It is told of a certain rabbi of old, that he used to walk up and down before any person who had wronged him, in order to give that person a chance to ask pardon. Instead of giving way to anger himself, he sought to bring the other person to repent. In this he was great like Abraham. Of men like these the Bible wisely says,

He that is slow to anger is better than the mighty;
And he that ruleth his spirit than he that taketh a city.
(Proverbs XVI, 32.)

And the rabbis sagely remarked, "Who is a hero? He who subdueth his own evil inclination".

In this, as in everything else, Abraham is typical of Israel. Frequently we hear it said, "Israel's mission is peace". While this is by no means all of Israel's mission, none the less it is a very important part thereof. Peace is the basis of human brotherhood, which Judaism proclaims. Without peace there can be no fellowship nor brotherly cooperation in the work of the world. In the face of the jealousy, rivalry and hostility of the nations and races into which the human family is divided, it is Israel's task to herald unceasingly the principles of peace, brotherhood, cooperation and unity as the foundation of true living. Peace, Judaism teaches, is God's supreme blessing. The Bible makes the pursuit of peace the highest duty of life when it says,

Come, ye children, hearken unto me;
I will teach you the fear of the Lord.

Who is the man that desireth life,
And loveth days, that he may see good therein?
Keep thy tongue from evil,
And thy lips from speaking guile.
Depart from evil and do good;
Seek peace and pursue it.

In ancient times, and even still today, one Jew would greet another with the words, *shalom alecha,* "peace be upon thee", and the answering greeting would be, *alecha shalom,* "and upon thee be peace". And in departing from the house of God the priests would invoke the divine blessing upon the faithful worshipers, closing with the beautiful words,

The Lord lift up His countenance upon thee and give thee peace. (Numbers V, 26.)

And the pious Psalmist pictured the supreme good which can come to Israel and to all men, as the time when

Mercy and truth are met together;
Righteousness and peace have kissed each other.
Truth springeth out of the earth;
And righteousness looketh down from heaven. (Psalm LXXXV, 11-12.)

Such is the teaching of peace, which Israel, following the example of Father Abraham, has ever proclaimed to the world. And through this teaching all the children of the one Father must in the end be united into one loving family, even as God intended.

Again we find evidence of true greatness in Abraham's answer to the king of Sodom. He had done the right and fought for the weak, and had rescued Lot and the other captives, not thinking of reward, but only of duty. It was a rich reward which the king of Sodom offered, and many might think that Abraham was entitled to it, and might have taken it without compunction. But Abraham did not hesitate an instant. Of course he had no right to refuse the reward for the three allies who had accompanied him; they must speak for themselves. But for himself, he would take not so much as a shoestring. It was enough to know that he had done his duty, and had made people happy. No rewards could tempt him. It reminds us of the question asked in one of our most beautiful psalms,

> Lord, who shall sojourn in Thy tabernacle?
> Who shall dwell upon Thy holy mountain?

and the answer,

> He that walketh uprightly and worketh righteousness. (Psalm XV, 1-2.)

This is only a part of the answer given there. Yet we may be sure from what we know of Abraham already, and what we shall learn later, that he would be among those who may dwell in the tabernacle of God.

Above all else, these two stories give further proof of Abraham's fitness for the great mission upon which God had sent him. He had stood the test of unquestioning faith in God, the first indispensable requisite for one who would do God's work. But that was not enough. One can serve God only by serving fellowmen loyally and usefully, entirely forgetful of self, and without thought of reward for the performance of duty. The story of Abraham and Lot had proved that Abraham could sacrifice his own interests in order to preserve peace and love with his kinsman, and the story of Abraham and the king of Sodom had proved equally, that in the discharge of duty Abraham could not be swayed by considerations of personal interest and reward. He had stood these first three tests nobly. But they were not enough; other and more severe tests were to follow.

Stories very similar in character are told of one of the wisest and noblest of the ancient rabbis, Hillel. He was renowned throughout all Israel for his quiet, even, peace-loving disposition. He was fond of using the saying, "Be of the disciples of Aaron, loving peace and pursuing peace, loving all men and bringing them near to the law (of God)". One day, it is told, two men made a wager, one betting that he could make Hillel angry, and the other betting that he could not. It happened to be just before the beginning of Sabbath, and Hillel was bathing himself and preparing to welcome the Sabbath in true Jewish spirit. The man who had made the wager came to Hillel's house and called out, "Is Hillel at home?" Hillel heard and clothed himself and came down. "What is it, my son?" he asked. "I would ask a question; "why have the Babylonians such pointed heads?" It was a very foolish question, but the man asked it purposely, thinking that Hillel would resent being disturbed for such a trivial thing. But Hillel answered, just as if it were a wise question, "It is because they have no good physicians, my son". The man departed and Hillel went back to his bath. But soon the man returned and again called out, "Is Hillel at home?" Again Hillel dressed and came down. "I would ask another question; why have the men of Tadmor (a famous city in the desert northeast of Palestine) such narrow eyes?" "Because they live in the sandy desert (and the glare of the sun forces them to always keep their eyes half closed), my son". Again the man went away and Hillel returned to his bath. But a third time the man came with another silly question, and once more Hillel clothed himself and came down. "Why have the people of Africa such big feet?" "Because they dwell in a swampy country, my son", was the patient reply. Then the man said, "I would ask many more questions, but I fear that thou mayest become angry". At this Hillel sat down and said, "Ask all thy questions, my son". Then the man himself became angry and said in a loud voice, "Art thou indeed Hillel, whom they call the Prince? Well, may there not be many more like thee in Israel". In surprise Hillel asked, "Why, my

son?"   "Because thou hast kept thy temper and hast caused
me this day to lose ,four hundred zuz (an ancient coin)".
But Hillel calmly answered, "Better, my son, that thou
shouldst lose thy four hundred zuz than that Hillel should
lose his temper".

At another time while deep in study, Hillel heard a knock
at his door.   He opened and found a young, heathen boy
standing there, with an insolent smile on his face.   "Teach
me the law", he said, "while I stand on one foot.   If you
do, then I will become a Jew".   His purpose was, of course,
to mock at the Jewish religion and its teachers.   He had
already tried the same trick upon Shammai, another famous
teacher of the time.   And Shammai, not noted for patience,
had become very angry and driven the boy away.   Of course
this was just what the boy wanted.   But instead of becoming angry, Hillel looked at him kindly for a moment, and
then answered, "What is hateful unto thee thou shalt not
do unto thy neighbor.   This is the whole of Judaism; everything else merely explains it".   We see from their conduct
that both Abraham and Hillel did nothing unto their neighbors which was hateful unto themselves; that instead, they
truly loved their neighbors as themselves.   Thereby they
showed their true greatness.   Our religion bids us all do
just this, love our neighbors as ourselves, speak the soft
answer which turns away wrath, and makes for peace and
love and true happiness.   Thereby we shall each be doing
our part in fulfilling the mission of Israel, of being a blessing unto all the families of the earth.

NOTES

The picture of Abraham and Lot here is one of nomads rather
than of city dwellers.   Their possessions consist of sheep, and probably also of camels.   They live in tents, and wander about from
place to place in search of pasturage and water for their flocks.
When these increase to a considerable extent, the pasturage and
water in a given district become insufficient.   In consequence their

shepherds contend for the same wells and pastures. The southern part of Palestine, in which Abraham is here represented as now dwelling, has always been better suited for grazing than for agriculture, chiefly because of its insufficient water supply. The sons of Jacob in Egypt were still shepherds. And out in the desert, before they entered Canaan, the tribes must have lived entirely as shepherds. In fact this is the only life possible in the desert. This fact of early desert, shepherd life had a far-reaching effect upon the subsequent life and religion of Israel.

V. 7. The Canaanites and Perizzites were two of the peoples who inhabited Palestine before its conquest by the tribes of Israel.

V. 12. "The Plain", i. e. the low-lying valley of the Jordan, of which the bed of the Dead Sea is the lowest part.

XIV, 1. Some modern scholars have tried to identify some of the names of the kings given in these verses with names of early Babylonian and Elamite kings known from other historical sources, but with questionable success. This is a legend pure and simple, without the slightest historical basis.

V. 2. Sodom, Gomorrah, Admah and Zeboiim were legendary cities in the lower Jordan valley, which, according to tradition, were destroyed by God, and whose sites are now covered by the Dead Sea. For Sodom and Gomorrah cf. XIX and also Lesson IX; for Admah and Zeboiim cf. Deuteronomy XIX, 22; Hosea XI, 8. These last two passages make it clear that a tradition about Admah and Zeboiim, similar to that about Sodom and Gomorrah, was current in ancient Israel. The probable site of Zoar is occupied today by a small Arabian village, still known by the similar and closely related name, Seghur; cf. XIX, 22f. and 30.

Vv. 5f. The Rephaim, Zuzim, Emim and the Horites were early legendary inhabitants of Canaan and Edom; cf. Deuteronomy II, 10-12; 20-23 (here the Zuzim are called by the fuller name, Zam-zumim).

The Amalekites were a nomad people inhabiting the desert south of Palestine. They were conquered by Saul and David (I Samuel XV and XXX). The Amorites were a people dwelling in Palestine and to the east of the Jordan before the Israelite conquest of the land.

V. 10. Numerous asphalt or bitumen wells are found near the Dead Sea. Some, in fact, exist in the bed of the sea itself, and in places where the water is not deep, the asphalt rises and floats upon the surface, where it is gathered by the Arabs of the neighborhood, who carry it to market and sell it. By "slime pits" such asphalt wells are meant; cf. note to XI, 3.

V. 14. His trained men, i. e. his herdsmen and other servants who were of course also warriors. This number, three hundred and eighteen, shows how wealthy and powerful Abraham was.

V. 15. A surprise attack at night is the usual method of nomad warfare in the desert. With this may be compared Gideon's victory over the Midianites and David's over the Amalekites.

"On the left hand", i. e. north. Among the ancient Semites directions were reckoned according to the position of a man facing the rising sun. Hence in Hebrew *kedem,* literally "in front", means "east", *ahar,* literally "behind", means "west", *s'mol,* "left", means "north" and *yamin,* "right", means "south".

V. 16. For the use of the term "brother" here and in XIII, 8, cf. the note to XXIX, 15.

VV. 18-20 in the Bible, giving the incident of Melchizedek, are an interpolation into the main story, difficult to understand, and serving only to confuse the real narrative. Salem is generally thought to mean Jerusalem.

V. 22. Oaths were usually confirmed by raising either the right hand or both hands on high, as if calling God to witness; cf. Deuteronomy XXXII, 40; Isaiah LXII, 8; Daniel XII, 7.

V. 24. "Their portion", according to common custom the booty really belonged to those who had captured it. This makes Abraham's magnanimity all the clearer, since it shows that he refused to accept that, to which he was by custom fully entitled.

VIII

ABRAHAM'S HOSPITALITY

(Genesis XVIII 1-16)

When he saw them he ran to meet them. (Genesis XVIII, 2.)

He that is gracious unto the poor lendeth unto the Lord. (Proverbs XIX, 17.)

Read Isaiah LVIII, 6-12.

Thus far Abraham had stood God's test. The incident with Lot had proved his willingness to make great sacrifices in order to preserve peace. Yet Lot was a near kinsman, and frequently we will do for those who are close to us things which we would be unwilling to do for others. Furthermore, the duty of preserving peace with Lot had, as it were, come of its own accord to Abraham's door, and could not be put aside. He had had to do something at once to maintain the old relations of confidence and affection, or these would have been severed forever. Indecision, or inaction, or shutting the eyes would not have helped.

But there are many duties in life, which do not seek us out, but which we must seek, if we would perform them. It is so easy to shut our eyes to duties like these, and refuse to see them, to fold our hands, and refuse to do them. These are only sins of omission, as they are called, and to many, if not most people such sins seem negligible, hardly sins at all. However, one of the wisest of the ancient rabbis used to say, "Be as diligent in the performance of a small duty as in the performance of a great one". He who would go upon the mission of God, and perform His service gladly and loyally, can not wait for duties to seek him out, nor discharge only those obligations imposed upon him by the ties of kinship. He must be fully conscious of that larger relationship, which, we have learned, Judaism teaches, the brotherhood of all the children of God. And he must be eager to perform all the duties of this larger brotherhood, to serve his fellowmen in every way possible. Not only must he discharge those duties which seek him out, but he must himself search out all possible forms of service, and when he finds them he must run eagerly to meet them. Whoever can not stand this test, can be no true servant of God. How did Abraham stand this test?

One day, while sitting at the door of his tent, Abraham saw three strangers coming towards him, dusty and foot-sore. It was just at noon, when the sun is hottest, and, in Palestine, beats down cruelly upon the head of the venture-some traveler, and consumes his energy and vitality. Then people generally seek refuge from the heat. But apparently these three men had no place whither they might turn, until Abraham ran to them and urged them to rest and refresh themselves in his tent. Then he prepared for them a sump-tuous meal, from the standpoint of that day a veritable ban-quet, and, as the final mark of respect, he waited upon them himself. The rabbis of old called attention to the fact that in his words Abraham invited the travelers to rest and re-fresh themselves with a piece of bread, but actually he offered them far more than he had promised. This, they remarked, is the best hospitality and the truest sign of worth, to promise little in words, but to give much in deeds.

Now why was Abraham so urgent that these travelers accept his hospitality? Of course, partly because his heart was touched by their plight; but even more, because hos-pitality is indeed a great virtue. Because of this incident, and many similar stories about him, Abraham has always been regarded, not only by Jews, but by all men, as the pattern of true hospitality. The wise rabbis used to tell that Abraham's tent was so situated that he could look out on all four sides to see if anyone was coming, to whom he might offer his hospitality. And he always kept the sides of his tent raised, so that he might not miss a single opportunity. Anyone who has ever traveled in the Orient, or has read extensively about travel there, will appreciate what this means. Until comparatively recently there were no hotels at all in the East. Instead people would take the stranger into their homes, and entertain him for as long as he would stay. In fact it was thought that the stranger had a right to be entertained. He might demand food and lodging from anyone, and it would be a contemptible churl who would refuse. Occasionally though there were such, and we shall hear of some in our very next lesson. But in the Orient they are not many, for hospitality is regarded as the highest virtue, and the rights of the guest and the stranger precede everything else.

But Abraham was not content merely to give the stranger his rights, or to wait until he might claim entertainment. He was eager rather to discharge the duty of hospitality on every possible occasion. Therefore, as the story emphasizes, he did not wait for the men to come to him, but he ran to meet them, and urged them to honor him by accepting his hospitality. It is another instance of Abraham's greatness and large-heartedness. It shows that he was not merely hospitable in the ordinary sense, but that he possessed this virtue in the highest degree. And even more, it shows that Abraham would not wait for duties to seek him out, but would run to meet and to serve his fellowmen in every possible way. This test, too, Abraham had stood.

Abraham had no idea who the strangers were; nor did he ask. It was enough that they were tired and spent. But

unconsciously he was entertaining God Himself, or at least
three angels. It illustrates well the beautiful proverb from
our Bible,

He that is gracious unto the poor lendeth unto the Lord.

Whenever we help the poor and show true hospitality, it is
as if we gave unto God Himself. And true hospitality
consists, not merely in giving food and lodging to friends,
but in opening heart and hand to all, not asking who they
are, in sharing what we have, what God has given us, with
all who need, in truly loving our neighbor as ourselves. We
have seen repeatedly that Abraham lived and acted in just
this spirit; therefore he has become the world's model of
hospitality and generosity.

But especially to us Jews is Abraham the model and
inspiration of true hospitality. Hospitality means brotherhood, and has always been a characteristic Jewish virtue.
Among our fathers the stranger was always welcome in
every Jewish home, and the household felt itself honored
when strangers accepted its hospitality. It was indeed a
poor and miserable household which, especially on Friday
night, when the Sabbath was ushered in with gladness
and rejoicing and with an unusually excellent supper, did
not have some stranger at the table to join in the gladness, and to share, and thereby enrich, the blessing of the
Sabbath. Nor was the guest asked who he was. Some,
too, will remember how at the Seder service, which ushers
in every Pesach festival, the door is opened in the hope that
the Prophet Elijah might enter and partake of the family
hospitality.

But it is no wonder that, with the example of Father
Abraham to inspire us, hospitality should have become a
characteristic Jewish virtue. In commenting upon this act
of Abraham, the rabbis told this beautiful story. A traveler was once journeying through the desert. He had wan-

dered for many days, without meeting anyone, or finding a
place where he could replenish his supply of food and
water. At last these were exhausted and he wandered
on despairingly, growing weaker and weaker. Suddenly
he found himself lying beneath a magnificent palm tree,
whose branches were laden with dates, and at whose foot
bubbled a softly murmuring spring. The traveler ate and
drank, and his strength returned. He filled his bottle and
pouch and prepared to depart. But first he turned to the
tree and said, "How can I reward thee for thy blessing? I
can not wish for thee anything that thou hast not already.
I can wish only that thy offspring may be like thee". So, in
departing from Abraham, God said, "What can I offer thee
for thy kindness, since already thou art rich and hast everything that thou dost want? I can grant only that thy descendants, the people of Israel, may be like thee". Thereupon He announced to Abraham and Sarah the birth of
their long wished for son, Isaac. And through Isaac the
people Israel, Abraham's descendants, came to be; and hospitality has been, just as God blessed Abraham, one of the
greatest Jewish virtues. In its spirit the Bible teaches that
among the acts of service most pleasing to God are,

> To deal thy bread to the hungry,
> And that thou bring the poor that are cast out to thy house.
> When thou seest the naked, that thou cover him,
> And that thou hide not thyself from thine own flesh.

And the rabbis taught that the table which feeds the
stranger becomes an altar, meaning that this is the same as
giving unto God, as if God Himself were the guest at the
table, just as, unawares, He was Abraham's guest. They
also taught, "Let thy house be wide open to the poor, and
let the poor be as the members thereof". It is told that the
Prophet Elijah once sternly rebuked a renowned rabbi for
having built a porch, so large and so magnificent that he

could no longer hear the poor who stood at his door and cried for help.

As the above story told, the reward of Abraham's hospitality was Isaac. Not that Abraham expected a reward. He had acted, just as in his dealings with the king of Sodom, without thinking of reward. Yet every good deed brings a reward of some kind, although not always immediately, and not always recognized as the reward for that particular deed. And Abraham's reward was Isaac. The rabbis told that on the day of Isaac's birth the sun shone more brightly than ever before or since, thereby proclaiming that he would be a blessing to all mankind, that he and his descendants would carry out faithfully God's command to Abraham to be a blessing. Therefore it was a day of great rejoicing for all mankind.

NOTES

The picture of Abraham sitting at his tent-door, and of the meal which is served, and of the manner of serving it in the open space before the tent-door, is typically nomadic. We have seen that Abraham is represented as living the life of a typical nomad, such as a wealthy Beduin sheikh would live today.

V. 2. There are various modes of bowing in the Orient. The Hebrew verb used here denotes a complete prostration of the body. In this the person bends the knees, and then gradually inclines the body until the head touches the ground; cf. XXIII, 7, 12; XLII, 6; XLIII, 26. This is the extreme form of bowing, and is indicative of the desire to accord the highest possible honor.

V. 4. In the Orient where only sandals are worn, washing the feet is one of the most indispensable acts of the toilet, and one of the most characteristic services of hospitality; cf. XXIV, 42.

The tree here is the largest and most striking tree of the grove, in whose shade Abraham's tent is pitched. Cf. note to XIV, 13.

V. 6. Bread or cakes (however, not cakes in our sense, but small, round loaves of bread), are in the nomad households not prepared in quantities and stored for several days, but are baked fresh for every meal. Here the bread is made from finely sifted wheat flour, the finest flour then known. This is further evidence of the high honor which Abraham shows his guests.

V. 7. Meat is eaten by the nomad only on very rare occasions. That Abraham takes a young calf, the choicest of meats, shows the honor he accords his guests and the extreme measure of his hospitality. The host usually kills and dresses the animal himself, just as here.

V. 8. In the Orient it is customary for the host to wait upon the guests whom he most honors. He himself eats later of what they leave.

V. 9. Sarah had remained in the tent, however, not because the nomad women were forbidden to show their faces to strangers (this custom is as a rule practiced only in the cities of the Orient, and practically never among the nomads. This seems not to have been an Israelite practice). But among the nomads woman is so lightly esteemed that her presence is negligible. That the strangers ask after Sarah is a distinct mark of honor.

V. 10. It is an altogether human trait of the story, that Sarah is represented as standing behind the door of the tent, i. e. a skin or rug suspended over the opening of the tent, curious to see and hear everything that goes on. The curiosity of the nomad women, manifested in ways such as this, is proverbial. Therefore Sarah is not at all confused when in vv. 12ff. it is discovered that she was behind the door. She merely denies that she had laughed.

The Bible tells that the tent door was behind the speaker, to show the supernatural knowledge and character of the latter. The three strangers had come to Abraham in the guise of ordinary wayfarers, and he had received them as such, without the slightest suspicion of their divine character. But this manifestation of supernatural knowledge, and the further evidence that, even though this stranger had never visited Abraham before, still he knew Sarah's name, and could ask for her, and also, although he could not normally have seen Sarah standing behind the tent door, he still knew that she was there, and furthermore, that she had laughed at his words, even though, as the Bible carefully states, Sarah had laughed only to herself, all these manifestations of supernatural knowledge cause Abraham to realize that he is entertaining no ordinary mortal being, but one who partakes of divinity. This truth, it is implied, dawns upon Abraham gradually, and leads him in the end to put complete faith in the stranger's promise of a son, and in the further revelation of the doom of Sodom and Gomorrah.

Vv. 12ff. The incident of Sarah's laughing here is intended to explain the name Isaac. This name in Hebrew means "he laughs". A parallel explanation of the same is given in XVII, 17, and still another in XXI, 6.

IX

SODOM AND GOMORRAH

(Genesis XVIII, 17—XIX)

Shall not the Judge of all the earth do justly? (Genesis XVIII, 25.)

The Lord, the Lord, God, merciful and gracious, long-suffering and abundant in goodness and truth, keeping mercy unto the thousandth generation, forgiving iniquity and transgression and sin. (Exodus XXXIV, 6-7.)

Read Psalm XCIV, 9-12.

We learned in the last lesson that Isaac was God's reward for Abraham's hospitality. From this we inferred, and experience proves it correct, that God always, sooner or later, rewards righteous deeds. Likewise, from the story of the flood we learned that God also punishes wicked deeds just as they deserve. God has placed us here, and has given us knowledge of right and wrong and many other precious gifts, in order that we may live rightly, and bring good and happiness to our fellow-creatures. To live thus and to do God's will is good, and brings reward from God. Not to live thus is disobedience of God, is wrong and sin, and must bring punishment from God. So, we believe, God rules the world in justice, noting the acts of men, and meting out reward and punishment as men deserve.

In significant contrast to Abraham's righteousness and God's reward therefor, the present story tells of the wickedness of the inhabitants of Sodom and Gomorrah, and of God's punishment of them. We have previously heard of these cities, of the beauty and fertility of their land, of their defeat by the four kings from the East, and of the rescue of their captured men and women and the restoration of the booty by Abraham. Tradition tells how very wicked these cities were. Because of the productivity of their land, they had become very wealthy. But unfortunately they had not learned from experience the truth of the wise saying of the rabbis, "Who is wise? He who rejoices in his portion." They had not learned to rejoice in their portion, good and pleasant though it was, but instead, as happens, alas, so frequently, their very wealth had made them dissatisfied and covetous. They did not understand that riches, too, are a gift of God, given by Him only to be used, like all His gifts, for some purpose of good, and never for injustice and oppression. Their greed had made them selfish, heartless and unscrupulous. Having much, they thought only of how they might get more. Nor did they care how they got it. They were, so the rabbis told, particularly wicked in their treatment of strangers. If a stranger came to their city, one man would take some small thing, of so little value that it would not be missed, or if missed, would not be worth complaining about. Another would do the same, and still another; and soon the poor stranger would be robbed of everything, without being able to blame any one person. Or if, perhaps, he did complain, it did not avail. For the judges themselves were wicked and corrupt, and always received a portion of the stolen goods. Therefore they invariably decided against the stranger.

And not only strangers did the Sodomites treat thus, but even the poor and helpless of their own city. The rich and powerful knew how to take advantage of them and despoil them. And from the judges the poor received the same treatment as strangers. In fact, we are told, a law had even been made, that whoever would give food or lodging or assistance to a poor man or a stranger, would be put to death. How different from Abraham's righteous conduct, and how contrary to the fundamental principles of justice and hospitality!

This had been going on for many years. Even their escape from the four hostile kings, and Abraham's noble example in refusing the rich reward which the king of Sodom had offered him, had failed to make them realize that there is something in life far better than mere wealth. So at last God felt that He must destroy them. But He remembered His promise to Noah, never to bring another flood to destroy all mankind. Instead He determined to punish only the sinners, but to spare all the righteous in the city.

First, as we know, the angels came to Abraham to enjoy his hospitality and to test him. Having tried and proved him, they announced to him the birth of Isaac. At the same time God revealed to Abraham His intention with regard to the people of the wicked cities. This was in reality another and a worthy test of Abraham's fitness for his great mission. Not the righteous and the well-doing have departed farthest from God, and therefore stand in greatest need of the ministrations and help and loving guidance of God's servants, but the wicked and the evil-doers. As we have learned, the principle underlying this service of God is that of eternal, human brotherhood. All men are our brothers, be they who they may, the righteous and the wicked alike. It is easy to preserve the consciousness of brotherhood with those who do well. But we are all too prone to condemn the wicked, to cast them off and leave them to their fate, and to feel that our relationship with them and our responsibility for them have ceased. But it is not true, and we are still our brother's keeper, and all the more the keeper of that weak brother who can not keep himself, and who, without our help, must be lost completely. He who would do God's service and go as God's messenger unto his fellowmen, must have a great heart, filled with love for those of his brethren who need him most. He must be slow to condemn and quick to excuse and forgive. He must never despair of the eventual regeneration of his brothers, no matter how hopelessly wicked they may seem, but he must have faith that with God's help his labors will not be in vain, and that in the end all men must come to know God truly and to live the life which He has appointed for men. Only he who possesses such boundless love and compassion for all his fellowmen is worthy to go upon the mission of God.

Now Abraham knew full well the wickedness of the people of Sodom and Gomorrah. Nevertheless his loving heart overflowed with pity and compassion for them, and the thought of their destruction moved him to intercede on their behalf even with God Himself. Possibly some righteous men might be found in the cities, fifty, or forty, or thirty, or twenty, or perhaps only ten. Yet for the sake of these ten the city should be forgiven. For, on the one hand, these few righteous men might yet convince the people of the evil of their ways, and cause them to repent and return to God. And, on the other hand, Abraham said, "Shall not the Judge of all the earth do justly?" And true justice must always be tempered by mercy. For if God should judge all men absolutely according to their merits, who could stand before Him in judgment? What man doeth good ever, and sinneth not? Everyone does wrong at times, for no man is perfect, but only God. And unless God forgives, all men, in strict justice, must perish. Surely not to punish is God's desire, but to forgive; not to chastise in anger, but to pardon and correct in love. So Abraham, we are told, pleaded with God. And when he had made an end, God caused all the generations of old, the wicked generation of the flood, and the generation of the Tower of Babel, and all those which came after that, to pass before his eyes. Then Abraham saw that he was pleading needlessly, that God had always judged, not in strict and absolute justice, but in that truer justice, which is ever tempered by love and mercy and forgiveness, and that He had punished, as in the story of the flood, only at last, when He saw that the people had become completely and hopelessly wicked and deaf to all thoughts of correction and repentance. Nevertheless Abraham had not pleaded entirely in vain. For this very pleading had proved again his fitness for God's service. Even the wicked inhabitants of Sodom and Gomorrah were still his brothers, and his heart was still filled with love and compassion for them.

After revealing God's purpose to Abraham, the angels went on, slowly and reluctantly, towards Sodom. So great was God's sorrow at the thought of destroying His children, even though they were wicked, and so eager His hope that at the last moment ten, perhaps, might repent, and thus justify His sparing the city, that the angels' journey, which ordinarily would have required but a short time, took many hours. Thus, the good rabbis taught, the feet of God's messengers hasten on errands of mercy and blessing, but on errands of punishment and sorrow they lag.

The angels reached Sodom just at dusk. But they did not destroy the city immediately. God would give the people one more chance to obtain forgiveness. So the angels determined to pass the night in the city, to see what the people would do. However, not a citizen of Sodom offered them hospitality, but only Lot, himself a stranger, and therefore in constant danger because of the Sodomites' habitual treatment of strangers. In fact, we do not know just how they happened to allow Lot to remain in their midst. Lot had learned the lesson of hospitality from Abraham. And in almost the same words as Abraham, he urged the strangers to become his guests. Thus good example and helpful influence always beget righteousness. Lot's conduct was in marked contrast to that of the Sodomites, for they tried to work their evil desires upon the strangers and even threatened Lot for protecting them. They had proved again how hopelessly sinful they were, and had forfeited their last opportunity to obtain forgiveness. So the destruction of the city followed. First, however, God provided for the safety of Lot and his family. But when Lot tried to persuade his sons-in-law to hearken to the warning and to flee with him, they refused and mocked at him. They shared completely in the wickedness of the city, and therefore merited destruction.

So, at last, God was compelled in justice, though in sorrow, to destroy the wicked cities. In contrast to the judges of Sodom, His was true justice. Yet, just as Abraham had pleaded, like all true justice it was tempered by mercy and the desire to forgive. So God always judges, our religion teaches. He delights to reward men for their goodness. Only in sorrow, and only late, does He punish for sin. Always He holds out the hope and opportunity for repentance, and always He longs for the return of the sinner. Always His patient love guides the affairs of men, and always He sends His word of truth and right and forgiveness unto them. In His great love He has given us our Yom Kippur, our Day of Atonement once each year. It is the constantly recurring symbol of His love, and of the opportunity He gives us to obtain forgiveness and begin anew a life of righteousness and of walking with Him. Upon it we may turn to Him in sorrow, and implore pardon for the sins of the past year, and earnestly resolve to live the new year better. Even more than this, the rabbis told, He fixed Yom Kippur ten days after Rosh Hashonah for a wise and loving purpose. On Rosh Hashonah all the world must pass for judgment before Him. The ten days from Rosh Hashonah to Yom Kippur are given for repentance and return to God. They are called the *asereth y'mai t'shuvah,* "the Ten Days of Repentance" or "Return". If, during these days, so the rabbis taught, one truly repents, the sentence passed on Rosh Hashonah is not recorded; forgiveness is his. But if not, the sentence is recorded, to be preserved for the final reckoning. But even this can be atoned for and averted by repentance and righteous deeds, for God's mercy and love endure forever, and ever, just as with the men of Sodom and Gomorrah, He would rather pardon than punish His beloved children. Therefore our new year begins with joyful thoughts and hopes of pardon and forgiveness. And in our prayers on Yom Kippur the beautiful words from our Bible occur repeatedly, "The Lord, the Lord, God, merciful and gracious, long-suffering, and abundant in goodness and truth, keeping mercy unto the thousandth generation, forgiving iniquity and transgression and sin".

But true repentance means not merely saying, "I'm sorry". It means not merely words of the lips, but also deeds of the heart and the hand. God holds out the hope of repentance and pardon. But man himself must truly repent, and show by his life that he deserves pardon. The responsibility for forgiveness rests, not upon God, but upon man alone. The rabbis told of a wise father whose son had committed a grievous sin. The father said, "My son, you have committed a great wrong and deserve punishment. Yet my love prompts me not to punish you now. I will try you again. If you never do wrong again, but learn from your sin to live nobly and usefully, the sin shall be forgiven and forgotten. But if not, and at last I see that you will not do right, then I must punish you for this and all your sins". So God, the loving Father, judges all His children, and rewards in love where He can, but punishes, though in sorrow, when He must.

We have learned how kind and generous Abraham was. Yet this kindness and love may not be compared with God's. One day, we are told, Abraham was sitting at his tent-door as usual, watching for whom he might entertain. Suddenly he saw an old, old man tottering along the road. Abraham ran to him, took him by the arm, and helped him to his tent. There he washed the old man's feet, clothed him in fresh garments, and set a generous meal before him. But to his surprise, the old man uttered no blessing over the bread, nor spoke any word of thanks to the Giver of all for the good he had received. Indignantly Abraham asked, "Old man, why do you not thank God for these blessings?" The old man replied, "I do not worship your God, but I pray to the fire". Then in wrath Abraham seized the old man and thrust him from the tent. There he lay all through the long, dark, stormy night, groaning and suffering. At dawn he slowly took his departure. Suddenly Abraham heard God's voice, "Abraham, why didst thou treat this poor, old man thus?" Abraham answered, "Because he would not worship Thee". But God replied, "He, too, is one of My children. I have borne with him for these one hundred years; couldst thou not have borne with him for a single night?"

So the wicked cities were destroyed by God in justice, for their wickedness and unwillingness to repent. Over their site, tradition tells, lies the Dead Sea, so salty that no living creature can exist in it, and no bird, it is said, ever flies across it. The land which once had been like the garden of the Lord is desolate now. So sin corrupts everything it touches.

And Lot, who had done God's will, escaped with his two daughters. Only his wife, who had disobeyed the angels' last command, was destroyed. And in time Lot's reward for his righteousness came. For among his descendants, as we shall learn later, were to be the great King David, and also, so the prophets and the rabbis told and many Jews still believe, the Messiah, who is at last to bring in the age when sin and sorrow and punishment shall be no more, but only good and happiness and love shall obtain, when all men shall truly walk. with God, and, in the prophet's inspired words,

> The earth shall be full of the knowledge of the Lord,
> As the waters cover the sea. (Isaiah XI, 9.)

NOTES

The question is frequently asked whether this story of the destruction of Sodom and Gomorrah is literally true. Many devout and enthusiastic travellers have laboriously sounded the waters of the Dead Sea for some trace of the lost cities. But all in vain. The reason is obvious. A little mature consideration must show that this is not history but mythology. Just as with the creation and flood stories, our ancestors laid hold of an ancient myth, adapted it to their own use, and made it the vehicle for expressing the fundamental principle of Judaism, of God's justice, tempered by His desire for mercy and forgiveness. Certainly it adds greatly to the value of the story to understand and interpret it in this light.

However, inasmuch as the topography of the country east of the Dead Sea, and probably also the deep depression of the Dead Sea itself, is due to very remote volcanic activity and other geological disturbances, it may well be that the ancient myth was based upon a dim reminiscence of this fact.

Chapter XVIII, 22. The confusion to be noted here, as well as in the earlier verses of this chapter, between God speaking as if alone and the three angels in human form, and the frequent, and otherwise inexplicable, change from singular to plural, are due to the fact that the story in its present literary form is the result of the combination by some skillful editor of two ancient versions of this myth. One version told that God alone visited Abraham, while the other told of the visit of three angels. Otherwise the two versions seem to have been practically identical.

Chapter XIX, 1. Lot was sitting at the gate of the city, through which, of course, all travellers had to enter. The rabbis inferred from this that Lot practiced hospitality in the same manner as Abraham. The gate of the city was and is still the common meeting-place in Oriental towns and cities and there very much of the public business is transacted; cf. XXIII, 10; XXXIV, 20; I Samuel IV, 8; II Samuel XV, 2; Psalm LXIX, 13; Proverbs I, 21; Job XXIX, 7.

V. 3. By "the broad place" the public square of the city is meant. The gate of the city generally opened upon this, just as here. It should be always borne in mind that, as the excavations have shown, with but very few exceptions the towns and cities of ancient Palestine covered comparatively small areas. Therefore the public square itself was never very large, nor, at the most, far from the city gate. Sodom seems to have been a larger city than ordinary, since, as v. 4 tells, it was divided into a number of quarters. Generally in large cities the people of various occupations had each their own quarter; cf. Isaiah XLVII, 15; Jeremiah XXXVII, 21.

V. 17. For "the Plain" cf. the note to XIII, 12. The mountains on either side of the Jordan valley rise quite abruptly to an average height of approximately 3,500 feet above the surface of the Dead Sea.

Vv. 18-23 are really an interpolation into the original story, and not an integral part of it. They were inserted probably to explain the etymology of the name of the village of Zoar, which seemed miraculously to have escaped the general destruction. Actually they have no relation to the story proper, and even seem to contradict some of its details. Zoar is represented as derived from the Hebrew stem *sa'ar*, "to be little."

V. 26. Very much has been told and written about this incident of the pillar of salt. Most of this is altogether fanciful, and without the slightest basis of fact or history. This verse is probably also an interpolation, similar to the Zoar episode. Near the southern end of the Dead Sea is a large hill of salt, today known to the Arabs of the vicinity as *Gebel Usdum* (Mountain of Sodom). It is, of course, the product of centuries of deposit of salt from the Dead Sea. Vivid imaginations have from the earliest times professed to see the likeness of a woman in the configuration of this salt hill. Gradually the tradition arose that it was actually a woman who had been changed into salt. Ancient Israelite folk-lore identified this woman with Lot's wife. Of course there is not the slightest historical basis to this tradition.

Vv. 27f. From the highlands of Judah one can easily look across the valley of the Dead Sea to the mountains of Moab on the east.

V. 29 is a late interpolation into the original story. It seeks to tell that God saved Lot, not because of his own merits, but altogether for Abraham's sake.

Vv. 30-38. These verses are. undoubtedly intended to be an account, from the Israelite standpoint of course, of the origin of the two kindred peoples, Moab and Ammon. Inasmuch as, throughout Israel's history, Moab and Ammon were among Israel's most constant and troublesome enemies, it is not at all surprising that Israelite tradition should ascribe to them this base and immoral origin.

X

HAGAR AND ISHMAEL

(Genesis XVI and XXI, 9-21)

And God heard the voice of the lad.   (Genesis XXI, **17.**)

My son, keep the commandment of thy father,
And forsake not the teaching of thy mother;
Bind them continually upon thy heart,
Tie them about thy neck.
For the commandment is a lamp, and the teaching is light,
And reproofs of instruction are the way of life.   (Proverbs VI,
    20-24.)

Read Psalm CXIV, 14-19.

The story of Hagar and Ishmael was probably first conceived to account for the well-recognized kinship of Israel
with the nomad, Ishmaelite tribes of the desert.   The tribes
of Israel, which later came out of the Arabian Desert and
settled in Palestine, were of the same, or kindred, stock as
the Ishmaelite tribes, which remained behind and continued
to live as wandering nomads with their sheep and camels.
The consciousness of this common stock continued until
comparatively late in Israel's history.   The present story
accounts for this relationship by tracing the descent of both
Ishmael and Israel from one common ancestor, Abraham.
The traditional relationship between Israel and Moab and
Ammon has already been accounted for by a similar tradition of descent from a common ancestor (XIX, 30-38).
We shall learn later another similar tradition which ac-
counted for the relationship between Israel and Edom.

But even more, the story of Hagar and Ishmael illustrates for us one of the simplest, yet also one of the most fundamental, beautiful, and eternal of human virtues, a mother's love. The picture of Hagar's love, and of her despair and anguish at the thought of the impending death of her child and of her helplessness to relieve his suffering, touches us to the quick. We may be sure that Hagar had spared no effort to keep her little one alive, and that she had denied herself of the food and water in order to give it to him. And childlike, he had accepted it unquestioningly, not understanding nor appreciating his mother's sacrifice, nor realizing that she was giving her very life for him. So children always do more or less. The fulness of a mother's love and a mother's sacrifice is too great to be appreciated ever. We begin to understand something of it only when we become parents ourselves, and make our own loving sacrifices for our own children. Yet even then we do not comprehend all that our dear parents have done for us, all the tender love they have showered upon us.

The more we read the story and the more we respond to its irresistible call for sympathy, the more, too, the realization grows, that Hagar and Hagar's love are types, types of true motherhood and true mother's love. Especially are they types of the Jewish mother and Jewish parental love and capacity for sacrifice. True, Hagar was not a Jewess by birth. But inasmuch as Jewish law and lore taught that the wife lives in the tent or house of her husband and follows completely after him, the Bible undoubtedly meant to imply that, despite the accident of Egyptian birth, Hagar was nevertheless a Jewess in thought and act. Similarly Joseph's wife was an Egyptian and dwelt in Egypt, yet her offspring, Ephraim and Manasseh, are represented throughout the Bible as quite as thoroughly Jewish as any of the sons of Jacob. So, too, here it is the God of Israel who cares for Hagar and her son. And the sentiments and virtues which this story illustrates have always been recognized by our ancestors and by the world as animating the Jewish people to an unusually high degree. As Hagar, so every Jewish mother, and every Jewish father, too, act, and of such sacrifice for their children they have ever shown themselves capable. Therefore the expression has become proverbial, "a mother in Israel", i. e., the true Jewish mother, the highest type of motherhood the world has ever known. It is indeed something to be proud of, that throughout all ages our Jewish mothers and fathers have set before the world the standard of true motherhood and fatherhood. Our Bible is rich in stories of Jewish fathers and Jewish mothers. It tells of Jacob and his undying love for his son Joseph, of the tender love of the mother of Moses for her little baby, of Hannah and her earnest prayer that God might bless her with a child, upon whom she might bestow her mother love, of the old king David, whose love for his son could not be quenched, even despite the latter's heartless treatment of his aged and trusting father. We shall hear all these stories in time, and therefore need not recount them here.

However, two stories, told by the rabbis of old, to illustrate how true and undying is a Jewish parent's love, may be related here. They told that when Joseph was sold as a slave, and was being brought down to Egypt, the road led past the tomb of Rachel, his mother, who had died when he was a mere baby. Just opposite the tomb he suddenly broke away from his captors, and ran and threw himself down upon his mother's grave and wept bitterly, and called upon her for help, even though he knew that she could not hear. But the rabbis told, and they were very wise and knew best, that still she did hear, for her love for her boy was not dead. And from out the tomb, it seemed to him, there came words of comfort and cheer, bidding him not despair, for this was all in accordance with God's will, and success and blessing were still in store for him. The story is true; a mother's love, at least, never dies. Long after

she has passed to her eternal reward, her love lives on and
on in the lives of her children, and her gentle words of counsel and admonition are a lamp, which guides them through
all the darkness upon the way of life. Therefore the Bible
says truly,

> My son, keep the commandment of thy father,
> And forsake not the teaching of thy mother;
> Bind them continually upon thy heart,
> Tie them about thy neck.
> For the commandment is a lamp, and the teaching is light,
> And reproofs of instruction are the way of life.

The other story told that when God called to Moses for
the first time, He did not speak in His own voice, for He
feared that this might frighten Moses. Nor would He use
too weak a voice, lest Moses should pay little attention, or
fail to recognize His true glory. So He called to Moses in
the voice of his father, for He knew that to this gentle
and loving voice Moses could answer only in accents of
respect and tender affection. If only we are observant, we
can see our father's love and our mother's love, and can
hear it, too, not only in their actions and in the many things
they do for us, but even in the sound and inflection of their
voices, when they speak to us or about us, and in the light
which shines in their eyes when they look at us, or even
think of us. This is the traditional love of Jewish fathers
and Jewish mothers, which has ever made them happy in
their many sacrifices for the sake of their children. Many,
many stories may be told of this love, and many examples
may be given. Each child, if only made to think for a moment, must know some instances of father love and mother
love from his own experience. And we can understand
that in wisdom and truth the Bible commands, "Honor thy
father and thy mother".

One more thought this story suggests. God had promised that Ishmael, too, like Isaac, should become the pro-

genitor of a numerous and mighty people. Yet despite this promise, it seemed at one moment that the child was on the point of perishing of thirst. In vain the distracted mother sought to still his cries; in vain she called upon God for help; in vain she besought Him to be mindful of His promise. It seemed to her as if God did not hear, or would not hear Small wonder if she doubted or lost faith. But just when it seemed that in another moment the child must die, God opened her eyes, and she beheld the life-giving well of water for which she had prayed. God had heard her cries; He was indeed a God of mercy and faithfulness, who cares for the suffering, the outcast, and the helpless, and none of His promises remain unfulfilled. Nay more, the well had been there continually, only in her blindness she had not seen it until God opened her eyes.

So it is with many people. Our eyes are closed to God's countless blessings, and we vainly call upon Him to satisfy our needs. Yet if we would but open our eyes and see all the blessings which God does shower upon us, all His bounties with which we may satisfy our needs, we would not doubt, nor murmur, nor cry for more, but we would bravely set to work to use what God has given us, and to strengthen ourselves thereby for the great tasks for which He has created us.

The word of God is sure. As one of the greatest of the prophets said,

As the rain cometh down and the snow from heaven,
And returneth not thither,
Except it water the earth,
And maketh it bring forth and bud,
And give seed to the sower and bread to the eater;
So shall My word be that goeth forth out of My mouth:
It shall not return unto Me void,
Except it accomplish that which I please,
And make the thing whereto I sent it prosper. (Isaiah IV, 10-11.)

The truth of this we learned in the story of the flood,

when God watched over all those in the ark, and though it
had neither sail nor rudder nor helmsman nor sailors, still
it floated along upon the mighty waters, safe and firm under
God's protection. We learn this truth, too, from the story
of the exodus from Egypt. Though the mighty Pharaoh
and his army shut the people in behind, and the beating sea
barred their way in front, and to go either backward or forward, it seemed, meant destruction, still God, in His mercy
and faithful to His promise, made a path for Israel through
the depths of the sea, and led His people on to safety and
freedom. We learn it also from the story of the prophet
Elijah. Though the whole land hungered because of the
drought, and though he had to flee and hide for his life
before the vengeful king and queen, none the less he was
safe in God's loving care, and was fed by the ravens who
did God's bidding. And we learn this truth, too, from this
story of Hagar and Ishmael, from the significant words,
"And God heard the voice of the lad", and from the name,
Ishmael, "God hears".

The wise teachers and rabbis in Israel used to tell many
wonderful tales, which showed God's never-failing providence and loving care of all His creatures. But far more
than in such stories and miracles, which seemed to exemplify
a special providence of God, they delighted in pointing to
the manifold instances of God's bounty and blessing, which
come to us ceaselessly day by day, and which alone make
living possible. They told, for example, that even though
the farmer wears himself out with plowing, harrowing, sow-
ing, pulling weeds, harvesting, binding the sheaves, and
threshing, still all his labor would be vain, did not God send
a little wind to help winnow the grain and separate the
wheat from the chaff. "And God heard the voice of the
lad". As the Psalmist said,

> He giveth to the beast his food,
> And to the young ravens which cry. (Psalm CXLVII, 9.)

He hearkens to our voice when we call upon Him; He satisfies our needs and gives us strength to do His work. Day by day His love watches over us and His providence never fails us. His countless blessings come to us constantly in overflowing measure, if only we open our eyes to see and our minds to understand. Again in the Psalmist's words,

> The Lord upholdeth all that fall,
> And raiseth all those that are bowed down.
> The eyes of all wait for Thee,
> And Thou givest them their food in due season.
> Thou openest Thy hand,
> And satisfiest every living thing with favor.
> The Lord is righteous in all His ways,
> And gracious in all his works.
> The Lord is nigh unto all them that call upon Him,
> To all that call upon Him in truth.
> He will fulfil the desire of them that fear him;
> He also will hear their cry, and will save them.

And the story suggests still one other thought. God's command had come to Abraham to send away Hagar and Ishmael. His heart was torn, for Hagar was his wife and the mother of Ishmael, and Ishmael was his son, and he loved them. Nay more, he felt a stern sense of duty to provide for them and protect them, just as the true husband and father always feels. But according to the standards and practices of those days, Sarah had the right to demand that Hagar, her handmaid, be put away because of her arrogant conduct, and her son, Ishmael, with her. And God had bidden Abraham do as Sarah had demanded. He was torn between two duties, the duty to protect and cherish Hagar and Ishmael, and the duty to do as Sarah, his first and chief wife, had the right to demand, and as God Himself had bidden him do. Which duty should he perform? His own desire and feeling for his offspring bade him keep Hagar and Ishmael, and care for them at all costs, even in defiance of Sarah's right and of God's bidding. A voice within kept

whispering, "This is your duty quite as much as that". But
another voice answered sternly, "Yes, that is a duty; but it
is a greater duty to hearken to God's word, and to give to
Sarah, who has the first claim upon you, and who has ever
shared with you, faithfully and loyally, all the hardships and
trials which have come to you, that which she has a perfect
right to demand." As the wise prophet told Saul, the king,
when the latter had disobeyed God's command, and had offered sacrifices which he thought would be pleasing unto God,

Hath the Lord as great delight in burnt-offerings and sacrifices,
As in hearkening to the voice of the Lord?
Behold, to obey is better than sacrifice,
And to hearken than the fat of rams. (I Samuel XV, 22.)

It is hard to resist temptation, when it comes in the
alluring garb of pleasure and gratification of desire. But it
is harder far to resist temptation when it comes in the guise
of duty, and bids us do it and neglect the greater, harder,
less pleasing, and more costly duty. Time and again we are
confronted with conflicting duties and are forced to make
our choice between them. A voice within keeps urging us to
choose the easier and more agreeable duty; after all, that is
duty, too, and little duties must be performed as well as
great duties; there is equal merit in both, and both are pleasing to God. But the other voice keeps insisting that this is
the greater and more urgent duty, and it must be performed first at all costs. It is the hardest choice in life to
make. Nevertheless we must all make this choice time and
again. How shall we decide? There is but one way, the
way which Abraham chose, to put aside all selfish considerations of ease and pleasure and personal desire, and determine honestly and uncompromisingly which is the greater
and more urgent duty, which is truly God's bidding, and
then to do that duty steadfastly and conscientiously, regardless of the cost. It is a hard and bitter trial, which must

come to all of us repeatedly, to prove our true worth and
fitness for God's service. It always means pain and sorrow,
and leaves a scar which never heals, as the mark of the
battle of the soul which we have had to fight. But all life
is in a very true sense a ceaseless battle in the cause of
duty, and we can not go through this battle unwounded and
without scars. It is the battle which tries and proves us,
and purges the evil of weakness, selfishness, and cowardice
from our souls, and makes us men and warriors and true
servants of God. This was another and a severe trial of
Abraham, possibly the most severe which he had had to
endure thus far. And again he had withstood the test
nobly, and had proved himself worthy to go upon the mission of God.

NOTES

A thoughtful question raised is, "Did Abraham do right in
yielding to Sarah's request, and sending Hagar and Ishmael away?"
Judging by modern standards, of course he did wrong. But it is
ridiculous, as well as unfair, to apply modern standards to ancient
conditions. According to modern standards it was wrong, also, for
Abraham to take more than one wife. But we know that it was in
full accord with ancient practice. Equally, Sarah's request that
Hagar and Ishmael be sent away, and Abraham's compliance, were
in accord with ancient law and standards. Certainly the Biblical
authors had no feeling that Abraham had done anything at all wrong.
The story betrays not the least indication thereof. On the contrary,
the Bible tells that Abraham was induced to hearken to Sarah's request by the very word of God, and by the divine assurance that God
would protect Ishmael and make of him also a great people. The
story depicts no more than Abraham's touching grief and solicitude
at the thought of sending his two loved ones away, and also represents Abraham as enduring another bitter trial and test of faith and
worth. It is good to know that the rabbis told that Abraham was
later reunited with Ishmael in a way (cf. Ginzberg, *The Legends
of the Jews,* I, 266), and that the Bible itself tells that at Abraham's
death Ishmael rejoined Isaac, in order to share with him the sad

but loving duty of laying the body of their father in its eternal rest-ing-place (XXV, 9).

For the general understanding of the story it should be borne in mind that in the Orient, and also in the true Jewish household, children are considered the supreme blessing. A childless couple is regarded as unfortunate and unhappy indeed. Hence the longing of Rachel and of Hannah for a child. It seems to have been a not uncommon practice for a childless woman to give one of her maids to her husband as a second wife, and to regard the children of this union as her own. The story of Jacob and Leah and Rachel fur-nishes another instance of this practice. The maid, in such case, continued subject to her mistress, even though she had actually born children.

XVI, 7. Shur is the district at the Isthmus of Suez on the border of Egypt.

V. 12 pictures the wild, tribal state of the nomad tribes in the Arabian Desert.

XXI, 6. Another attempt to account for the name Isaac; cf. note to XVIII, 12.

V. 8. In the Orient children are weaned generally at about the age of three years. This is usually an occasion for rejoicing and feasting, just as is described here.

V. 9. The rabbis told that Sarah beheld Ishmael mocking Isaac as he wept; hence her sudden hatred of the boy.

Vv. 13 and 14 are very difficult of exact translation, and their meaning is altogether uncertain. They picture the most primitive conception of the deity in ancient Israel, that of a god who lives in one fixed place, and whose power extends only over the immediate vicinity of his abode. Such a god was ordinarily conceived of as dwelling in a spring, a rock of unusual appearance, or a tree of extraordinary size. Here the deity is represented as being actually the god of the well; hence the peculiar name of the latter, "The well of the Living One who seeth me". The story in its original form implied that not only did Hagar not see the well at first, but also that she had no intimation that a god dwelt in this spot until he revealed himself to her. A strikingly similar idea is contained in the original form of the story of Jacob at Bethel, XXVIII, 10-22. This primitive conception of local gods Israel outgrew at a com-paratively early period of its religious evolution.

V. 19. "And God opened her eyes", i. e. caused her to see the well, which had been there constantly, but which she had somehow not noticed. It does not mean that God suddenly created this well.

V. 20. The Ishmaelites were supposedly renowned archers.

V. 21. The Wilderness of Paran was the ancient name for the desert of the Sinaitic Peninsula. The Bible represents it as the traditional wandering ground of the Ishmaelite tribes. Actually, however, these tribes wandered over the northern half or two thirds of the vast Arabian Peninsula. The Mohammedan Arabs claim descent from Ishmael, and Mohammedan tradition holds that the well which God revealed to Hagar was the sacred well of Zemzem at Mecca, the holy city of the Mohammedans.

It is now recognized by scholars that XVI and XXI contain, not the accounts of two separate flights of Hagar from Sarah's household, but two independent versions of one and the same event. This is clear from the fact that the same incidents, such as the announcement of the glorious future of Ishmael and his descendants, are found in each version.

A few discrepancies and anachronisms are readily apparent, such as that in the opening verses of XX Ishmael is represented as a lad of thirteen years, and therefore practically grown to man's estate, according to Oriental standards, whereas in the story proper he is still an infant, unable to care for himself, and cast away, helplessly, to die under a bush. Of course these two passages are the work of two different writers and belong to two originally distinct versions of the Ishmael story.

XI

THE SACRIFICE OF ISAAC

(Genesis XXII, 1-19)

Here am I.   (Genesis XXII, 1.)

For My thoughts are not your thoughts,
Neither are your ways My ways, saith the Lord.
For as the heavens are higher than the earth,
So are My ways higher than your ways,
And My thoughts than your thoughts.   (Isaiah ~~IV~~ 55, 8-9.)

Read Psalm CXXI.

As was stated in the Introduction, one central theme runs
through the entire Abraham cycle of stories.   It is the
thought that God tried Abraham repeatedly, to prove his fitness for the great task for which he had been called.   Each
trial thus far had tested Abraham in a different way.   He
had stood the first test of faith; he had proved his ability to
subdue his own inclinations and passions in order to preserve peace with kinsmen and fellowmen; he had shown
conclusively that he would serve for the sake of duty alone,
and without thought of reward; he had demonstrated his
hospitality, generosity, and consciousness of brotherhood, his
eagerness to pursue after duty, as well as to perform it
when it came to him, his all-embracing love and compassion
for his fellowmen, even when they were sinners, his readiness to put duty to God above everything else.   But one test
more was necessary to complete God's trial of Abraham.
Would he give up at God's behest that which was to him the
very dearest thing in all life?   The story of the sacrifice of

Isaac is the answer to this question. It is the climax of the Abraham cycle of stories.

This story, like that of the garden of Eden, is recognized as one of the classics of the world's literature. The author's art is incomparable. Although the story proper is told in only fifteen short verses, it is complete and perfect in every detail. The little artless child, with his simple, naive questions, trusting so implicitly in his old father, and the father, silent and grief-stricken, yet steadfast in his faith in God, command our admiration and sympathy. We constantly ask ourselves, "Will the old man actually sacrifice his beloved son, and will God allow him to do so?" Isaac's simple question, "Where is the lamb for the sacrifice?" is dramatic in the extreme. It expresses the very point of the story. And equally dramatic is Abraham's answer, "God will provide the lamb". For all unconsciously, in these words, as well as in those to the two servants, "I and the lad will go yonder; and we will worship and come back to you", Abraham has hinted at the real outcome of the story. He thought at the moment that he alone would come back. But actually both were to return. The ancient rabbis said that through prophetic inspiration Abraham foretold the true end of the journey. But had Abraham thus foreseen the outcome of this adventure, there would have been no real trial of his faith, and no point to this story. And so we know that the dramatic effect of his words is due entirely to the author's consummate art.

But besides surpassing artistic merit, the story itself is, because of the spiritual lesson it conveys, sublime and inspiring to the highest degree. Hardly any other story in the Bible equals, and certainly none surpasses it in this respect. Partly because of this, this chapter has become the traditional passage from the Torah read in every synagogue on Rosh Hashonah.

Historically the story had a twofold purpose. On the

one hand, as has been stated in the Introduction, it was designed to combat what was in the 9th, 8th and 7th centuries
B. C. an ever-growing evil, the horrible practice of child-
sacrifice. The Books of Kings tell how prevalent this practice was in Israel at this time. This story was first conceived
and written down in the 9th century B. C. as a strong
protest against this awful custom, and to show that God
does not demand child-sacrifice, but, at the most, only some
fitting animal, as, for instance, a ram or a lamb. And on
the other hand, the story was in time expanded and spiritualized, and made to show that dearer to God than even the
richest animal sacrifice is the sacrifice of the heart, perfect
faith in Him and willingness to obey His word, readiness to
answer His call, even before its purpose be known, with the
unfailing "Here am I", and to give up for Him what is best
and dearest, even one's only, beloved child. As the Psalmist
said,

> Offer the sacrifices of righteousness,
> And put your trust in the Lord. (Psalm IV, 6.)

How well the story succeeded in its twofold purpose, is self-
evident.

When God had commanded Abraham to leave forever
birthplace and father's house and loved ones at home, and
wander forth, he knew not whither, it had been a severe
trial. It had been a more severe trial when God had bidden
him hearken to Sarah's word, and send Hagar and Ishmael
forth into the barren wilderness, to what fate he knew not.
But this trial was harder far, for now God demanded his
and Sarah's only son, for whom they had hoped and prayed
for so many years, and who had been granted to them only
in old age, after they had long given up all hope. Now,
after but a few years of happiness, in which they had learned
to idolize the boy, and had conceived the fondest hopes for
his future, came the command to sacrifice him. It meant

the end of all their hopes and happiness; it meant that their old age must be dark and cheerless, and that, when at last their end would come, there would be no loved one to follow them sorrowfully to their last resting-place. Surely they could hope for no more children. Small wonder had they hesitated, and even refused to make the sacrifice. But Abraham did not falter nor question God's will. His faith in God was stronger even than his love for his son. Slowly and sorrowfully he obeyed the divine command, and never once did he doubt or seek to turn back on his sad and hopeless journey.

It might be asked, "Why should God try Abraham again, and so cruelly? Was not the first hard test of his faith, which he had stood so well, sufficient?" It is a difficult question to answer. We can not understand, nor judge, nor even question God's motives and God's ways. This story brings home the full truth of the prophet's words,

> For My thoughts are not your thoughts,
> Neither are your ways My ways, saith the Lord.
> For as the heavens are higher than the earth,
> So are My ways higher than your ways,
> And My thoughts than your thoughts.

We can not understand God's ways, nor dare we even question them. We can only trust with absolute faith that He knows best, and that His purpose is good and wise, even though we may not understand, and even though it may seem hard and harsh. This is what Abraham did, and he has deservedly become Israel's and the world's inspiring model of true faith in God.

Yet the rabbis did ask themselves, "Why did God try Abraham again and again?" And they gave a very wise answer. "When the potter bakes his vessels in the kiln, which does he test to see if they are well made, the best or the worst? Surely the best, from which he expects the most. So, too, God tried Abraham severely, just because He expected so much from him and from his descendants, the children of Israel".

But not only Abraham did God try thus. He tries everyone in some way. Some He tries just as severely as He tried Abraham. Others, from whom, perhaps, He expects not quite so much, He tries less severely. But all people must be tried in some way, and their fitness for God's service proved. A wise and good rabbi of old, it is told, suffered very much. He was blind and crippled in hands and feet, and was dependent upon others for everything. Many additional misfortunes, too, befell him. Yet of everything he said, *gam zu l'tovah,* "This, also, is for good". That was complete trust in God.

The following story is told of his pupil, the well-known Rabbi Akiba. He was compelled by persecution to leave his home and wander about in a sparsely settled country, with only an ass, upon which he rode, a cock which would wake him in the morning, and a lamp, by the light of which he used to study the Torah until late into the night. Once, just at nightfall, he came to a village and asked for lodging. But the churlish people, very much like the inhabitants of Sodom, refused, and Rabbi Akiba was compelled to spend the night shelterless in a nearby wood. He consoled himself with the thought, "God is just; no doubt, as my beloved master taught me, this, too, is for good". He lit his lamp and prepared to study. But scarcely had he commenced, when a sudden gust of wind blew out the light, and he could not rekindle it. So he lay down to sleep. Soon a wolf came and killed the cock; then a lion carried away the ass. But Rabbi Akiba piously remarked, "This, too, must be for good", and he thanked God for having spared his life. Early in the morning he arose and went back to the village to purchase food. But to his surprise, he found not a single person alive. During the night robbers had killed all the inhabitants and carried away all their property.

*good
ib.*

Then Rabbi Akiba understood, and once more he thanked God for having saved his life. For he said, "Had they not refused me lodging, I would have been killed with them. And had not the wind put out my light, and the animals killed my companions, the robbers might have seen me studying, or heard the cock crow or the ass bray, and would have captured me. Praised be God, who does everything for good".

God tries everyone in some way. Nor must we imagine that, as with Abraham, at the last moment our sacrifice will not be required. Generally our sacrifice is accepted. And the real test is in the way we offer our sacrifice, the willingness with which we give up what is dear, the perfect faith in God which we still preserve, and which keeps us from doubting His wisdom and goodness.

At times God even demands the very same sacrifice which He asked of Abraham, dearly beloved children, or even an only child. Of course He does not ask that the parent sacrifice his child with knife in hand. Nevertheless it is a sacrifice indeed to give up a darling child or some other loved one at God's behest, probably the very greatest sacrifice. Just as with Abraham, it is always the hardest test of faith. Some make the sacrifice, not willingly, of course, but with resignation and perfect faith that God knows best, even as Abraham did. Others doubt and question, and say, "God can not have done this", or "God is unjust and cruel", or "There can be no God, for, otherwise, He would not have let this sorrow befall me". But we must remember that we can not understand God's motives nor His ways.

> As the heavens are higher than the earth,
> So are My ways higher than your ways,
> And My thoughts than your thoughts.

This is the true faith, which enables us to endure all trials and stand all tests, and prove ourselves fit and ready for the great work for which, sooner or later, God calls everyone of us.

To everyone some trials must come. We may not realize that they are trials, and we may rebel and refuse to make our sacrifices; and we, too, may doubt whether God has done this, or whether a just God could allow this misfortune or unhappiness; or we may ask complainingly, "What have we done to deserve all this?" But if we would only think, "Perhaps God is trying us, to see how much of real faith and real manhood we have, and how fit and ready we are to do the great and worthy tasks which He has in store for us; perhaps this, too, is for good, even though we can not understand it fully", if only we would think this, it would help us bear our burdens and grow stronger, better, and wiser from all our trials.

One other thought suggests itself. God has placed us here, we have learned, not for mere pleasure, but for a definite purpose, to do His work and make the world better and happier. God's purpose is sure. And we are the tools with which He accomplishes His purpose. Now, have you ever stood before the watchmaker's shop, and seen him wield his little, delicate tools so softly and so gently that they barely seem to move or to feel his touch? And then have you stood before the blacksmith's shop and seen him lift his heavy hammer aloft, with muscles stretched and taut, and bring it down with all his might, until the sparks fly in all directions, and both hammer and anvil ring and quiver? We are, all of us, the tools in God's hands, some, perhaps, the little, watchmaker's tools, which He wields so softly and gently that we barely feel His touch, and our trials and sorrows are light and easily borne. And others are the blacksmith's hammer and anvil, with which He deals His mighty blows, and we, too, must suffer and writhe and groan at the stroke. But neither hammer nor anvil nor watchmaker's tool can know the purpose of its master, why it is used as it is; nor can we know the purpose of our Master, why some He tries so lightly that they barely feel His touch, and to others He deals His heavy blows, blow upon blow, until they tremble and writhe and cry out in pain. Yet the Master's purpose is sure, is wise and good, and laden with blessing for all mankind, greater far than all our suffering. Of this we may be certain, and in Him we should ever trust. And perhaps, as the rabbis suggested, those whom He is calling for His greatest work, He tries most severely, to see if they are ready and fit.

And, as the story implied, not only Abraham was tried, but also Isaac. For it must have been indeed a severe trial and test of Isaac's faith and courage, when he felt himself bound upon the altar, and beheld the knife in his father's hand, upraised to take his life. In that moment he might well have doubted his father's love, and questioned God's wisdom and providence. But the rabbis told that, although only a lad, Isaac never faltered nor lost faith, not even for a single moment. Bravely and loyally he urged his father to be steadfast in the performance of his duty, and to strike the blow which would sacrifice him at God's command. Thereby he proved himself a worthy son of Abraham, equal to his father in faith in God and unflinching devotion to duty, and fit to become his successor in the service for which God had called Abraham and his posterity.

And not Abraham and Isaac alone has God tested by this most bitter trial, but also their descendants, the children of Israel. All Israel God has called as His servant, and charged to do His work and be a blessing unto all mankind, even as He called to Abraham. And all Israel God has tried continually, to learn whether they were ready and fit. Israel has suffered greater hardship and oppression than any other people upon the earth. For thousands of years Israel has been driven from place to place, homeless, friendless, and persecuted. Time and again Jewish fathers and mothers have had to sacrifice even their beloved children, and time and again they have made the sacrifice unhesitatingly and unquestioningly, in the spirit of Abraham of old. Israel has never lost faith in God. Ever it has trusted and ever it has repeated, "This, too, is for good; this, too, is God's will, and in accordance with His divine purpose of wisdom, goodness, and love for all men". Ever, when the clouds seemed darkest, and their sufferings too heavy to bear, they comforted themselves with the thought of God's protection and promise, and repeated in perfect faith the words of the Psalmist,

> I will lift up mine eyes unto the mountains:
> From whence shall my help come?
> My help cometh from the Lord,
> Who made heaven and earth.
> He will not suffer thy foot to be moved;
> He that keepeth thee will not slumber.
> Behold, He that keepeth Israel
> Doth neither slumber nor sleep.

This has ever been Israel's faith in God, exemplified in this beautiful story of Abraham, our great father.

And on Rosh Hashonah, our sacred New Year's Day, the blasts of the Shofar remind us of Abraham's sacrifice, and of God's promise to him. According to tradition, the Shofar was first made from the horn of the very ram which Abraham sacrificed in place of Isaac. Therefore the Shofar on New Year's Day proclaims, unto Israel and all mankind, peace and forgiveness, and a new period of life and faith in God.

The spot on Mt. Moriah where Abraham erected his altar became later, so the rabbis told, the field of the two brothers, about whom we have already heard. and the site of the glorious Temple of Solomon. The spot which was sanctified by Abraham's faith and devotion, and by the mutual love of the two brothers, was deemed worthy of becoming the place where Abraham's descendants might later bring their sacrifices to God, and consecrate themselves to His service, just as Father Abraham did of old.

NOTES

V. 2. The land of Moriah; presumably in the vicinity of Jerusalem, where, in historical times, Mt. Moriah, the Temple mount, was located.

Here, too, just as in the story of his call, Abraham does not know exactly whither he is going. But he relies on God's word, that at the right moment He will point out the proper mountain upon which to offer the sacrifice. The rabbis told that as Abraham drew near the end of his journey, he saw the pillar of fire, in which God was later to lead Israel through the desert, upon the top of one of the mountains. He asked Isaac if he saw it too, and Isaac answered that he did. But the two servants, when questioned, replied that they saw nothing. Then Abraham realized that this was no ordinary mountain, but the one destined for the sacrifice, and that the pillar of fire symbolized God's presence, revealed to him and Isaac alone. It is a beautiful thought that God's presence is revealed to those who live and work in perfect faith in Him, and who seek Him with their whole heart.

V. 3. The saddle consisted only of a small piece of cloth fastened to the animal's back. Elaborate saddles with stirrups were unknown in the East. As is still customary in the Orient, only the old man rode; the others accompanied him on foot.

V. 6. It was necessary to carry fire from the hearth at home, since in those days fire was not easily kindled. Wood, too, had to be carried with them, since in Palestine wood is very scarce, and so not easily gathered.

V. 13. The rabbis told that this ram had been one of the things created by God at twilight of the eve of the Sabbath of creation. It was created, they told, just that it might offer itself at this moment for sacrifice in place of Isaac.

Vv. 14-18 are really an interpolation into the original story, and, on the whole, rather detract from than add to the merit of the narration. The story is much more complete and artistic if we read v. 19 immediately after v. 13. This must have been the original form of the story.

XII

THE DEATH OF SARAH

(Genesis XXIII)

And Abraham came to mourn for Sarah, and to weep for her. (Genesis XXIII, 2.)

The memory of the righteous shall be for a blessing. (Proverbs X, 7.)

Read II Samuel XIX, 1-5.

It is told of a rabbi of old that he boasted, "Never have I called my wife 'Wife' nor my home 'Home', but I have always called my wife 'Home' and my home 'Wife'". It is indeed a beautiful thought, for above all else, our Jewish women, our Jewish wives and mothers, make the true Jewish home, recognized by all the world as the truest, noblest, and most beautiful and inspiring example of all that the home can and should be. All the love and holiness and inspiration, which radiate from our Jewish wives and mothers, sanctify our homes, and make of them temples hallowed by God's very presence.

An ancient, rabbinical legend beautifully illustrates the influence of the wife and mother in the home. While the father goes to the synagogue on Friday eve to offer homage unto God, and to thank Him for the blessings of the past week, and to implore His protection and favor for the week to come, the mother usually remains at home to supervise all preparations for the joyous Sabbath, and just at dusk to kindle the Sabbath lights, the symbols of Sabbath gladness and Sabbath blessing in the home. Then she and the children wait expectantly to greet their loved one. And as he enters the home and feels its holy spirit of love enfolding him, reverently he lays his hand in blessing, first upon the head of his wife, and then upon each child, and silently he thanks God once more for all this love and blessing. But, the wise rabbis told, the man never returns home alone; two angels always accompany him, his angels of good and of evil. If he finds the table beautifully spread, as it should be, the Sabbath candles kindled, and wife and children in festive array and festive spirit, joyfully awaiting his blessing, then the good angel says, "May this Sabbath and all thy Sabbaths be for blessing. Peace be on this house, peace and joy to every soul therein". And the angel of evil must respond, "Amen". But if the house be not ready, if the table be not spread, nor the Sabbath lights kindled, and if wife and children be not waiting with the smile of love upon their lips, then the angel of evil speaks, "May this Sabbath and all thy Sabbaths be for sorrow, and may no blessing abide within this home". And to this the angel of good must sadly whisper, "Amen" Truly it is the wife and mother who makes our Jewish home all that it is, and brings the manifold blessing of love and happiness to it. And when God, in His wisdom, takes her unto Himself, then it seems that all that was good and precious in life has departed.

So Abraham must have thought when the moment of separation from his beloved Sarah, the wife of his bosom, the companion of his trials and perils, the partner of his love and grief, she who was his own other self, and dearer to him than self, came. The whole story is told in one little sentence, "And Abraham came to mourn for Sarah, and to weep for her". Yet the little sentence overflows with meaning. We feel all Abraham's grief and sense of loss and loneliness. The rabbis told that with Sarah's death the cloud which symbolized God's presence, which had hovered over the tent of Abraham and filled it with the blessings of contentment and peace, departed; the light which Sarah had kindled on the Sabbath eve, and whose radiance glorified the tent throughout the entire week, was extinguished; the blessing which had rested upon the dough and other food, and ensured plenty and abundance for both the inmates and the stranger who might seek its shelter, ceased; and the doors of the tent, which had ever stood wide open for the poor and needy, inviting and summoning them to hospitality and protection, were closed tightly. She who had sanctified the tent by her presence, and had made of it a true, Jewish home, was gone. And Abraham grieved.

Yet even in his grief he did not complain. Still he trusted in God and His goodness, and still he realized that this, too, must be for good. He thought of all the long, happy years he and Sarah had had together, and of the great blessing which had come to them in their old age, in the person of their beloved son, Isaac. And he realized that all this happiness and blessing had come from God, that Sarah herself, and her love and companionship had been given to Him by God as the greatest blessing of his life. And so he must have murmured, as has every pious, God-fearing Jew since then,

> The Lord gave, and the Lord hath taken away;
> Blessed be the name of the Lord. (Job 1, 21.)

These words, our Bible tells us, were first spoken by the greatest sufferer of all. And ever in sorrow and separation, our fathers have trustingly repeated them, and thanked God for all the blessing which was theirs from Him for so long a time. It is a beautiful view of life, and the truest view too.

All that is good and precious, even the love of dear ones, comes from God, is but lent to us for a time, and must be given back when He in His wisdom, demands. Not even our loved ones may we keep with us forever. Yet when the moment of separation comes, instead of complaining, or doubting, or questioning, should we not thank God for all the love and blessing which He has given us for so many years; and should we not still trust in Him, as did Abraham, and believe that even this, hard though it be, must also be for good, even though we can not understand? We may grieve and mourn, as Abraham did, but still we must trust in God, and thank Him for all His goodness and love.

The following story is told of Rabbi Meir, the greatest disciple of Rabbi Akiba, and his beloved wife, Beruria. One Friday evening Rabbi Meir came home from the synagogue, expecting to be met at the door as usual by his beloved wife, and their two boys, the idols of their eyes, all waiting to receive his Sabbath blessing. But on this evening Beruria alone welcomed him. In answer to his question where the boys were, she said that they had gone away for a moment, but that they two would meanwhile eat their evening meal. So they sat down together. Suddenly Beruria said, "Rabbi, I must ask a question. Some time ago a friend entrusted to me some priceless jewels for safekeeping. I had them so long that I thought he would never want them again, and that I might keep them forever. Now he has demanded them back. Must I return them?" "Surely you must", said her husband. Without a word she took him by the hand and led him into the next room, where, upon the bed, cold in death, lay the two boys, the priceless jewels which the Friend of all had entrusted to them for a time, and had taken back when He needed them. The wise rabbi understood, and together they bowed their heads and thanked God for the love and happiness He had given them in their boys during all these precious years. Truly the Lord giveth, and taketh away again, and truly for all this, for all the happiness and blessing, which come with the love and companionship of our dear ones, may the name of the Lord be praised.

One more lesson this story teaches, a truth upon which

Judaism has ever laid great emphasis. The Bible tells that Abraham came to mourn for Sarah, and to weep for her. But it tells, too, that after the first strong passion of grief was spent, "Abraham rose up from before his dead". True grief is beautiful and sacred. It is the token of thankful appreciation of the rich blessing, which God has given us for a time in the love of our dear ones; our tears are the tender tribute of affection for those who might be with us but a while. True grief hallows and ennobles and clears the vision, so that we may see deeper and with greater understanding and broader sympathy into the problems and sorrows and needs of life.

But grief, indulged in too long, becomes base, ignoble and selfish. It loses its sanctifying power; it narrows and obstructs the vision, and confines and stunts the soul. We become self-centered; we think only of our own grief and our own sorrow, and indulge ourselves in them, until this becomes the normal course of our life, and to depart therefrom is difficult and painful, and causes unrest and discontent. We refuse to believe that others have grief and sorrows, too, like ours, or even surpassing ours, and we cease to feel for them and to think of them. We wrap ourselves up in the dark, forbidding cloud of our grief, and live apart by ourselves, and lose entirely the consciousness of brotherhood with our fellowmen and of the duty of serving them. We forget that God has created us for a purpose, and that this purpose is not to indulge ourselves in grief, but like Abraham, after the first bitter pain of sorrow has passed, to rise up from before our dead, and resume the ordinary tasks and duties of life, to live in the world among our fellowmen, and bring unto them help and cheer and blessing. We are here on this earth, not to grieve too much, but to serve. And though our loved ones were precious to us, and our grief is sincere and deep, and can never cease completely, nevertheless it is our duty to thank God for the love which was ours, to rejoice in the hallowing memory of our dear ones, which abides with us forever, and to approach the tasks of life, which still exist for us, with stronger faith, deeper insight, and holier consecration to the service of God. Thus alone can we rear unto our loved ones an imperishable monument in the hearts and lives of men, so that their memory shall be for a blessing, even as the Bible says.

So Abraham mourned and grieved. But bravely he faced the years of loneliness ahead, and prepared to bury his beloved Sarah. It must be a fitting sepulchre. So he bought the Cave of Machpelah in Hebron for four hundred shekels of silver, a very large sum of money for those days. Thus the Cave of Machpelah passed into the possession of Abraham and his descendants, and there not only Sarah, but Abraham, too, and his children after him for three generations, were buried. Ever since the Cave of Machpelah has been a place of veneration for the descendants of Abraham, and ever they have pilgrimed thither and shown their reverence for the memory of their great and noble ancestors.

And our religion teaches that after all, death is not the end, but only the beginning of another existence. When one of our great ancestors passed away, the Bible says, "He was gathered to his fathers", not only in the family sepulchre, where their bodies were laid to rest, but in the great, eternal life of the spirit, which knows no end and no separation, but only God's reward and God's blessing. And somehow, even here on earth, death is not the end. The rabbis said of Jacob, "Jacob, our father, never died". And in a sense this is true of every righteous man. For the blessing he has wrought during lifetime still continues among those who knew and loved him, and his memory lives on for years and generations, inspiring all to lives of nobility and usefulness similar to his. Truly our Bible says,

The memory of the righteous shall be for a blessing.

And when our time comes to go hence and stand at last in the presence of our Maker, may we go like Sarah and Abraham and Jacob and all the patriarchs of old, leaving behind us some to mourn for us and to weep, and a memory which shall be for a blessing unto those who come after us. Then we shall not have lived in vain, but shall have realized the purpose for which God placed us here on earth and gave us life; then through us will all the families of the earth be blessed.

So Sarah died and Abraham mourned for her. And so every Jew has mourned who has lost the companion of his days and the source of his truest blessing. And to this day when the husband comes home joyous and expectant on Friday eve from the sanctuary of the synagogue to the even greater sanctuary of the home, reverently and thankfully he lays his hand upon the bowed head of his wife with the softly-murmured words, "May God make thee like Sarah and Rebekah, like Leah and Rachel".

NOTES

In ancient Palestine it was customary to bury the dead in caves. There are many famous, ancient sepulchres in Palestine, visited by thousands of pilgrims today. But the most famous of all is the Cave of Machpelah near Hebron. Until the war in 1918 it was in the possession of the Mohammedans, who believe themselves descendants of Ishmael and consequently also descendants of Abraham. Therefore they have quite as much veneration for the place, as we Jews. And unfortunately, being very fanatical in their religious beliefs and practices, they have allowed none but Mohammedans to approach the sepulchre. They regard it as a sacred shrine and have erected a sanctuary over it. Into this none but Mohammedans were for many centuries permitted to enter. Perhaps Jews will soon be once again allowed to approach close to the sepulchre of Father Abraham and there show their reverence for his great memory. *Machpelah* means "double". Actually the Cave of Machpelah consists of two parts, one of which projects from the other.

Arba" (Joshua XIV, 15) or, probably better, "city of the four" (either four heroes [cf. the names of the three heroes in Judges I, 10] or four quarters).

V. 3. "The children of Heth"; in early, pre-Israelite times the Hittites overran northern Babylonia and western Asia as far south as the border of the desert, below Hebron. They were a non-Semitic, warlike people, whose original home was in the highlands of Asia Minor, where they had established a powerful kingdom. Several excavations have been conducted on the site of the ancient Hittite capital, and valuable finds have been made. The Hittites were gradually pushed back and eventually driven out of Palestine in the 14th and 13th centuries B. C. E. by the great kings of the powerful nineteenth dynasty of Egypt. In the early period, to which the story of Abraham is assigned, Hebron may have been an important Hittite settlement.

V. 8. In the Orient a bargain is seldom concluded between the two parties to the transaction directly. Almost invariably the services of one or more mediators are invoked by each side. All then participate in the haggling and chaffering, seeking, on the one hand, to reduce the price demanded, and, on the other hand, to induce the prospective purchaser to increase his offer. Finally, after considerable time and much excitement, the bargain is concluded to the satisfaction of all concerned. Thus Abraham now entreats the Hittites to act as his mediators with Ephron.

V. 10. Ephron is sitting among the other elders of the city at the city gate. There the elders were wont to gather, and there business transactions were carried on, court was held, and the public life of the city was administered; cf. note to XIX, 1.

V. 16. In the ancient Orient, since the art of coining money was unknown, money was weighed instead of counted (cf. Jeremiah XXXII, 9f; Zechariah XI, 12). The word *shekel* literally means "weight". Silver was the metal regularly employed for currency. The silver shekel was the standard of value in ancient Israel. Its value varied at different periods (cf. *Jewish Encyclopedia* XI, 257f.).

As has been said, this was a very large sum of money for that time. Ephron seems to have made a very good bargain. The scene is typically Oriental. The Oriental loves a bargain more than anything else. In commercial transactions it is still customary for the seller when first asked the price of an article, to offer to give it to the would-be purchaser. When this offer is refused and he is pressed for the price, he names one greatly in excess of the real value of the article. Then begins a process of haggling until the price is finally reduced to what seems reasonable to both parties. Here, too, Ephron begins in the usual manner. At first he is unwilling to part with his field and cave, he says, and then when pushed, he offers to give it to Abraham. When this offer, too, is refused, he names a price probably far in excess of the real value of the property. Abraham's generosity and magnanimity are shown in that he immediately accepts this first-named price, even though he must feel that it is probably excessive.

V. 17. Everything in the field is specified as being included in the sale. This is still customary in the Orient. One of best authorities on Eastern life has written, "The contract must mention everything that belongs to it (the lot), and certify that fountains or wells in it, trees upon it, etc., are sold with the field. If you rent a home, not only the building itself, but every room in it, above and below, down to the kitchen, pantry, stable and hen-coop, must be specified". (Thomson, *The Land and the Book,* II, 383.)

V. 18. To be binding contracts in the ancient Orient had to be duly witnessed. Ancient Babylonian contracts have been unearthed, to which the names of ten or even more witnesses are affixed. So here, all who are passing by at the moment are made witnesses to this contract.

XIII

THE WOOING OF REBEKAH

(Genesis XXIV)

And Isaac brought her into his mother Sarah's tent—and he loved her. And Isaac was comforted for his mother. (Genesis XXIV, 67).

A woman of valor who can find?
For her price is far above rubies.
Her children rise up, and call her blessed;
Her husband also, and he praiseth her:
'Many daughters have done valiantly,
But thou excellest them all'. (Proverb XXXI, 10 and 28f.)

Read Proverbs XXXI, 10-31 (selected verses).

The story which we consider today is the first real romance which we have found in our study of the Bible, and one of the oldest and most beautiful of the many love idyls of the world's literature. It, too, is a classic of narrative art, comparable in every way with the stories of the Garden of Eden and of the sacrifice of Isaac. The author was particularly happy in his delineation of the characters of the faithful, devoted, efficient, old servant, and of the young, virtuous, tender-hearted, high-minded maiden, ready at the call of love to leave home and kindred, and to journey forth into the strange world, to meet the husband who had sent for her, and who was also her own choice. We are face to face with a real heroine, whose beauty, charm, and nobility command our admiration and love.

She seems more real, human and sympathetic than Sarah, and eminently fit to be the wife of Isaac and the successor of Sarah as the second great mother in Israel. As the Bible

says so beautifully and expressively, "Isaac brought her into
his mother Sarah's tent, and he loved her". In her answering love he found solace for the loss of his mother. And, as
the rabbis told, the cloud, symbolizing the presence of God,
which had hovered over the tent throughout Sarah's lifetime,
but had departed at her death, once more returned; the
light which Sarah had kindled on the eve of every Sabbath,
again shone forth; the blessing which had rested upon the
dough was renewed, and the doors of the tent were again
opened wide for the needy. Once more God's blessing of
love and happiness rested upon that home, and radiated far
and wide to all who came under its influence. It was the
type of what the true Jewish home has ever been, just as
Sarah and Rebekah were the types of the true Jewish wife
and mother. Of them, as of every such wife and mother
in Israel the beautiful words of Proverbs are eternally true,

> A woman of valor who can find?
> For her price is far above rubies.
> Her children rise up, and call her blessed;
> Her husband also, and he praiseth her:
> 'Many daughters have done valiantly,
> But thou excellest them all'.

For as was said in the last lesson, it is above all else
our Jewish wives and mothers who make the real Jewish
home. From them radiate all our sacred home love and
joy and blessing, and all the noble influences which help
to make of their sons and daughters true Jewish men and
women. As they kindle the Sabbath lights on Friday eve,
they symbolize all that it pure, noble, and holy in our individual lives and in the collective life of the Jewish people.
The Kiddush ceremony on Sabbath eve in every pious Jewish
household is a sanctification, not only of the home, but of
the wife and mother, the guardian angel who makes and
protects and blesses the home, who keeps far from its doors
all evil and defilement, and permits only beauty, holiness, and

joy to enter.˙ And as in the Kiddush service the beautiful
chapter from Proverbs is read, and those sacred words ring
forth,

> A woman of valor who can find?
> For her price is far above rubies.
> Many daughters have done valiantly,
> But thou excellest them all.

every Jewish husband and every Jewish child knows full
well that it is to just his wife and his mother that these
words apply so truly. Our Jewish wives and mothers and
homes are the greatest blessings which God has given unto
His Jewish people, and, more than aught else, they have
served, through all Israel's long years of trial and sorrow
and persecution, to keep the light of hope and faith and
devotion to the God of our fathers burning in our hearts,
even as they have kept the Sabbath light of peace and joy
and sanctity burning in our Jewish homes.

Many true, beautiful and inspiring stories of Jewish
mothers, and of their nobility, idealism, and capacity for
sacrifice for husband and children might be told. However,
the following romantic story of Rabbi Akiba and his faithful
wife will suffice. Rabbi Akiba, during the first forty years
of his life, was a poor shepherd, uneducated and ignorant.
He kept the sheep of Kalba Sabua, a man renowned for
wealth and philanthropy. And, as is so often the case, he
fell in love with Rachel, the gentle and beautiful daughter
of his master, and his love was returned. Unknown to her
father, they were married. But first Rachel made Akiba
promise that he would study and become a wise man and
a leader in Israel; for she had already recognized his latent
ability. When her father heard of the marriage he was
furious. He cast his daughter from his house, and vowed
that she should never again receive aught from him.

Then began pitiful days, days of want and hunger, especially hard for the young wife, reared in plenty and lux-

ury. Still her love and faith in her husband buoyed her up
and made her happy. But Akiba's heart was torn with grief
as he saw his loved one suffering so bravely and uncom-
plainingly, and thought of all that she had sacrificed for his
sake. They were compelled to live in a miserable hovel and
sleep upon a couch of straw even in midwinter.

One cold day they heard a knock on their door. A poor
man, trembling and in rags worse than theirs, asked for a
little straw, that he might have a bed for his sick wife.
Then they realized that there were human beings even poorer
and more wretched than themselves, and they thanked God,
despite their poverty, for all His blessings. The poor man,
so the rabbis told, was the prophet Elijah, who had come
in this guise to comfort and encourage them in their misery.

And he had encouraged them. Up to this time Akiba
had not had the heart to leave his beloved young wife, to
go and study in the great schools. It seemed hopeless for
a man of forty to begin to study. Nor had his brave, young
wife been quite brave enough to bid him leave her. Now
courage came to both. Bravely she sent him forth, and
bravely he set out to study and learn, and to become a wise
man, teacher and leader in Israel. It was a difficult undertaking. He had to begin with the little children to learn his
letters. But the thought of his noble wife and of all her
loving sacrifice spurred him on. And at last, at the end of
twelve long years, he thought he had learned enough to
warrant his returning to her.

Meanwhile things had gone badly with her. Sternly her
father had kept his vow. Time and again she was on the
verge of starvation. Yet she labored on and sent all that
she could earn in one way or another to her husband, that
he might continue untroubled at his studies. And one win-
ter, when her earnings had been less than usual, she even
stole forth into the market place and sold her beautiful, long
tresses, that she might send him some assistance.

At last Akiba was coming back with joy in his heart at the thought of being once more united with his devoted wife, and being able to alleviate her hardships and give her happiness in return for all her deprivations and sacrifices. But just as he set foot within the door, he heard his Rachel in conversation with a neighbor, and the latter say, "It serves thee right for having married beneath thee; thy husband has forsaken thee and will never return". And the brave Rachel answered, "If only he would hearken to me, he would remain away another twelve years in order to study and grow, and become the leader in Israel that I know he can be". When Akiba heard these brave words he thought, "I will do her bidding; surely this is her desire". So without a word he went away again, and remained another twelve years. During these years his knowledge grew in every direction, and the fame of the new rabbi spread far and wide. His teachers and colleagues came to respect his opinions and seek his advice, and at last he was looked upon by all who knew him as the wisest man and the true spiritual leader of all Israel. But his real name was as yet unknown.

Then one day word came that the great rabbi was coming to the city in which Rachel dwelt. The news penetrated even to her hovel, and with it her heart beat fast. Somehow the thought grew upon her, that this great rabbi would prove to be her husband, gone now these twenty-four years. Trembling and expectant she went out with the crowds to greet the master. At last she beheld him among all his disciples, and lo, it was he. Sobbing for joy she fell to the ground and kissed his feet. Indignantly the disciples sought to push the seeming beggar away. But the master raised her in his arms before all the people and kissed her tenderly and reverently. And softly the words fell from his lips, "Let her be. All the knowledge which I have, and all which you have, are due to her alone". So Rachel's husband came back to her, the great Rabbi Akiba, the wisest man of his

day, the leader of Israel in the period of almost its greatest
trial. And Rachel had her reward.

But this was not the end. Among the crowd who had
come to greet the great rabbi was Kalba Sabua. Little did
he dream that the man whom he sought to honor was his
own son-in-law, whom he had driven away in anger. He
had intended to ask the great rabbi to free him from his
cruel vow, if this were possible. His heart had gone out
to his daughter in all her misery, and he longed to help her,
but his vow held him back. Now perhaps the wise rabbi
could find some way to release him from the vow. And
when he asked the rabbi, and the latter answered, "Hadst
thou known that thy son-in-law would become a renowned
rabbi, wouldst thou have made thy vow?" he replied, "Had
I thought that he would be able to learn even one chapter
of the Torah, I would have been satisfied". "I am thy son-
in-law", said Rabbi Akiba simply. For a moment the rich
man stared in amazement. Then he, too, threw himself at
the feet of his son-in-law and begged forgiveness. But
Rabbi Akiba raised him up with words of comfort and
cheer. "It was all God's will", he said, "all for the best".
And thereafter they lived happily together. The fortune of
Kalba Sabua became Akiba's and Rachel's in time. The
poverty and suffering of their early days were succeeded by
plenty and happiness. Nor did they fail to give of their
abundance to the poor. Of Rabbi Akiba we shall hear from
time to time. But of his noble wife, Rachel, we know no
more. Nor do we need to learn more. Her story and her
example are typical of the Jewish wife and mother, just as
are those of Sarah and Rebekah. And of her, and of them,
and of all true Jewish wives and mothers we may say,

> Many daughters have done valiantly,
> But thou excellest them all.

But to return to Rebekah. Not every maiden, even among

the relatives of Abraham, was worthy to become the wife of Isaac. The task of being a blessing unto all the families of the earth was to descend from Abraham to Isaac as a precious birthright. Isaac was to become God's servant and messenger of truth and blessing after his father. In this task his wife must share. And quite as much as Isaac, she, too, must possess all the qualities and virtues indispensable for the fulfilment of the mission, kindness of heart, generosity, hospitality, tireless industry, willingness to serve and to satisfy the needs of even the humblest of God's creatures. And so the wise servant determined upon a test, which should adequately measure the maiden's real worth and· fitness to become the wife of his young master. If, in answer to his request for water, she should bethink herself also of his thirsting camels, and if she should respond whole-heartedly and generously to his appeal for entertainment for himself and his attendants, and should not spare herself in the sincerity of her hospitality, it would prove that this maiden was worthy in every way to become the wife of Isaac, and to share in the glorious birthright of service which was to be theirs. How well Rebekah stood this test, the story tells.

But a word of caution must be spoken here. This motive of the test, and particularly of Rebekah's watering the camels, is the most striking incident of the early part of the story, and its moral lesson is obvious. But this is not enough. This is by no means the main theme of the story, and certainly the author intended it to be no more than a passing incident in the larger narrative. Therefore to over-emphasize this thought means to miss the real point of the story, and to fail to bring out its essential Jewish message.

Second only to Rebekah in effectiveness of portrayal and in the interest and sympathy evoked in the mind of the reader, is the faithful, old servant. Loyally and efficiently he discharges the responsible mission upon which he has been sent. His thoughts are not for himself at all, but only for his master's welfare. Even before he will touch a morsel of food or satisfy his other physical needs, he will tell his errand. His faith in God is unbounded; he is sure, even as Abraham was, that his journey can not be in vain, but that it is in accordance with God's will and will be under God's guidance.

Far too frequently the term, servant, is thought to be indicative of inferiority and degradation. We would all be masters; but few are willing to be servants. Yet we have learned that God has created us, not to be masters, but to be servants, to serve Him and our fellowmen loyally and faithfully, like this servant of Abraham, without thought of reward, but with the consciousness of duty in our hearts and the fear of God upon us. Only by serving can we realize the purpose of existence. And "servant of the Lord" is the proudest and most honorable title the world can know. This title God bestowed upon Israel, when he spoke through His prophet,

Ye are My witnesses, saith the Lord,
And My servant whom I have chosen.   (Isaiah XLIII, 10.)

and again,

Remember these things, O Jacob,
And Israel, for thou art My servant;
I have formed thee, thou art Mine own servant.   (Isaiah XLIV, 21.)

And just as Abraham sent his faithful servant upon a difficult and responsible journey, and assured him that God's angel would go before him to guide him upon the way, so has God sent His servant, Israel, upon a long and difficult and exacting mission, and charged him to serve fearlessly and faithfully, until his work shall be accomplished and his mission of service and blessing shall be fulfilled.

But thou, Israel, My servant,
Jacob whom I have chosen,

The seed of Abraham, My friend;
Thou whom I have taken hold of from the ends of the earth,
And called thee from the uttermost parts thereof,
And said unto thee: 'Thou art My servant,
I have chosen thee and not cast thee away';
Fear thou not, for I am with thee,
Be not dismayed, for I am thy God;
I strengthen thee, yea, I help thee;
Yea, I uphold thee with My victorious right hand.   (Isaiah XLI
    8-10.)

NOTES

V. 2. The servant here would seem to be the same Eliezer mentioned in XV, 2. "Elder of the house" is probably a technical term for steward or chief servant.

Vv. 2-3. Solemnizing an oath by putting the hand upon the loins or the thigh of the person to whom the oath was given, was a common practice in the ancient Semitic world. It was probably based upon the conception of the peculiar sanctity of certain parts or members of the body. Cf. also XLVII, 29.

V. 4. In the Orient a man's parents generally choose a wife for him. Cf. XXI, 21; XXVIII, 1f; XXXVIII, 6.

An interesting and illuminating parallel to this mission of the servant to secure a suitable wife for Isaac from the relatives of his father, is to be found in Blunt, *A Pilgrimage to Nejd.* The Blunts undertook a long and dangerous journey from Tadmor, the site of an ancient and important city in the wilderness of northern Syria, to Nejd in central Arabia, partly in order "to secure for a young Arab attendant whom they valued, a wife from among his blood relatives, the Ibn Arooks, whom he had never seen."

V. 10. Aram Naharaim, i. e. Mesopotamia, the country lying between the Euphrates and Tigris rivers. The name means "Aram of the two rivers". The city of Nahor here referred to must have been located somewhere in the northwestern part of Mesopotamia, in the vicinity of the large and important city of Haran.

V. 11. Camels kneel for their riders to mount or dismount, and to be loaded or unloaded.

As has been said before, in many parts of the Orient water is scarce. Frequently a village or city gets all its water from one well. And since cities are generally located on the tops of hills for pur-

poses of defense, and the wells or springs, from which they draw
water are usually at the lowest point, at the foot of the hills, it
happens frequently, as here, that the wells are outside the city walls
or limits. Often the water must be carried for considerable distances.
This work generally falls to the women or girls. As a rule they go
for water once or twice a day, generally, as here, in the evening,
or in the morning and evening; hence the expression, "at the time of
evening the time that women go out to draw water".

V. 15. The full genealogy of Rebekah is given in XXII, 20-24.

V. 16. Not infrequently the water of wells or springs does not
rise to the level of the ground, and must either be drawn up laboriously by buckets, or, if the opening of the well be large, steps lead
either all or part of the way down to the water. Here the steps
seem to have led down to the water's edge, so that the jars could be
filled by hand.

V. 23. In accordance with the principles of oriental hospitality
the servant does not ask whether he may pass the night in Rebekah's
house. This is self-understood, provided of course that there be
room. Hence his question.

V. 25. Rebekah answers that not only is there room to lodge,
but also provisions for himself, and even for his animals. It must
have been a large and well-provided household which could at a
moment's notice shelter and feed a stranger with ten camels and the
number of servants necessitated by these.

V. 30 seems to imply that in significant contrast to Rebekah's
sincere and generous hospitality, Laban was influenced by consideration of the rich gifts which his sister had received and the desire
to obtain similar presents for himself. This is an effective hint at
Laban's avaricious nature, of which we shall have further instances
in the Jacob story.

V. 31. In the typical semi-nomadic home, such as is here pictured, still today as in ancient times, animals are housed, not in
separate stables, but in the very house in which the family resides.
Usually the floor of such a house is divided into two parts, one for
the animals, and the other, a few steps higher than the first, for
the family.

V. 32. Laban furnishes the provision for the camels and the
water for the men.

In the Orient, where only sandals are worn, washing the feet is
the first act of hospitality; cf. XVIII, 4.

V. 33. A part of the regular procedure of securing a wife for a
young man in the East, as described by Trumbull, *Studies in Oriental*

Social Life, 18, is as follows; "Arriving at the house, the deputy asks if 'the father of Maryam'—or whatever the young woman's name may be—is at home. When the latter appears to greet his guests, he is told that the deputy will speak for the party. As coffee is proffered, the deputy says that the visitors have come upon a very important mission, and that they can neither eat nor drink until that mission is accomplished. It is now as it was in the days of Abraham."

V. 47. In the Orient, still today as in ancient times, women commonly wear rings in their noses.

V. 50 implies that Laban and Bethuel are conscious of divine intervention in this incident, and therefore are willing to forego the usual right of parent or brother of disposing of the daughter's or sister's hand, and to leave the matter to Rebekah herself. At the same time it should be understood that in Israel women always enjoyed rights and privileges unusual in the modern Orient. From a considerable mass of evidence we infer that it must have been not uncommon in Israel to secure the maiden's consent before giving her in marriage. Nor do the present-day oriental customs of the harem and of the veiling of women seem to have been common in ancient Israel. Throughout the Bible we hear constantly of the high position, power, and privileges of women.

V. 53. In the case of a betrothal, such as this was, presents to the bride and her family from the side of the groom were, and still are, the rule. They serve to bind the marriage contract, as it were.

V. 55. It is customary in the Orient to urge a departing guest to remain longer and enjoy further hospitality. Here, of course, this sentiment is coupled with the thought that they might never see Rebekah again, in consequence of which they were loathe to let her depart.

V. 59. In the Orient the nurse in childhood remains a woman's personal attendant and confidant throughout life. Cf. XXXV, 8.

V. 64. To alight from the animal or chariot upon which one is riding, in the presence of one who is walking, is considered in the Orient a mark of respect. Cf. Joshua XV, 18; Judges I, 14; I Samuel XXV, 23; II Kings V, 21.

V. 65. In the East the bride should not be seen by the groom unveiled before marriage, or at least between betrothal and marriage. Therefore Rebekah lets down her veil.

V. 67. Sarah's tent was nothing more than the women's apartment of the principal tent of the encampment; cf. XVIII, 9f and

Judges IV, 18. Occasionally, however, when there was more than one wife, and particularly when the relations between them were not altogether amicable, a separate tent was assigned to each; cf. XXXI, 33.

Bringing the bride into the tent or house of the groom has always constituted the essential marriage ceremony in the Orient. Religious rites, such as we observe today, were unknown in ancient Israel. The removal of the bride's veil by the groom, when they were left alone together for the first time, was the culminating rite of the marriage ceremony.

It should be remarked, also, that in ancient Israel, as in fact throughout the entire Semitic world, marriage between cousins was regarded as the highest type of union. Occasionally a man was thought to have an inalienable right to his cousin's hand, and she could marry no one else until he had publicly waived his right. We shall have another instance of marriage of cousins in the story of Jacob and Leah and Rachel. Readers of *The Arabian Nights* will remember numerous instances of this same custom in that work, so illuminative of oriental customs and manners.

XIV

THE WELL OF THE COVENANT

(Genesis XXVI, 12-33)

Let there now be an oath betwixt us, even betwixt us and thee, and let us make a covenant with thee. (Genesis XXVI, 28.)

Hatred stirreth up strifes;
But love covereth all transgressions. (Proverbs X, 12.)

Read Micah IV, 1-4.

The thoughtful student of the Bible can not but observe that although the last portion of the Abraham story implied that Isaac was destined, under God's providence, to play an important role in the history of Israel, actually the Bible tells very little of Isaac's life and work. In only one story is he the chief actor. Otherwise his is a role second to those of Abraham, Rebekah, and Jacob, the three persons with whom he is most intimately associated.

And even this one story duplicates in almost every detail what has been previously told about Abraham. The story itself consists of two episodes, that of Rebekah passing as the sister of Isaac, and that of Isaac's covenant with Abimelech. Two other versions of the first episode occur in the Bible, in XII, 10-20, and XX, in both of which, however, Abraham and Sarah are the chief actors. It is noteworthy that in the second of these two versions Abimelech of Gerar plays the same part as in this Isaac-Rebekah version. It is altogether unlikely that so unpleasant an event could have occurred in one family on three separate occasions, and that one king should have twice played the same unfortunate and discreditable role. More probably we have here an instance of the well-known fact, that very frequently one and the same tradition attaches itself in slightly varying forms to several historical figures. In this case it would seem that, inasmuch as the central motive of this episode is that the wife passes as the sister of her husband, and since the Bible tells that Sarah was actually Abraham's half-sister (XX, 12), whereas Rebekah was only Isaac's cousin, this portion of the story was originally told about Abraham and Sarah, and came only secondarily to be told of Isaac and Rebekah also.

Similarly the episode of Isaac's covenant with Abimelech has its complete parallel in the account of Abraham's covenant with the same king (XXI, 22-34). One significant fact proves conclusively that XXVI does not imply that Isaac merely renewed the covenant with Abimelech which Abraham had made previously, but that it states clearly that Isaac's covenant with Abimelech was the first such covenant made. XXI tells of a well which had been dug by the servants of Abraham, but which the servants of Abimelech had seized. Abraham proves his title to the well, and in token thereof he gives to Abimelech seven ewe-lambs. The Hebrew words for "seven" is *sheba*. It is closely akin to *shebuah*, "oath" or "covenant". Therefore the story says, Abraham called that well *Beer-sheba*. The story is somewhat confused as to whether this name should be interpreted as "the well of the seven", i. e., the seven ewe-lambs, or "the well of the covenant". On the other hand, XXVI tells that Isaac dug four wells, at the last of which he made a covenant with Abimelech. Therefore Isaac gave to this well, which his servants had just dug, the name *Beer-sheba*, here meaning unmistakably, "the well of the covenant". This story implies both that this was a new well, just discovered by the servants of Isaac, and also that this spot had never been called Beer-sheba· before, but first received this name from Isaac. It knows nothing, therefore, of a well previously dug by Abraham at this same place and given this same name by him. It is clear that these are actually two different and independent versions of the story of the covenant with Abimelech; the one version tells that Abraham made the covenant, and the other ascribes this role to Isaac. Since the Isaac version of the story is apparently more complete, and explains the name Beer-sheba, more logically and satisfactorily than the Abraham version, it is probable, though by no means absolutely certain, that in the original form of this story Isaac played the leading role, and that this was ascribed only secondarily to Abraham also. If so, then, as has been stated, this is the only story in the entire Bible in which Isaac is really the principal actor.

It is interesting to note that some late Biblical writer sought to harmonize these two versions by telling that Isaac merely reopened the wells which Abraham had previously dug, and which the Philistines had filled up. Accordingly he inserted vv. 15 and 18 into XXVI. Not only do these two verses confuse the story and disturb its continuity, but this writer failed also to insert a third verse, necessitated by his attempted harmonization, stating that Isaac merely renewed the covenant with Abimelech which Abraham had made before him. Manifestly this writer did not succeed in his task. Certainly the story in XXVI reads more smoothly without vv. 15 and 18.

But while it is true that the Bible records only this one original Isaac story, and even in this, as in everything else, it makes Isaac the counterpart of his father, nevertheless by this very fact it voices a significant truth. God had called Abraham to be His servant, to be a blessing unto all the families of the earth, and to bring to them the knowledge of Him and His law. He had tested Abraham by bitter trials, and had proved his fitness for this exalted and exacting mission. After Abraham's death this mission of service had descended to Isaac as a precious birthright. The same duties and obligations which had rested upon Abraham, now devolved upon Isaac. He must possess the same qualities and virtues as Abraham, if he, too, was to be fit for God's service. And so the Bible tells that some of the same trials which Abraham had endured, also befell Isaac, and that he, too, withstood them as his father had done. But even more than this, the Bible implies that just because he was Abraham's son, and had been brought up by his father, and had lived in intimate association with him, he had inherited Abraham's virtues. We have already learned that the rabbis called attention to the fact that Lot greeted the angels and proffered his hospitality in almost the same words with which Abraham had greeted them earlier in the day. They explained this remarkable coincidence by saying that Lot had learned the lesson of hospitality from Abraham. Similarly Isaac must have acquired his virtues, which made him so like his father, as the result of the latter's gentle but compelling example and influence. The rabbis used to liken good deeds and helpful influence to a lamp whose flame can kindle one thousand other lamps yet grow not one whit smaller or weaker thereby. Or as our own poet, Lowell, has put it,

> As one lamp lights another, nor grows less,
> So nobleness enkindleth nobleness.

This story shows how completely Isaac had inherited his father's peace-loving disposition. When the shepherds of Abraham and Lot had quarreled, Abraham had yielded to Lot, and had allowed him to choose the more desirable land. Here, too, the shepherds of Isaac quarrel with those of Abimelech for the wells of water. But this case was more aggravated. For Isaac's servants had discovered and dug the wells, and according to desert practice the wells belonged to them. But the servants of Abimelech claimed them, probably upon the rather questionable grounds that the land belonged to them. But the story implies that this was no valid claim, and that Isaac had by far the better right to the wells. Nevertheless he yielded his rights, as Abraham had done, in order to preserve peace.

Peace is the greatest blessing of life. When all men shall live in perfect peace with one another, then they will also live completely in accordance with God's law. The fundamental task of the servant of the Lord is to preserve and promote peace at all costs. And whoever does this is a true servant of the Lord. Rights are precious, and should be guarded most jealously. Yet more precious at times even than the safeguarding of rights and mere, mechanical justice is peace; and men, and nations, too, must learn to make sacrifices and yield rights once and yet again for the sake of peace.

Doubtless it was not easy for Isaac to yield. It would have been far more natural, and possibly more agreeable, too, to say at the very commencement of the trouble, "This well is mine, for I dug it, and I shall defend my rights at all costs". Not improbably, too, he could have defended himself successfully, had the men of Gerar attacked him, for he had many servants and followers. But he was mindful of the teaching and example of his father and of his precious birthright of service. Therefore he resisted the temptation to hold the well at all costs, and yielded; and not only once, but a second and a third time. Thus he proved himself a man of peace like his father, and worthy of his birthright. And thus he established peace and friendship with his neighbors, the people of Gerar. As the Bible says,

> Hatred stirreth up strifes;
> But love covereth all transgressions.

Here, just as in the majority of cases, hatred and opposition would have meant strife and bloodshed and eternal enmity; it would have meant that Isaac brought, not peace, but warfare to his fellowmen, and was unworthy to be the servant of the Lord. But love and forgiveness and patient forbearance meant peace and fellowship and an eternal covenant of brotherhood. The weak and selfish are only too prone to fight; only the strong and generous can forgive and yield. The wise rabbis used to say, "If one refrains from sin once, twice and thrice, God will guard him thereafter, and he will triumph over sin". So it was with Isaac.

A charming story about Rabbi Meir, the greatest disciple of Rabbi Akiba, shows the limits to which the true servant of the Lord will go in order to preserve peace. Rabbi Meir used to hold his lectures until late in the evening. A certain woman, whose soul thirsted for knowledge of the law of God, used to attend his lectures. One evening she returned home from the school later than usual, and found her husband there before her, and enraged because she was not yet at home and the evening meal had not been prepared. He was a boor, altogether without appreciation of the Torah, and thought only of his appetites and pleasures. When he heard that she had remained away so long just to listen to Rabbi Meir's lecture, his rage became extreme, and he drove her from the house and vowed that she should never return until she had first spat in the face of her revered teacher. In sorrow and shame the woman left the house. Almost unconsciously her feet carried her back to the school, whence she had departed so joyously only a short time before. Slowly and sadly she entered the room where the great teacher still sat with a few of his chosen disciples. Now the prophet Elijah had appeared to Rabbi Meir, and had revealed to him how the cruel husband had treated his wife. When Rabbi Meir saw the woman, he began to blink his eyes and to rub them as if they troubled him. Then he called out, "Does not someone here know a remedy for sore eyes?" In those days it was a common belief that if certain persons would spit upon sore eyes, they would be healed. Therefore Rabbi Meir called out what he did. At first there was no response. But when he had called again the woman came forward, trembling and abashed, and said, "Master, I can heal thine eyes". "Do so", said Rabbi Meir. With that she spat in his eyes, and immediately he ceased to blink. He looked at her for a moment mildly and benevolently, and then he said, "Go home and tell thy husband that thou hast spat in the face of Rabbi Meir".

It is also told that at one time the people of Jerusalem were divided into two factions, which hated each other bitterly and sought each other's destruction by every possible means. At this time there was in Jerusalem a man named Onias, who belonged to neither party. He was very old and frail, and so pious that it was commonly believed that his prayers were certain to be answered by God. One day the leaders of one of the parties dragged him from his home and bade him pray for the destruction of the other faction. They offered him rich rewards if he would do their bidding, and threatened him with dire punishment, should he refuse. But the old man knew only how to supplicate God for good and not for evil. Unmoved by either promises or threats, he quietly kneeled down amid the surging mob, and with eyes raised aloft he prayed, "O God of Israel, since these are Thy children, and those are Thy children also, hearken to the evil prayers of neither the one nor the other, but grant them all Thy blessings of peace and love". His prayer was drowned by the shouts of the angry mob. Stones fell thick and fast about him, and the life was speedily crushed from the frail body. He died for the sake of the peace for which he had prayed. Thus do the true servants of the Lord ever strive to preserve peace.

Like Abraham, Isaac, too, is typical of Israel. His love of peace and his willingness to yield his rights repeatedly, exemplify the love of peace which Israel has constantly exemplified among the nations of the earth. Even as the Philistines envied and hated Isaac because they saw that the Lord was with him and had blessed him, and bade him depart from their land, whither they cared not, even out into the burning desert, if need be, to perish of thirst and hunger, so, too, the nations have again and again envied and hated Israel because the Lord was with it, and have bidden it begone, they cared not whither nor to what fate. And time and again Israel has yielded its rights to the wells of life-giving water which it has dug, and has moved onward and ever onward. It has cost it dear, and its sufferings have been bitter. But God has always been with it, and it has always found new wells from which it might drink; and not it alone, but the whole world might drink with it. For Israel has dug wells, not for itself alone, but for all mankind. It is Israel's sacred task, imposed upon it by its religious genius, to dig the spiritual wells which the world shall seize, and from which it shall drink. Israel yields its wells for the sake of peace and of the knowledge of God. And still we repeat reverently the time-honored prayer of our fathers, "Grant us peace, Thy most precious gift, O Thou eternal source of peace, and enable Israel to be a messenger of peace unto the peoples of the earth".

And today, it seems, the wells of "Contention" and "Enmity" have been left far behind, and we are drawing close to *Beer-Sheba,* "The Well of the Covenant", where all the world will come together and say, "Let us make with one another a covenant of peace and brotherly love, whereby we shall no more seek one another's hurt nor disadvantage, but we shall ever dwell together in peace and unison, helping one another, and living the life which God has meant that we should live". It seems as if this blessed time is approaching slowly but surely. And if only Israel remains worthy of its birthright, and performs its God-appointed task faithfully and loyally, then God will continue to be with it as He was with the patriarchs of old, and in the end Israel's mission must be fulfilled, and the world be filled with peace and love and knowledge of God.

NOTES

V. 1. In time of famine it was not uncommon for the people of Palestine to migrate in search of food. Usually they sought refuge in Egypt, or, as here, in the fertile Philistine plain. The monuments of ancient Egypt record many instances of Semitic peoples coming down to Egypt for this purpose. Similarly the Bible tells that Abraham went down to Egypt in time of famine (XII, 10), as did likewise Jacob and his sons (XLV, 9ff), and that on a similar occasion Elimelech and his family sought refuge in Moab (Ruth I, 1).

The Bible commits a very noticeable anachronism here in calling Abimelech king of the Philistines. From a great mass of evidence, much of which is derived from the Bible itself, we know that the Philistines were not natives of Palestine, but like the Israelites entered the land as strangers and invaders, and conquered the southwestern portion of the country and settled there. They came over the sea from the west, and seem to have been of Cretan, and therefore non-Semitic stock. They entered Palestine probably during the 12th century B. C., shortly after the great body of Israelite tribes had gained a firm foothold in the country. Consequently they could not have been in the land already in the time of Abraham. XX is historically more correct in omitting all reference to the Philistines and calling Abimelech simply king of Gerar.

The exact location of Gerar is unknown. It was, however, probably located near the southeastern border of the Philistine plain, touching upon the desert (cf. *Jewish Encyclopedia* V, 629f). It was not a large kingdom, but only a small town, whose dominion extended over the immediately adjacent country. The boundary-lines of such a little city-state were rather elastic; therefore the shepherds of Gerar ventured to claim the wells which Isaac had dug, as being within their territory, even though they were probably outside of the normal boundary-lines.

V. 7. As was stated in the lesson proper, XX, 12 says that Sarah was actually Abraham's half-sister, being the daughter of his father, but not of his mother. In very ancient Israel marriage between half-brother and half-sister on the father's side was not unknown. II Samuel XIII gives an instance of the possibility of such marriage as late as the time of David. However this form of marriage was ultimately forbidden in Israel (cf. Leviticus XVIII, 9)

V. 12. A crop of a hundredfold was exceedingly large .

"In the same year"; the year began in the fall. The seed was planted shortly after new year's day, and the grain was harvested in the spring of the same year.

V. 19. By "living water" (Hebrew, *mayim hayyim*) the Bible means a spring or well which bubbles up out of the earth.

V. 20. The names of the wells are symbolic of Isaac's relations with the people of Gerar. *Esek* means "contention," *sitnah*, "enmity," and *rehoboth*, "room, expansion'.

V. 25. Cf. note to XII, 7.

V. 30. Among the ancient Semites a covenant was frequently solemnized by the contracting parties partaking together of a meal. So Isaac now prepares the covenant meal for himself and Abimelech. Cf. also XXXI, 46 and 54.

V. 33. "Unto this day", i. e., of course, until the time of the writer of this narrative.

In addition to the two explanations of the name *Beer-sheba* cited in the lesson, the rabbis suggested a third explanation. They said that this was the same well which, so XXI, 25 tells, Abraham had dug. According to their tradition Abraham had had to dig in three different places before he located this well. And according to XXVI this was the fourth well which Isaac had dug; hence the name *Beer-sheba*, "The well of the seven diggings". They also said that this well accompanied the patriarchs upon all their wanderings, and is also to supply Jerusalem with water when the Messiah shall come and establish his kingdom there. (Cf. Ginsburg, *Legends of the Jews*, I, 324). Of course this tradition is altogether without historical and philological grounds, and is purely fanciful.

It has been frequently suggested that there were originally seven wells at this spot, and therefore the place received its name, *Beer-sheba*, i. e. "the seven wells". However, while it is true that there are a number of wells, some three or four, at this place, there is not the slightest evidence that there were ever as many as seven. Nor does *Beer-sheba* mean "the seven wells", but at the most, only "the well of seven".

XV

THE UNITY OF THE JACOB STORY

As was stated in the Introduction (pp. 1-13), the Jacob cycle of stories consists of a group of ancient traditions and legends, which center about the figure of Jacob. These traditions were originally independent of each other, and arose at different times, in different localities, and for different purposes. Thus, for example, the story of Jacob wrestling with the "angel" (XXXII, 25-33), told originally of an evil spirit of the night, which attacked Jacob and sought to kill him, but Jacob proved more powerful than it and wrested a blessing from it.[1] However, Jacob did not emerge from

---

[1] Arabic tradition records an interesting and significant parallel to this legend. Damîri tells in the *Musnad* that one of the companions of the Prophet Mohammed met one of the genii, who wrestled with him and sought to throw him to the ground. The man said to him; "I see that you are slender as though your arms were the forelegs of a dog; are all you genii like this, or are you alone among them so?" To this the genius replied, "I alone am so strong; but resume the contest, and if you throw me down, I shall teach you something beneficial to you". They wrestled again, and the man threw the genius to the ground. Thereupon the latter said, "Recite, 'Allah, there is no deity but him, the living, the self-subsistent!' There is no house in which you recite this, but out of it Satan will come, and will not reenter until morning". Damîri, *Ḥayāt al-Ḥayawān*, Trans. Jayakar, I, 463.

the contest unscathed. He was wounded in the hip and limped. Therefore his descendants, the children of Israel, do not eat the sinew of the thigh. Quite a number of Arab tribes, who are of the same Semitic race as Israel, and have many similar customs, still today do not eat the chief muscle of the hindquarter out of superstitious fear that it will make them ill.[1] The same custom was practiced by certain North American Indian tribes, who accounted for the origin of this rite by a very interesting story.[2] There can be no doubt that this same practice existed in Israel from antiquity so remote that its real origin and purpose were forgotten at a comparatively early date, and that this tradition of Jacob limping after his bout with the evil spirit of the night arose in time to account for it.

[1] Musil, *Arabia Petraea*, III, 150.

[2] The story as recorded by Frazer (*The Golden Bough; The Spirits of the Corn and the Wild*, II, 265), is as follows: "Once upon a time a man found a burrow of porcupines, and going down into it after the porcupines he lost his way in the darkness, till a kind giant, called 'He who sees before and behind', released him by cleaving open the earth. So the man, whose name was 'Fireless and Homeless', lived with the kind giant, and the giant hunted elans and beavers for him, and carried him about in the sheath of his flint knife. 'But know, my son,' said the giant, 'that he who uses the sky as his head is angry with me and has sworn my destruction. If he slays me the clouds will be tinged with my blood; they will be red with it, probably.' Then he gave the man an axe made of the tooth of a gigantic beaver, and went forth to meet his foe. But from under the ice the man heard a dull muffled sound. It was a whale which was making this noise because it was naked and cold. Warned by the man, the giant went toward the whale, which took human shape, and rushed upon the giant. It was the wicked giant, the kind giant's enemy. The two struggled together for a long time, till the kind giant cried, 'Oh, my son! cut, cut the sinew of the leg.' The man cut the sinew, and the wicked giant fell down and was slain. That is why the Indians do not eat the sinew of the leg. Afterwards, one day the sky suddenly flushed a fiery red, so Fireless and Homeless knew that the kind giant was no more, and he wept". Cf. *ibid.* 264-267 for further instances of the same custom.

A few of these traditions were local in character. Thus the story of Jacob asleep in the field, of his dream and his subsequent realization that this spot in which he had inadvertently lain down to sleep was a sacred place, in which the (or a) Deity was present (XXVIII, 10-22), arose to account for the origin and sanctity of the great northern national shrine at Bethel. The story implies that Jacob discovered the presence of the Deity at Bethel, and therefore set up the sacred stone pillar there, and founded the original sanctuary, and instituted the practice of bringing tithes thither.

The story of the covenant between Jacob and Laban (XXXI, 22-54), centers about the place east of the Jordan, probably known as Mizpeh in Gilead, which marked the boundary line between the territory of Israel, typified by Jacob, the traditional ancestor of Israel, and the territory of the Syrians or Aramaeans to the north, typified by Laban the Aramaean. Such a treaty was, in all likelihood, actually made between Israel and Syria during the reign of Ahab (875-854 B. C.). This story must have had its origin in this period.

The story of Jacob at Shechem (XXXIII, 18–XXV, 4), probably arose to account for, or to justify, Israelite possession of the important and powerful Canaanite city of Shechem in central Palestine. Since Shechem was still a Canaanite city, and had not yet passed into Israelite hands in the days of Gideon and his son Abimelech (Judges IX), it follows that this story, at least in its present form, could not have been conceived until after that time, at the very earliest, therefore, not before the 12th century B. C.

Likewise XXXII, 2-3, tells of a place east of the Jordan to which Jacob gave the name Mahanaim. This place later became the seat of government of the petty kingdom of Ishbosheth, after the death of Saul and his other sons at the hands of the Philistines (II Samuel II, 8ff.). The verses tell that Jacob called the place *Mahanaim,* i. e., "the two camps", because he was met there by angels, and when he saw them he said, "This is God's camp". It is clear that these angels did not merely meet Jacob, but that something must have transpired on the occasion, and that there must have been not one, but two camps. In other words, there must have been a considerable legend of Jacob at Mahanaim, and of what befell him when he was met by the angels, or whatever these may have been in the original legend, to which the compilers of the Jacob cycle of stories merely refer, but which unfortunately, for some unknown reason, they do not preserve in full.

A moment's consideration suggests also that the stories of Jacob securing his brother's birthright by selfish cunning, and of his obtaining, likewise by cunning and deceit, the blessing of his father, which was intended for his older brother, were originally parallel versions of one and the same incident. There is actually little or no difference in practical effect between the birthright and the blessing. Both were intended for the older son, and both secured for the recipient the same advantages, lordship over the other brother and an undue portion of the bounties of the earth.

It is clear, therefore, that, as has been stated, these various Jacob traditions and legends arose independently of each other, at different times and places, and as the result of varying forces and conditions in ancient Israel, and that the present Jacob cycle is the product of a process of literary compilation and editing, rather than of creative authorship. We have already learned that the creation-flood and the Abraham cycles of stories were also the products of similar processes, and that in both the compilers did their work in accordance with set plan and purpose, in order to give concrete expression to what they conceived to be fundamental principles of Judaism. Inasmuch as the Jacob cycle is the product of a similar process of compilation, it is to be inferred that it, too, is not the result of random, unsystematic effort, but is animated by a definite purpose and one central theme.

One important fact must be noted at the outset. This Jacob cycle of stories differs in a very essential respect from either the creation-flood cycle or the Abraham cycle. In the Abraham cycle the various stories are but loosely connected. Almost any one, with the possible exception of the stories of the call of Abraham and of the sacrifice of Isaac, might have been omitted without having seriously impaired the unity of the Abraham story as a whole, and without our being conscious that anything was lacking. Thus, for example, all the stories referring to Lot might have been rejected by the compilers, and while it is true that thereby the accounts of several trials of Abraham would have been lost, and the story would thereby be much poorer spiritually, nevertheless the Abraham cycle as a whole would have presented a perfectly complete and well-rounded story.

To a somewhat less degree this is true of the creation-flood cycle also. A slight dependence of one story upon its predecessor is manifest there. Thus the story of the Tower of Babel would be almost meaningless except as the sequel, as it were, of the story of the flood. Yet the dependence here, and throughout this creation-flood cycle, is a dependence of thought rather than of incident. Each story is in itself a unit of narration, which can be told by itself and convey the impression of completeness. The unity of the creation-flood cycle is purely a unity of the Jewish thought and doctrine which animate and correlate all these stories.

But the Jacob cycle is different. While the unity of thought is not immediately apparent, the unity of narration becomes manifest at once. Hardly a single incident of the Jacob story could be told by itself and be perfectly intelligible. One event flows out of another, and in turn leads up to something else. For example, to tell the story of

Jacob's winning of Rachel without having first told of Esau's hatred of Jacob and of the latter's consequent flight from home, would be tantamount to beginning a long serial story in the middle without knowing anything of the causes and events which preceded and paved the way for this episode. Or, even more indicative, the story of Jacob's final meeting and reconciliation with Esau would be absolutely unintelligible without a full knowledge of their previous relations. In other words, unlike the creation-flood and Abraham cycles of stories, we have here, in the present Biblical form, not a group of independent Jacob stories, united by a common theme, but one single Jacob story, which is a unit of narration as well as of thought.

The procedure of the compilers is easily perceived. They took the old, independent Jacob traditions, and wove them together into one complex and highly dramatic narrative. The legend of the struggles of the two brothers in the womb of their mother serves as an effective introduction or prelude to the story, in that it foreshadows dramatically the future relations of the two men. The story of the father's blessing, originally, in all likelihood, a parallel version of the birthright story, they presented as a subsequent and supplementary incident in the relations of Jacob and Esau. Thereby they heightened the dramatic effect of the situation and brought out the contrasted characters of the two men more pointedly and emphatically. Esau unspiritual, rash, lacking in foresight and judgment, revengeful, animal in his uncontrolled desires and passions, yet not without the saving grace of loving consideration for his father. And Jacob restrained, foresighted, selfish, cunning and deceitful, unscrupulous in securing his ends, yet managing always to justify himself in some way, and to secure illegitimate gains by dubious, yet superficially legitimate methods. Hence Esau hates his brother, and Jacob must flee for his life. But at the very beginning of his journey God reveals Himself to him and promises to be with him upon the journey, and in time to bring him back to his home land and to his father's house. And, as these writers constantly imply, God does not manifest Himself to individuals out of mere personal interest in them or solicitude for their individual welfare, but only because He has some deep, yet unrevealed purpose with them.

Already a change is manifest in Jacob. He had been willing to hazard his relations with his family in order to secure his own selfish ends. But now his one desire and prayer are that he may return, and in peace, to his father's house. He seems vaguely conscious that this journey, the real duration of which he can not suspect, is to be the necessary preparation for this return and reconciliation. His mother had bidden him leave home for a few days, until his brother's anger should have passed. Little did either imagine that these few days would become twenty years, and that they should never see each other again. The ironic tragedy of the situation is readily apparent.

But even more is implied in this situation, and in the words of Jacob's prayer (XXVIII, 20-22). God had said that He would be with Jacob on all this journey. The subsequent story shows how faithfully God kept His word. It tells also that only at the end of twenty years did God bid Jacob return to his home land and to his father's house. It implies thereby that Jacob had remained away all these years under God's providence and in accordance with God's will and purpose. What God's purpose was, must be determined later.

The story continues with the account of Jacob's meeting with Rachel and their mutual love. The delicate touch of romance, which the compilers understood so well how to employ, is apparent in the picture of Jacob serving seven years for Rachel, and in the words, "And they seemed unto him but a few days, for the love he had to her" (XXIX, 20).

Another dramatic situation, of which the compilers did not fail to take full advantage, exists in the substitution of Leah for Rachel, and in the simple, yet direct and forceful words, "And it came to pass in the morning that, behold, it was Leah" (XXIX, 25). This is really the reversal of an earlier situation of the story. Just as Jacob had impersonated his brother to secure the coveted blessing, which belonged by right to Esau, so here Leah impersonates her sister to secure for herself the husband who should have been Rachel's. This motive of the deceiver being deceived is common in all literature.

Furthermore, we have learned that in ancient Israel marriage with a cousin was considered the highest type of marriage. The story of Isaac's obtaining his cousin Rebekah, artistic and spiritual though it is, is nevertheless in itself an independent incident of the Abraham cycle of stories, without which the unity of the Abraham story would nevertheless have been complete. It is merely the connecting link between the Abraham cycle and the Jacob cycle, and shows that the patriarch Isaac found the very best possible wife, and that his descendants sprang from a marriage of the highest type. But here the motive of Jacob's marriage with, not one, but two cousins, is integral and vital. Without it the story would limp exceedingly, or would, in fact, be no story.

And still more is implied. God had said that He would be with Jacob upon this journey. Jacob must have regarded his meeting with Rachel at the very moment of his arrival, and the love which immediately sprang up between them, as a sign that God was true to His word. Time and again the story affirms that Jacob knew with ever-increasing conviction that God was with him. He could not but see in the deception whereby the hated Leah had become his wife, instead of the beloved Rachel, only the counterpart of his own deception practiced upon his unsuspecting brother. How would he bear this deception? Would he seek revenge as Esau had done, or would he regard it as merited, and submit without further question or strife? The story tells that Jacob chose the latter course, and implies that he was conscious that in this, as in everything, God was with him, and that this was a part of God's discipline.

Then follows the account of Jacob's marriage with Rachel also, and of the children which were born to him. Thus passed the first two seven-year periods in the service of Laban. With the third period a new moment in the drama of Jacob's life begins. In his distress Jacob had learned to rely upon God's promise to be with him, and to see God's hand in everything which befell him. But these last years of satisfied desire and family happiness had tended to reawaken the old dormant Jacob, to make him once again self-centered, self-reliant and self-seeking. As his family grew, the conviction became stronger that he must himself begin to provide for them and their future. Material thoughts and desires once more filled his mind, and he knew of only one way to satisfy them. Laban had deceived him in regard to Leah, yet Jacob had held his peace. But now Jacob in turn practiced a trick upon his uncle, whereby he secured for himself an undue portion of the flocks. It was a trick, the secret of which seemingly was known only to him, and therefore it could not be detected. But it was a deception none the less. True, Laban met this deception with faithlessness, and changed Jacob's wages repeatedly. Yet Jacob, it is implied, knew always how to gain the advantage. Thus his wealth increased exceedingly, until Laban's sons began to eye him enviously and suspiciously, and it seemed that they could not abide together much longer. Then God's command came to return to his home land and to his father's house.

But how does Jacob return? He might have expected, in the normal course of things, to depart honorably and in peace. Ostensibly he had fulfilled his compact with Laban. Yet he slinks away in fear and unknown to Laban. And when Laban at last overtakes him, and chides him for having stolen away, Jacob can offer only a lame excuse. Yet in the end, after Laban had failed to find his stolen gods, they make a covenant and part in friendship, to Jacob's great relief.

Here, too, the dramatic sense of the compilers is readily manifest. Jacob had said, "With whomsoever thou findest thy gods, he shall not live" (XXXI, 32). Unconsciously he had pronounced the death sentence; and upon whom?—here again is real tragedy—upon his beloved Rachel. When Laban fails to find the stolen gods, the danger seems past. But divine retribution can not be escaped, and the words of an oath, such as Jacob had uttered, must, according to ancient belief, be fulfilled. And so the story tells in its sequel, that Rachel died in childbirth, shortly before the end of the journey (XXXV, 16-20). Without this conclusion the story would be incomplete.

Furthermore, just as Laban's earlier relations with Jacob but mirror the latter's previous relations with Esau, so now Jacob's later relations with Laban foreshadow the reception which he might expect from his brother. Jacob had deceived Laban; but Laban had first deceived him. But if Laban had been so enraged at having been deceived, even though he must have felt that it was not altogether unmerited, how must Esau feel, who had been so innocently and cruelly deceived by Jacob?

During the first part of his sojourn with Laban, Jacob had relied upon God's promise that He would be with him, and he had been fortunate and happy. But during these last six years increasing prosperity had led him to trust more and more in his own strength and cunning. And materially he had prospered thereby, even though he had

almost perished at Laban's hands, and would have perished
had not God intervened.

Now that the danger was past, Jacob must prepare for
the greater danger of the meeting with Esau. We would
expect that now he would remember God's word that he
should return in peace to his father's house. But the habits
of the last six years were too strong to be shaken off in a
moment. He failed to realize that only through God's intervention had he escaped this last danger, and his mind was
full of plans how he might meet Esau, and avert his wrath
with as little sacrifice as possible. He would send messengers to apprise Esau of his coming, and with instructions
to notice carefully and bring back speedy report of how
Esau received this news, and what were the prospects of
reconciliation. They might hint, too, that Jacob had prospered exceedingly, and would make due compensation, if
necessary, for the wrong done to Esau. And at the actual
meeting with his brother, Jacob would act warily and
craftily.

Unfortunately for Jacob, his plans miscarried from the
outset. The messengers brought back word that Esau was
hastening to meet him with four hundred men. Their purpose was unmistakable. It was too late to flee with all his
family and possessions. Esau could have overtaken him as
easily as Laban had done. Nothing remained but to meet
him, and to take every possible precaution. And now, in his
distress, when all his planning and scheming had availed
naught, Jacob bethought himself of that other source of help
and protection, whom he had well nigh forgotten during
these six years of material prosperity, God. And he turned
to Him with a fervent prayer, acknowledging his littleness
and unworthiness, and imploring help and protection in this
moment of peril. Yet how could he tell whether his prayer
would be answered? Prosperity through deceit during these
six years had dulled the edge of his faith. If God would

save him, well and good; but if not, then all the more must he endeavor to save himself. So he prepared his present for Esau, and marshalled it to best advantage, and sent it on before him. His wives and children and the entire camp he set over the stream. He himself remained alone upon the farther bank.

The Bible gives not the slightest intimation of why Jacob remained alone upon the farther bank, instead of crossing with the rest. Clearly he wanted to be alone. But why? The next morning he must surely meet Esau. If he would still escape, it was his last chance. Obviously here is the climax of the story.

There follows that mysterious incident of Jacob wrestling. The compilers have purposely changed the original evil spirit of the night into a man, as they call it. Yet he, too, must be gone by dawn. Unconsciously we feel that it is no real man, but a supernatural something, which, if conquered. can be made to bestow blessing. We do not know what it was, nor just how the compilers themselves conceived of it. We know only this, that Jacob emerged from the conflict a different man, weary and limping, yet victor withal. And in symbol thereof, and in true blessing, his name was changed from Jacob (*Ya'akob*) "the Deceiver", to Israel (*Yisra'el*), "the Conqueror", "for thou hast striven with God and with men, and hast prevailed" (XXXII, 29). Unconsciously we feel that the words, "thou hast striven with God and with men, and hast prevailed", refer not merely to this one night of combat, but also to the past twenty years, of sojourn with Laban, and the purgation and preparation which he had undergone there. The effects of the last six years are shaken off, and the old Jacob is gone forever. The new, purified Israel now steps forth, and humbly now, and supplicatingly he goes to meet his brother, prepared to accept unresistingly whatever his brother might put upon him.

But to his glad surprise his brother meets him, not in anger, but in peace. He, too, has prospered, and he, too, seeks only reconciliation. So Jacob returned in peace to his father's house, and God was with him and fulfilled His word. But it was no more the old, deceitful Jacob, but a new, purified Israel, "the Champion of God".

Such is the Jacob story in its present form. It is no longer a mere collection or cycle of stories, but the skillful hands of the compilers have welded it together into one single story, or, possibly better, in view of the marked dramatic, and at times even tragic, note, one single, powerful drama. In fact, it might well be arranged for dramatic presentation thus:

Prelude—The pre-natal struggles of the brothers.
Act I, Scene 1—The birthright.
         Scene 2—The father's blessing.
Act II—Jacob's vision of God at Bethel.
Act III—Jacob's family, and the beginning of his purification during the first fourteen years with Laban.
Act IV—Jacob and Laban.
Act V—The night of wrestling and the morning thereafter.

This scheme shows the unmistakable, unified, dramatic form and character of the Jacob story.

It is inconceivable, as has been said, that these compilers should have done their work aimlessly, or moved only by inner compulsion to satisfy an artistic and dramatic impulse. The creation-flood and the Abraham cycles have shown that they were actuated by deep religious purpose and conviction, and that dramatic effects were merely incidental products of their unmistakable artistic genius. The Joseph story will prove this even more conclusively. And did the Moses story come within the province of this work, it would add convincing and irrefutable proof thereto. The compilers of the creation-flood and the Abraham cycles, and of the Joseph and Moses stories, were likewise the compilers of the Jacob story. Unquestionably in this drama they were animated by a like purpose.

After having analyzed the Jacob story and proved its essential unity, it is not at all difficult to determine what the purpose of the compilers was. The central figure is Jacob. The story begins with his deception of his brother, and concludes with their reconciliation. Jacob had wronged Esau because of his own deceitful nature and selfish impulses. He was enabled to become reconciled with Esau only by having battled with, and having at last triumphed over his base impulses, or, as the story puts it very literally, by actually becoming a different man, no longer Jacob, "the Deceiver", but Israel, "the Champion of God". Throughout his twenty years' sojourn in a foreign land, God had been with him, not merely to protect and prosper him in material things, but, by allowing trials, disappointments, deceptions, and sufferings to befall him as a necessary part of his discipline, to help him purify himself of his base inclinations, and to transform him from the old Jacob to the new Israel. During the last six years of his sojourn with Laban, Jacob had thought that he could rely upon his own efforts and cunning, and the old Jacob had reasserted himself. But this had led him near to destruction. Just in time did he come to realize that only by trusting implicitly in God's promise, and in following the course, which, it seemed, God had marked out for him, could he prosper truly, and could lasting happiness and blessing be his. The climax of the story is that dramatic scene where Jacob wrestles through all the long, dark night, and as the dawn breaks, he emerges from the combat victorious, with the old Jacob gone forever, and the new Israel ready now to live the life which the true servant of the Lord, who inherited the birthright of Abraham and Isaac, must live. The story of Jacob is the unmistakable, powerful, and convincing drama of a repentant and regenerate soul.

The stories of the flood, of the Tower of Babel and of Sodom and Gomorrah have taught much about the Jewish conception of sin, repentance, and atonement. But they have all presented this thought from the standpoint of God. God desires not the death of the sinner, but that he return and live, and He constantly holds out to man the possibility of repentance and pardon. But how may men repent? Is it easy or difficult, accomplished in a moment, or requiring days and years of trial and purgation? In ancient Israel the belief was universal that repentance was an easy thing, and a matter of ritual alone. Let one but offer a sacrifice, a sin-offering, and the Deity would be immediately placated. Or, if not immediately, then let him continue to offer sin-offerings in sufficient measure, and to pour out prayers, and acknowledge his iniquity ceaselessly, and in the end the Deity must surely be appeased.

It was the prophet Hosea who, about 735 B. C., first taught the truth, till then unheard in all the earth, that repentance is no easy nor speedy thing. It requires a long and bitter period of trial and purification and constant testing, until the dross of evil inclination be purged from the soul, and we can return to God, not merely with words of repentance on our lips, but with sincere, humble, and contrite hearts. Repentance is not a matter of mere, mechanical prayer and sin-offering, but of purification of character, motive, and deed, a remaking of the old, sinful self into a new being, whether that old self be an individual man or a whole people. Nor does this true repentance mean momentary righteousness and service of God, which permits of later relapse into the old, evil habits and practices. Half-righteousness and partial purification are but futile shams. True repentance must reach to the very depths of the soul, and purge and purify of every inclination to evil. Thus

Hosea contrasts the old, popular, false idea of ritual repentance with the true repentance and spiritual regeneration, which he was the first to proclaim. He pictures the people as saying in their shortsightedness,

> Come, and let us return unto the Lord;
> For He hath torn, and He will heal us,
> He hath smitten, and He will bind us up.
> After two days will He revive us,
> On the third day He will raise us up, that we may live in His presence.
> And let us know, eagerly strive to know the Lord,
> His going forth is sure as the morning;
> And He shall come unto us as the rain,
> As the latter rain that watereth the earth.

And to all this sham, artificial repentance the prophet represents God as answering with infinite longing and pathos,

> O Ephraim, what shall I do unto thee?
> O Judah, what shall I do unto thee?
> For your goodness is as a morning cloud,
> And as the dew that early passeth away.
> Therefore have I hewed them by the prophets,
> I have slain them by the words of My mouth;
> And thy judgment goeth forth as the light.
> For I desire mercy, and not sacrifice,
> And the knowledge of God rather than burnt-offerings. (Hosea VI, 1-6.)

Even more drastically the prophet Micah, a generation or so later, proclaimed in the southern kingdom,

> Wherewith shall I come before the Lord,
> And bow myself before God on high?
> Shall I come before Him with burnt-offerings,
> With calves of a year old?
> Will the Lord be pleased with thousands of rams,
> With ten thousands of rivers of oil?
> Shall I give my first-born for my transgression,
> The fruit of my body for the sin of my soul?

It hath been told thee, O man, what is good,
And what the Lord doth require of thee:
Only to do justly, and to love mercy, and to walk humbly with
thy God. (Micah VI, 6-8.)

Just this conception of repentance the Jacob story illustrates concretely, dramatically, and convincingly. Repentance
is no easy thing to be won in a day. Twenty years of bitter
trial and suffering and purgation in a foreign land are not
too much. Nor can a half-won repentance, even though it
endure for fourteen years, when followed by a relapse into
former evil habits, suffice. The purification must be complete and permanent. But with him who would truly repent,
God is ever present, strengthening and helping him to overcome and to conquer in the struggle through the long, dark
night with the evil power which seeks his destruction. And
at last, with the dawn of the new day, which ushers in the
new life of righteousness, he must emerge a regenerate man,
no longer Jacob, "the Deceiver", but Israel, "the Champion
of God", strong in the knowledge of God which has come
to him, and ready and eager to do God's service. That is
the true repentance, which the Jacob story illustrates so
forcibly. In this way alone may repentance be worked.

There can be no further question that this is the central
theme of the story in its present form. Its compilers must
have been followers of the prophetic party who worked in
the spirit of Hosea, and sought in their own way to illustrate
his message concretely, and to enforce it practically. They
must have lived somewhat later than Hosea, and in all likelihood in the southern kingdom of Judah, since the northern
kingdom of Israel was overthrown by the Assyrians in 722
B. C., shortly after Hosea's time. The southern kingdom
had become the spiritual and cultural heir of its more advanced sister kingdom. Many, though undoubtedly not all,
of the literary treasures of the north had come into the possession of the south. A group of northern Jacob stories

came in time to be fused with a number of similar stories about the same patriarch current in the south, and these were later recast by these prophetic compilers into our present Jacob story. It is interesting to note in this connection that Hosea himself refers to various traditional episodes in the life of Jacob, and denounces the patriarch for his deceitful nature and his wrongful treatment of his brother (Hosea XII, 4, 5 and 13). Of course to the prophet Jacob symbolized the whole nation Israel.

And these compilers had still more in mind. In their hands not alone the Jacob story became a unit, nor also the creation-flood and Abraham cycles, and the Joseph story, but, in a very positive sense, the entire Book of Genesis and even the entire Torah. Their ultimate aim was to show how Israel was chosen by God as His servant, was given the Law, and was disciplined and prepared for his mission as the herald of this Law and of God's truth unto mankind. They had told how God had called Abraham and had bidden him become a blessing unto all the families of the earth. They had told, too, that Isaac had received the birthright from Abraham. Now they told that the birthright descended in turn to Jacob. True he acquired it by taking base advantage of his brother's need and weakness of character. But as the Bible so carefully emphasizes, Esau despised the birthright; it implies thereby that Jacob eagerly desired it. By thus despising the birthright and by his weak and passionate nature, Esau had proved his unworthiness of the birthright. And although Jacob was far from perfect, none the less the implication is that he was more worthy of this birthright than was Esau. What was this birthright, as these compilers conceived it?

It was not merely the right to a double portion of their father's estate, the usual privileges of the firstborn. The Bible nowhere states that Jacob received this, but implies that he acquired all his wealth during his sojourn with

Laban. On the other hand, the Bible states that Esau, too, had become wealthy at home, as if he had had the enjoyment of his father's property. No, the birthright was something other than this, something which the materialist and sensualist Esau despised. To these compilers, writing in the prophetic spirit from the standpoint of Israel as God's chosen people, the birthright could have meant nothing other than the mission of Abraham, the right to become God's servant and messenger after Abraham and Isaac. It was this which Esau despised and which Jacob eagerly desired. And of this Jacob's regeneration, these compilers would have us understand, made him worthy. He was to be transformed from Jacob, "the Deceiver", into Israel, "the Champion of God", in order that he might truly contend with evil gods and with men, and triumph over them in God's name and for God's cause. All this these compilers sought to teach, and they adapted the old, loosely connected Jacob traditions and legends to their purpose. How well they succeeded is best evidenced by the dramatic unity, power and conviction of the story itself.

However, with all their artistic and dramatic powers and definite purpose, certain difficulties confronted them which could not be fully overcome. To them Jacob, Esau, and Laban were types, quite as much as Abraham, Isaac, and Ishmael. To the prophet Hosea, Jacob had been less a single, historical, or even traditional, individual than the type of all Israel. Time and again Hosea denounced Israel for its sins under the name Jacob. In the minds of these compilers, too, Jacob stood for Israel, but not as with Hosea, only as a deceitful people, faithless to its God, but as the future servant of the Lord, who was to be made fit and ready for His service by spiritual regeneration. Laban, too, was the type of the arch-enemy of the northern kingdom, Syria, the Aramaean state. The very name *Arami,* the Aramaean, probably suggested to Israelite minds a connection with the word *ramaï*, "deceitful". The covenant at Mizpeh, as has been stated, depicts the relations between Israel and Syria during the reign of Ahab.

On the other hand, Esau typified the nation traditionally descended from him, Edom, still in the compilers' days the arch-enemy of their own nation Judah. In their task they were too much patriotic Judeans to be altogether prophetically objective. They could not do as Hosea had done, and paint Jacob in hopelessly black colors. They could not but feel, too, a certain sense of national gratification in picturing Jacob's triumph over Esau and Laban, even while at the same time from a purely moral standpoint they condemned Jacob's deception. Even today deception within the limits of international law is often regarded as praiseworthy diplomacy. These compilers were too much children of their own times not to exult a bit in the picture they had drawn of Jacob the Israelite outwitting and triumphing over Esau the Edomite and Laban the Aramaean.

But this caused the one great weakness of their drama. For after Jacob's regeneration and reconciliation with Esau, they still represented him as not trusting Esau implicitly, and outwitting him once more by promising to join him in his home land, Seir, and then instead journeying on elsewhere. It is an illogical sequel to the story. We would expect it to conclude with the perfect reconciliation of the two brothers and their mutual trust in each other, their return together to their father's house and subsequent dwelling together in peace and love. Probably the compilers would have concluded their story thus had they been able. But actual historical conditions made this impossible. Judah and Edom did not dwell together, nor were their relations peaceful and brotherly. Instead they dwelt apart in different lands, and were constantly divided by mutual distrust, hatred, and strife. And so the most these compilers could do was to make Jacob and Esau meet and part again amicably. And even here national pride impelled them to picture Jacob as finally triumphing over Esau. Israelite chauvinism whispered to them that the Edomite might not be trusted too implicitly, and so there could be no harm in making Jacob realize this and be on his guard. It was an insurmountable obstacle for them. But we must admit that it has weakened the otherwise wellnigh perfect drama.

One other difficulty confronted them and tended to render their story somewhat obscure. In a certain sense they were historians; not objective historians it is true, whose task was to record all the events of history in proper sequence and proportion, but rather prophetic historians, who sought to reinterpret the facts and traditions of Israel's history in such manner as to illustrate and enforce the message of the great prophets. Nevertheless they had a certain historic consciousness which bade them make some reference at least to all traditions which centered about the figure with which they were dealing. They could not resist the temptation to introduce certain traditions which had no direct connection with the main story other than that they, too, dealt with Jacob, and which actually impede and obscure the logical and dramatic evolution of plot and thought.

Thus the Mahanaim incident has no connection with the main story. As students of Jewish history and tradition, we are grateful for the reference, and regret only that the complete tradition has not been preserved. But we must admit that the Jacob story as a piece of narrative or dramatic literature would be more complete and perfect without it. This is true also of the brief reference to Reuben's incest with Bilhah, his father's concubine (XXXV, 22).

And to a far greater degree is this true of the episode of Jacob at Shechem. The natural and logical course of the story would have been for Jacob, immediately after his reconciliation with Esau, to proceed to his father's house, for which he had so eagerly longed and prayed. This protracted sojourn at Shechem is disturbing and disappointing in the extreme. On the one hand it interrupts the continuity of the story, and delays unnecessarily, illogically and undramatically the visiting of divine retribution, in accordance with Jacob's words, upon Rachel, for having stolen her father's idols. And on the other hand, it accords but poorly with the rest of the story. This told that Jacob had been but twenty years with Laban, and had married Leah only after seven years. Therefore his oldest child could have been at this time not more than twelve years of age, and the others must have been correspondingly younger. Yet the Shechem episode makes all the children of Jacob, including Dinah, the daughter, of adult age. This proves that the Shechem episode was not a part of the original story, as arranged by these compilers, but was inserted later, probably because of the impulse of some quasi-historian to preserve a Jacob tradition from oblivion.

Facts like these obscure the meaning and purpose of the main narrative somewhat. But when they are stripped away, the main Jacob story stands out clearly and unmistakably as a unit of both narration and thought, the central theme of which is easily determined. With this introduction we are ready to consider the Jacob story in detail.

XVI

THE BIRTHRIGHT

(Genesis XXV, 27-34)

So Esau despised his birthright. (Genesis XXV, 34.)

For I am become a father to Israel,
And Ephraim is My first-born. (Jeremiah XXXI, 9.)

Read Ecclesiastes, VII, 1, 8, 9, 11, 12.

The episode of the birthright constitutes the opening act in the Jacob drama. It introduces the two principal characters, and establishes their relations with each other. They are twin brothers, presumably starting in life with similar, and almost equal endowments. Yet how different were their lives to be. The rabbis said that Jacob and Esau were like the myrtle and the thornbush respectively, which at first resemble each other closely. But after they are fully grown the thorn-bush puts forth only destructive and poisonous thorns, while the myrtle sends its fragrance far and wide.

As twin brothers their relations should have been particularly intimate and loving. But already at birth they had striven together, and this but augured the contention of later years. Now, when the story opens, they have already grown far apart, and have developed characters and habits diametrically opposed to each other. "Esau was a cunning hunter, a man of the field; and Jacob was a quiet man, dwelling in tents". Esau the hunter and Jacob the shepherd, two contrasted types. Esau was the man of the chase; of quick, unpremeditated, improvident action; seeking speedy returns from everything, and ready to stake all life's prospects upon the uncertain chances of the chase; eager to satisfy the appetites of the moment, regardless of the cost; with no eye to the future and no power to govern his inclinations or restrain his passion; rash, impetuous, vengeful, possibly even cruel, or at least pitiless, as the pursuit of the chase was apt to make him; and above all else, unspiritual, materialistic, with no appreciation of the privilege of the birthright, but despising it because it could not fill his belly when hungry, and only laid obligations upon him.

And Jacob was the man of the tents, quiet and home-abiding, and therefore beloved of his mother; able to control his appetites and to govern his passions in order to secure a desired end; with a keen eye to the future, carefully weighing all chances, and deliberate and patient in the attainment of ambitions; all admirable qualities indeed, provided they be applied to right aims and uses, and destining their possessor for great things either in good or evil, whichever he might choose. Unfortunately at this moment Jacob applied these powers to base uses. He combined them with cold, calculating selfishness, cunning, and deceit, pitiless disregard for the rights and sufferings of others, and ignoble willingness to take advantage of their weakness, need, and indulgent love, in order to secure his own selfish desires.

But one quality Jacob did possess, at present undeveloped, yet capable under proper unfolding and guidance of becoming productive of great good. "Esau despised his birthright", the Bible says; and it implies thereby, and develops this thought in the story itself, that Jacob eagerly desired it. This birthright was, as we have intimated, not merely the usual privilege of the firstborn, of a double portion of the paternal estate, and the right to act as the clan leader and priest, but rather the spiritual heritage of being the servant and messenger of God, and of bringing blessing unto all the families of the earth. For this God had called Abraham. And the Bible told that Abraham had purposely sent Ishmael and his later children away, after providing for them properly, in order that they might not inherit along with Isaac (XXI, 10ff.; XXV, 5f.). In the case of Ishmael this meant, of course, that the right of firstborn fell to Isaac. Now Esau and Jacob must divide their father's estate, and the birthright with it. There was but a few moments' difference in their ages; yet Esau was nominally the elder, and to him therefore the birthright formally belonged.

But Esau despised his birthright. He had no appreciation of spiritual things, no desire to bring blessing unto all the families of the earth, and no ambition to become a benefactor of the human race. Perhaps he might have been willing to accept his birthright, had it been an easy thing, and laid no burden upon him. But it was no easy thing; it meant endless toil and sacrifice, and bearing the burdens of others, and infinite love for fellowmen. And of these Esau was incapable. And "so Esau despised his birthright", but Jacob eagerly desired it.

In all likelihood Jacob, too, had at this moment no full appreciation of the true nature of the birthright and of the obligations it entailed. True, it meant service, sacrifice, and blessing for others, but it also meant dignity, honor, leadership, and privilege for himself, a worthy reward indeed. Probably Jacob thought at first rather of this reward than of the service he might render. It is a common trait of self-centered and ambitious youth. Nor is there anything discreditable in this; rightly disciplined and directed, the ambition for leadership may become an unqualified blessing. It was not that Jacob's desires and ambitions were altogether wrong, but rather that the means he chose to gain his ends, were ignoble and blameworthy. The story of Jacob is the best proof of the truth that the end never justifies the means. All Jacob's sufferings, and those he brought upon others, were but the outcome of the means he employed to gain his ends. Ultimately what he had gained was established as his.

But before he could become worthy of the birthright, he had first to be purified of the base impulses which prompted him to employ such ignoble means.

The compilers of the Jacob story have done their work well, and have displayed artistic powers of the highest order. With a few masterful strokes they have depicted the two characters most effectively. The Jacob story does not stand by itself. It is the continuation of the Abraham and Isaac stories. The birthright is the connecting link. God's word to Abraham and his descendants must be fulfilled. The birthright of Abraham and Isaac must descend to that son who is the better fitted for it. The compilers of the Jacob story have drawn the two characters with this one thought in mind. Esau's character is simple, and stamped him as unfit and hopeless for the acceptance and fulfillment of the obligations of the birthright. He is a materialist through and through, without the slightest possibility of such change of character as might fit him for the birthright.

On the other hand, Jacob's character is complex. Two forces are already struggling within him for the mastery. If the evil, selfish, deceitful nature prevail, Jacob is destined by his very powers to become a curse to mankind. But if the more spiritual side of his nature, his ambition for leadership, power, and honor, can be purified of its selfishness, and can be applied to proper ends, he is destined to become a blessing unto mankind, and truly worthy of the birthright of his fathers. At the present moment the evil nature is in the ascendancy, and the prospects of his regeneration seem dark and hopeless. The episode of the birthright, and its sequel, the episode of the father's blessing, constitute a most effective and dramatic introduction to the whole story of Jacob's purification and preparation for the real birthright.

It might be asked, why did not God make Esau a good and noble man from the very beginning, or at least make Jacob so? The rabbis anticipated this question. It might in fact be answered by the equally appropriate question, why did not God create men so that they would always do right and enjoy happiness? God has, we know, purposely created man as he is, in order that he may be forced to strive to become perfect, and not be perfect unavoidably, and without ambition or effort on his part. Perfection must be worked for and striven for. And still, even if men are not perfect, God does not reject them nor refuse to use them for His purposes. If we have a broken tool, yet need it for our work, we first mend it and then use it. It was so with Jacob. He was the very tool which God selected, to carry on the mission of service for which He had called Abraham. And just because he was not perfect, we shall see that God mended him first, or rather helped him to mend himself, and then at last, when he was ready and fit, used him for His purpose of blessing.

One thought in particular this story of Jacob suggests. The Book of Ecclesiastes says:

Better is the end of a thing than the beginning thereof.

Far too often we pride ourselves on vain things and boast of trivial achievements. We are prone to judge by beginnings and promises rather than by ends and results. We parade the accomplishments of children and prophesy great things for them; and it often happens in consequence that the child's head is turned, and his powers are checked in development by injudicious praise. We make much of early success, and fail to realize that it is only a part of our training for greater things, when our powers shall have reached their full growth. We are ever ready to measure our strength and our achievements with those of our superiors in experience and wisdom. And we loudly proclaim that this is the age of the young man, and do not see that thereby we seal our own death warrant, and condemn ourselves to a long and inglorious middle and old age of decreasing usefulness and wisdom, and increasing burden upon society.

The story of Jacob should indeed give us pause. Were we to judge the patriarch by these first two incidents of his life, or even by some which follow, we should condemn him unqualifiedly as a villain and a scourge to society. But all life is not measured by the years of childhood and youth alone, nor is it to be judged only by early inclinations and promises. A life's true worth can not be ascertained until its complete course is run, and its full work is done, or left undone. Then alone may we say, "This life was well lived, and this was not; this one brought blessing to mankind, and this one was a burden and a curse. The world is better for this one's having lived, and worse for that". And even though we start wrong, as Jacob, and the evil nature, the voice of earth within us, it seems, must triumph, none the less it is possible, with wisdom, courage, and strength of will, and with God's help, to purge ourselves of the evil inclination, and become true servants of the Lord, worthy of the birthright of service and blessing which is ours. Wisely, therefore, does the Bible say:

> A good name is better than precious oil;
> And the day of death than the day of one's birth.

The rabbis likened life to ships which sail the troubled sea. One sails forth from the harbor upon a long and hazardous voyage, and every one is anxious, for they know not what the outcome will be, nor even whether the ship will ever return. And another ship sails slowly and quietly into port, weatherbeaten and worn, yet stately withal; and every one rejoices, for the voyage is done, and the ship comes home laden with precious stores. Truly

> Better is the end of a thing than the beginning thereof.

So it was with the life of our father Jacob.

One thing above all must be clearly understood, that just as Abraham, Isaac, and Ishmael, so Jacob and Esau, too, are types. Jacob is the type of Israel and Esau of Edom.

Not that the compilers of the story meant to imply that all the evil qualities which they ascribed to Jacob in the beginning were characteristic of Israel. They had to depict Jacob thus in order to bring out their thought of the nature and power of repentance and spiritual regeneration. But they meant to imply that in their contrasted qualities Esau and Jacob were types, Esau, the Edomite, the violent hunter, the materialist and sensualist, who despised his birthright and thought only of filling his belly; and Jacob, the Israelite, the "quiet man, dwelling in tents", who desired the birthright and was ready to restrain his passions and make all necessary sacrifices to obtain and keep it. The virtues attributed to Jacob here are really qualities which Israel has always possessed and cherished, though in a loftier way and for a nobler purpose. Israel, too, has aspired to spiritual dignity, honor, and leadership. Israel, too, has ever preferred the quiet life of the home to the wild life of the chase, camp, or battlefield. Israel, too, has ever cared for the inmates of its homes, for parents, wives, and children, provided for their comfort and happiness, and ministered to their needs and sufferings. Israel, too, has at times had evil inclinations, and now and then has employed its powers for selfish ends. But under God's guidance, Israel has been purified, generally through bitter suffering and punishment, and has come to appreciate its real purpose in life and the true meaning of its spiritual birthright. And so God has, we believe, taken Israel to be His people, and confirmed the birthright unto him, and spoken of him lovingly, "Israel is My son, My first-born" (Exodus IV, 22); and again,

> For I am become a father to Israel,
> And Ephraim is My first-born.

Israel is God's firstborn of the spirit. And to us, the children of Israel, have descended not only the privileges of the birthright of the firstborn, but also its duties and responsibilities, to be a blessing unto all mankind, likewise God's children and our brothers.

In rabbinical tradition Esau and Edom came to symbolize Rome, the colossal, temporal, material power, which sought to crush nations, which overran the earth with warfare and bloodshed, and found its highest pleasure in murderous gladiatorial combats. And Jacob continued to represent Israel, the spiritual people, the servant of the Lord, whose mission was to bind up the bleeding wounds of cruelty and oppression, and to bring law and order, peace and brotherhood, and the knowledge of God unto all mankind. Rome has perished; its temples and palaces are heaps of buried ruins; and the order of things and the standards of life and conduct, both individual and national, which it championed, are rapidly passing. Israel lives on; its law is beginning to reign supreme in the hearts and lives of men; and its dream of universal peace and brotherhood and love is fast becoming a living reality. Though conquered by Rome physically, Israel has triumphed over Rome spiritually. And in its history the words of the Bible are again verified,

Better is the end of a thing than the beginning thereof;
And the patient in spirit is better than the proud in spirit.

NOTES

XXV, 22f. This ancient tradition was employed by the compilers of the Jacob story to show that the conflict between the two brothers began at, or even before their birth. Since it foreshadows the actual future relations of the brothers, it is an integral part, and a highly dramatic introduction or prelude to the Jacob story.

V. 22. "She went to inquire of the Lord", i. e. she went to consult the oracle at some important shrine. In ancient Israel the belief was general that the oracle was one of the means by which the Deity revealed His will; cf. Exodus XVIII, 19; II Kings I, 2. The Urim and Tummim were one form of the oracle (Exodus XXVIII, 30; Leviticus VIII, 8; Deuteronomy XXXIII, 8; I Samuel XIV, 41 [note in particular the fuller Septuagint version of this chapter];

XXVIII, 6). That the oracle was usually consulted through the mediation of a priest is certain, but beyond this we know nothing of the procedure.

V. 23. This verse contains a fragment of a very ancient Hebrew poem, which, seemingly, forecast the destinies of the two nations, Israel and Edom. It is significant that already at the very remote period when this poem was composed, Jacob and Esau were conceived of as two nations, rather than as two individual men.

V. 25. The tradition that Esau was covered with hair already at birth, was probably based upon the common by-name, *Seir*, for the country of Edom. *Seir* seems to be derived from the stem *sa'ar*, "to be hairy", and therefore to mean "the hairy one".

Similarly the tradition that Esau was ruddy, was, in all likelihood, derived from the by-name, *Edom*. This was thought to be related to the stem *adam*, "to be red". V. 30 records a parallel tradition, that Esau was given the by-name, *Edom*, because he said to Jacob, "Let me swallow some of this red, red pottage" (*adom*).

V. 26. The tradition that Jacob was born holding fast to his brother's heel offers one explanation of the name Jacob. The Hebrew word for heel is *akeb*. The verb *akab* therefore means (a) "to follow on the heel" (hence *Ya'akob*, "he who follows on the (his brother's) heel"), (b) "to supplant" (hence Jacob as the supplanter of Esau; cf. XXVIII, 36), and (c) "to deceive" (hence *Ya'akob*, "the Deceiver"). Thus the Bible itself accounts for the origin of the name Jacob by these three different and mutually contradictory traditions.

V. 27. "Dwelling in tents", i. e. a semi-nomad, and consequently a shepherd, just as Abraham is also pictured (XII, 8; XVIII, 1).

V. 31. In ancient Israel the firstborn was thought to possess an undue portion of his father's nature (cf. XLIX, 3). Therefore he received a double portion of his father's estate (Deuteronomy XXI, 17). Above all he enjoyed the privileges of succeeding his father as the head of the family or clan, and of functioning as its priest and the arbiter of its life and policies.

V. 32. A bargain was usually confirmed and made binding by an oath.

V. 34. The rabbis told that this transaction between Jacob and Esau took place on the day of the death of Abraham. Jacob had been as a boy the favorite companion of his grandfather during the latter's last years, and was with him at the very moment of his death. And understanding the true nature of the boy and his latent possibilities, Abraham had charged Isaac that the birthright descend to him rather than to Esau. They told further that Jacob was preparing this dish of lentils for Isaac as a pious duty, because since lentils were thought to symbolize immortality, it was customary to give them to mourners to eat.

XVII

A FATHER'S BLESSING

(Genesis XXVII)

"Bless me, even me also, O my father."   (Genesis XXVII, 34 and 38.)

A wise son maketh a glad father;
But a foolish son is the grief of his mother.   (Proverbs X, 1.)

Read Psalm XXIV, 3-5.

The story of Isaac's blessing carries us one stage further in the unfolding of the Jacob drama. It completes the opening picture of the relations of the two brothers, and the presentation of the problem with which the drama deals. The iniquitous conduct and selfish and deceitful nature of Jacob are clearly portrayed, and the question is suggested, "Can Jacob be purified of his evil inclination, and be made fit for, and worthy of the birthright; and if so, how?" The succeeding acts of the drama offer the positive answer to this question.

The story of the birthright pictured Jacob as a selfish schemer, ready to take advantage of another's weakness and need, and to drive a hard bargain, and that other his twin brother. Yet the entire transaction was strictly within the law, and Jacob had nominally given full value for what he had received. The story of Isaac's blessing reveals the full possibilities of Jacob's evil nature. He is guilty of a sin greater far than that of selfishness and unbrotherliness. He is ready to deceive a blind, helpless, trusting father, to rob an innocent brother of that which is dearest to him in life, while the latter is absent upon a mission of mercy and love, and to take selfish and base advantage of a mother's love, and allow a curse, bringing misfortune and sorrow, to come upon her, provided only that he himself escape unharmed. Lower than this a man can hardly sink.

Yet this merely shows how great and true his final repentance must have been, that from such depths of iniquity he could rise to such heights of manhood. It shows, too, the greatness and eternity of God's love, that He can pardon one who had sinned as Jacob had, and ever desires the return of even the vilest sinner, rather than to punish him for his sin. It bids us realize that in God's sight no one can ever be so bad, as to be beyond hope of betterment; even the basest may still repent and return to God, and become an instrument for good. It bids us realize, too, that we are all brothers, even of the lowest and most wicked, and that it is our duty ever to be ready to forgive, like God, and ever to help our brothers live noble, righteous, and useful lives.

In ancient times the belief existed, and in a way still exists today, that a solemn word of blessing, spoken at sacred moments, particularly just before death, by someone close and beloved, was more than a mere wish. It was thought that at such times a person stood in intimate communion with God. Therefore words of blessing possessed a mysterious power, which made them certain of fulfillment. Accordingly it was customary for a man, just before death, to bestow his blessing upon his children, and particularly upon his firstborn son. In fact, the blessing of the dying father was often regarded as the actual right of the firstborn. So it was in this case.

Just as Jacob desired the birthright, so also he coveted Isaac's dying blessing. The birthright he had obtained through selfishness and hard bargaining. The blessing became his through falsehood and theft. True, Rebekah helped Jacob, and even suggested the plan, by which he might obtain the blessing. But this does not justify nor mitigate Jacob's offense. Besides, Rebekah was blinded by her passionate love for Jacob. What she did, was not done for herself at all. She was even willing that the curse should come upon her, if need be, in order that Jacob might have the blessing. Her action was wrong in every way. But while we can not excuse Rebekah's conduct, we can still sympathize with her to an extent. We shall see, too, how grievously she had to pay for her share in this sin.

And just as Rebekah was made to sorrow because of her love for Jacob, so, the rabbis told, Isaac also suffered because of his love for Esau. Probably in order to justify Jacob somewhat, they told, what the Bible nowhere implies directly, that Esau was very wicked. And God had made Isaac blind as a blessing, that he might not see how wicked Esau was. Probably Isaac did not count it a blessing. We do not always know what is really for our good, or that blessing may come even with grief and pain. Could Isaac have seen all the evil which Esau wrought, he would have grieved even more than he did because of his blindness. So, frequently, loving parents must suffer because of the evil deeds of their children. Therefore the Bible says truly,

> A wise son maketh a glad father;
> But a foolish son is the grief of his mother.

Esau's conduct contrasts most effectively and dramatically with Jacob's. Whereas the latter was willing that a curse befall his mother, just so that he secure the blessing, Esau was engaged upon a task of affection and kindness for his blind father. His love for his father was sincere and unfailing. Even though his hatred of Jacob was all-compelling, none the less it did not equal his love for his father. For once this enabled him to control his passion, and prompted him to defer his vengeance upon his brother until after Isaac's death, in order that the latter might be spared the grief and suffering which the knowledge of the strife of his two sons would otherwise cause. The dramatic pathos of Esau's cry, when he returns from the chase, and the quiet satisfaction of having found the food his father loves, and being able to satisfy the old man's craving, and to receive his blessing is changed to dismay when he learns that his brother has treacherously supplanted him, "Hast thou but one blessing, my father? bless me, even me also, O my father", can not escape even the most obtuse reader. Our sympathy, for the moment at least, is with Esau, and not with Jacob.

As has been said, the rabbis purposely represented Esau in the worst possible light, as guilty of every conceivable crime, partly to justify Jacob, and partly because to them Esau typified the dread, oppressive power of hated Rome. Nevertheless they were compelled to show him a certain measure of justice. And so, they told that although Esau broke every other commandment, this one, "Honor thy father", he kept most piously. He was ever kind and considerate of Isaac, and thought chiefly of his comfort and happiness. He brought him always the best portions of the animals which he killed in hunting, and prepared them always just as he knew his father liked them best. Moreover, the rabbis told that the reason why Rebekah gave Jacob Esau's garments to wear, was not merely to help deceive Isaac, but because Esau was accustomed, whenever he brought food to his father and waited upon him, to show his respect by putting on his finest raiment. For he said to himself, "In my eyes my father is a king, and it would become me ill to serve him other than as I would serve a king, with my very best". Such was the honor and love of Esau for his father. And the rabbis told that God spared his descendants much hardship and suffering as the reward for this one good act.

This, too, bids us realize that no one is wholly bad; that

some good can be found in everyone, if only we look for it. Ofttimes the man who has been the worst criminal or the basest sinner, when given another chance, shows himself a hero and a benefactor. In fact, as we have indicated, it happened so with Jacob himself. It warns us to be careful in judging others, and not to be too hasty to condemn them or think them wholly bad. Be quick to think good of others, and slow to think evil. This is an excellent motto, which must greatly multiply human happiness and brotherly love. Hillel used to say, "Judge not another until thou hast stood in his place". Who can tell whether we should do better under similar conditions? The story is told that the home of Rabbi Meir was surrounded by evil neighbors, who greatly annoyed the good rabbi and his noble wife. One day, when particularly vexed, Beruria exclaimed, "Would to God that all sinners might perish from the earth!" But the gentle rabbi mildly rebuked her, "Pray not to God that the sinners perish, for they are still thy fellowmen. But pray to Him that sin may perish from the earth, for then sinners will be no more". This is the mission of Israel, not to judge and condemn sinners, but to labor and to teach, that sin may at last perish from the earth, and all men be united in a covenant of peace, righteousness and love, to do the will of God.

Esau's loving conduct towards his father reminds us strongly of Isaac's trusting love in, and obedience to his father Abraham. It reminds us also of another charming story of the rabbis. In the city of Askelon, in ancient Palestine, lived a young man named Dama, who dealt in precious stones. One day some of the elders came to buy a certain stone for the breastplate of the highpriest. They offered one thousand gold pieces. Dama went to the inner room, where his jewels were kept, to get the stone. But in a moment he returned and told the elders that he could not let them have it. They thought that they had not offered enough, and since they needed the stone, they doubled their offer. When this did not induce Dama to change his mind, they offered still more, even ten thousand gold pieces, but all in vain. So they left the shop. Later in the day, however, they returned and renewed their offer of ten thousand gold pieces. Without a word Dama went into the inner room, brought out the stone and handed it to the chief of the elders. "Here is the stone", he said; "you may have it for your first offer of one thousand gold pieces". Unable to explain this strange conduct the elders asked what he meant. He answered, "When I went this morning to get the stone, I saw that my father was asleep with his foot upon the box in which the stone was. He is old and needs his sleep, and I would not disturb him for ten times the amount you offered. Now he is awake, so here is the stone". The wise elders, struck by this reply, urged him to take the ten thousand gold pieces, which they had offered. But he refused; for he said, "I was satisfied with the first price, and will not make any profit from my love for my father". So the elders paid one thousand gold pieces and took the stone. But first they laid their hands in blessing upon his head. "For surely", they said, "the son who honors his father thus, merits God's choicest blessing". So, the rabbis taught, did Esau also honor his father.

When we contrast Jacob's conduct in this one instance with Esau's, we can not but recall the beautiful words of the Psalmist:

> Who shall ascend into the mountain of the Lord?
> And who shall stand in His holy place?
> He that hath clean hands and a pure heart;
> Who hath not taken My name in vain,
> And hath not sworn deceitfully.
> He shall receive a blessing from the Lord,
> And righteousness from the God of his salvation.

Jacob had deceived his father and gained his blessing.

But it brought with it sin and sorrow and suffering for him and all his family. But to him who doeth righteousness and worketh good, who lifteth not up his soul to falsehood nor sweareth deceitfully, nor taketh God's name in vain, who honoreth father and mother, and bringeth peace and kindness to brothers and fellowmen, to him cometh the greatest blessing, the blessing of God, the Father of all men. And he is fit to ascend into the mountain of the Lord, and to stand in God's very presence.

NOTES

V. 13. A curse, like a blessing, if once uttered, could not be recalled. But it might be diverted to some person other than the one for whom it was intended, particularly if that second person were willing to take it upon himself. Therefore Rebekah says, "Upon me be the curse". These words alone sufficed to turn any curse which Isaac might utter against Jacob upon her. And Jacob selfishly permitted this great sacrifice on the part of his mother.

V. 21. This verse seems to imply that Isaac suddenly became suspicious of Jacob, of course, as the next verse tells, because his voice sounded so little like Esau's. But the rabbis told that the reason for Isaac's suspicion was because Jacob had mentioned the name of the Lord (v. 20), which Esau had never done.

V. 22. The expression, "The voice is the voice of Jacob, but the hands are the hands of Esau", has become proverbial for any harsh, deceitful act which follows fair promises.

V. 23 tells that Isaac blessed Jacob even before his suspicions were completely quieted, and before he had eaten of the food which Jacob had brought. It is clear that this verse comes too soon, and disturbs the continuity of the story, and is therefore a late insertion. The blessing is recounted in its proper place in vv. 27ff.

V. 28. In Palestine, where the rainfall is frequently deficient, the heavy dewfall is of extreme importance in agricultural life. Hence the reference to the dew of heaven here. Palestine is primarily an agricultural country; and this first verse of the blessing invokes agricultural abundance.

V. 29. By "mother's sons" and again by "brethren" in v. 37 is meant not brothers other than Esau, for there were none such, but only other relatives and descendants. Similarly Abraham calls Lot his "brother" (XIII, 8), and the same term designates the relationship between Laban and Jacob (XXIX, 12 and 15), although in both cases they were actually only uncle and nephew. Kinship is very frequently expressed in this manner in the Semitic Orient.

The last portion of Isaac's blessing reminds us strongly of God's word to Abraham, "And I will bless them that bless thee, and him that curseth thee will I curse" (XII, 3). The implication would seem to be that by these words God's blessing of Abraham is transmitted to Jacob.

V. 30. The dramatic effect of the statement that Esau comes in just as Jacob goes out after receiving the blessing, is readily perceived. The implication is that had Esau come but a moment sooner, he might still have circumvented Jacob and secured the blessing for himself. "A moment too late" is a common motive in drama.

Vv. 32 and 37 imply that a blessing once uttered, could not be recalled or altered.

V. 36. For the play upon the name Jacob here, cf. the note to XXV, 26.

V. 40 has been thought by historians to refer to the revolution by which Edom succeeded, during the reign of Joram, about 849 B. C. in casting off the yoke of Judah and gaining its independence (II Kings VIII, 20-22).

V. 41. The implication of this verse and of the entire story is that the death of Isaac is imminent. This is in contrast to XXXV, 29.

V. 46 and XXVIII, 1-9 introduce an altogether new and disturbing element into the story. They are the direct continuation of XXVI, 34f. They imply that Jacob left his home, not because of Esau's hatred and desire for vengeance and at the bidding of Rebekah alone, but at the bidding of Isaac, and after having peacably received, or received a second time, his father's blessing, because Isaac and Rebekah disapproved of Esau's marriage with Hittite women, and wished to ensure Jacob's making a proper marriage with some kinswoman, just as his father had done. This version is, of course, a protest against intermarriage. This and other incontrovertible evidence make it certain that this entire passage was not a part of the original narrative, but was inserted during, or shortly after the Babylonian exile, about which time opposition to intermarriage first became acute in Israel. The passage is contradictory of the main narrative, and disturbs the continuity and obscures the real question at issue. XXVIII, 10 is the direct continuation of XXVII, 45.

XVIII

GOD IS WITH US

(Genesis XXVIII, 10-22)

Surely the Lord is in this place; and I knew it not. (Genesis XXVIII, 16.)

The Lord is nigh unto all them that call upon Him,
To all that call upon Him in truth. (Psalm CXLV, 18.)

Read Psalm XXIII.

So, because of his sin against his old, blind father and his twin brother, Jacob had to leave home and dear ones, even his beloved mother. She had sinned that he might gain the blessing; in his happiness and success she would find her own greatest joy. But happiness and pleasure which come through sinning are never real nor lasting. The pleasure of a moment must be succeeded by long hours of sorrow, suffering and endless regret. It is a part of God's punishment of sin.

Jacob had gained his father's blessing as Rebekah had wished. But to both it brought only suffering and separation. She had expected that he would be gone but a few days. But neither was to see the other again. It was a hard punishment indeed. Perhaps it was harder upon Rebekah, because of her great, unselfish mother love. We can picture her sitting at the door of her tent almost every day toward evening, looking out steadily in the direction in which Jacob had gone, and from which he must come again; looking out day by day with ever-growing hopelessness in her eyes, wondering if he would ever come back, that once more, before she died, she might feel his strong, loving arms about her. He never came; and at last she closed her eyes and was laid to rest, without her beloved son present to receive her last kiss, and to shed a tear as the doors of the tomb were closed above her. She had gained for Jacob a father's blessing; but she had lost thereby the opportunity to give unto him all of a mother's love and a mother's blessing. It was hard indeed, yet it was just, as God's decrees are always just.

But it was hard for Jacob, too. As he went forth from his home, not knowing what fate was in store for him, nor whether he should ever return thither, he began to realize all that he had lost, a mother's love and a father's love and a brother's love, all sacrificed to selfish, wicked ambition. As he wandered on, ever farther from his father's house, he felt more and more alone in the world. It seemed as if there was no one at all to care for him, to cheer him in his trials, to comfort him in his grief, to help lighten the journey he must go, and lift the burden for a moment from his tired shoulders. He must have thought of his beloved grandfather, Abraham, who had, years ago, gone over this same road, though in an opposite direction. Yet how differently had Abraham journeyed. He had had with him his beloved Sarah and Lot, his nephew, and all his household. Above all he had journeyed on at God's command, and strong in his faith that God was with him. And God had been with him. But with him, Jacob, it was different. He was all alone, and even God, he felt, must have forsaken him, because of his sin. Now he realized as never before, the full wrong he had done to his brother. He must have thought, too, of Cain, driven out because of his crime against his brother, from the presence of God and men, and forced to wander on and on, solitary and hopeless, until death at last overtook him. He was like Cain, not like Abraham, and God had forsaken him, too, and left him to his fate.

So he wandered on throughout that long and bitter day. At last darkness came upon him in a wild, desolate, forsaken spot. He looked anxiously about him. Rocks on all sides, as far as eye could see, and no sign of living being in any direction. More than ever he realized his loneliness; and fear, too, began to lay hold upon him of what might befall him in this awful place, with not even God to protect him. So the sinner always fears, when the consciousness of his sin dawns upon him, and he feels that even God has forsaken him.

But at last weariness overcame fear, and he fell asleep, with his head pillowed upon a great stone. But it was no easy, restful sleep. The consciousness of his sin, the realization of all that he had lost, and the longing for his loved ones were still upon him, and his fears still troubled him. But suddenly a glorious vision came to him in a dream. He saw a ladder reaching up to heaven from the very spot upon which he was lying, with angels ascending and descending, and God Himself standing above him. And he heard God's words addressed to him, "I am the Lord, the God of Abraham thy father, and the God of Isaac. The land whereon thou lièst, to thee will I give it, and to thy seed. And thy seed shall be as the dust of the earth, and thou shalt spread abroad to the west, and to the east, and to the north, and to the south. And in thee and in thy seed shall all the families of the earth be blessed. And, behold, I am with thee, and will keep thee whithersoever thou goest, and will bring thee back into this land; for I will not leave thee, until I have done that which I have spoken to thee of". And with these words there came to Jacob peace and rest, and he slept quietly until morning.

When he awoke the dream was still with him. He felt that it must have been sent by God, to make him realize that God had not forsaken him, even despite his sin; that He was still with him, and would be with him throughout

his long and weary journey, and would bring him back in
His own time to this very land, perhaps even to his father's
house. Desolate as this place seemed, and forsaken of all
living creatures, none the less God was here too. "Surely
the Lord is in this place; and I knew it not". So Jacob
spoke. And unconsciously he had uttered a great, eternal
truth. For God is in every place; this whole universe which
He has created is filled with His presence. As the Psalmist
has said:

> Whither shall I go from Thy spirit?
> Or whither shall I flee from Thy presence?
> If I ascend up into heaven, Thou art there;
> If I make my bed in the netherworld, behold, Thou art there.
> If I take the wings of the morning,
> And dwell in the uttermost parts of the sea;
> Even there would Thy hand lead me,
> And Thy right hand would hold me.
> And if I say; 'Surely the darkness shall envelop me,
> And the light about me shall be night';
> Even the darkness is not too dark for Thee,
> But the night shineth as the day;
> The darkness is even as the light.   (Psalm CXXXIX, 7-12.)

God is in every place and at all times. He is with all
His children to care for and guide and protect them, and
lead them ever in His path, as long as they will but hearken
to His gentle word and follow His loving call. In the
words of the Psalmist:

> The Lord is my shepherd; I shall not want.
> He maketh me to lie down in green pastures;
> He leadeth me beside the still waters.
> He restoreth my soul;
> He guideth me in straight paths for His name's sake.
> Yea, though I walk through the valley of the shadow of death,
> I will fear no evil,
> For thou art with me;
> Thy rod and Thy staff, they comfort me.

This was the truth which Jacob now realized, that even in this desolate spot, which had seemed in the gathering gloom like the very valley of the shadow of death, God was still with him, and though he had lain down in fear and trembling, God still watched over him.

Jacob is the type of all Israel. Israel, too, has learned this truth through bitter experience. Time and again he has had to leave home, like Jacob, lest he suffer and perish at the hands of those who should have been his brothers. And he has wandered forth into the strange world, not knowing whither he was going, nor whether the journey must be long or short, nor whether he should ever find rest and peace. At times he must have doubted and wondered, as did Jacob, whether God was with him, or whether he was not alone in the world, forsaken of God and men. But it was only for a moment. Always the conviction returned, stronger because of the moment's doubt, that God was in this place, too, although he knew it not, that He was still with him, and had not forsaken him, nor would ever forsake him, that He would be with him upon the long and bitter journey which he must go, and at last, when the goal should be reached and his mission be fulfilled, he would, through God's blessing, find the rest and peace and reconciliation with his brethren for which he craved. In this quiet trust and undying faith in the God of his fathers, though enemies raged and danger threatened, and he must wander on and on, Israel has repeated those inspiring words of the closing verse of the beautiful Hebrew song in our prayer-book:

My spirit in His hands I trust,	*B'yodo afkid ruhi*
Both when I sleep and when I stir;	*B'eth ishan v'o'iro;*
My body, too, this frame of dust:	*V'im ruhi g'viyothi.*
The Lord is with me, I do not fear.	*Adonoi li, v'lo iro.*

But even more had Jacob realized; not merely that God

is everywhere and with all his children at all times, but
even with His sinning children He is ever present, yearning
for their repentance, seeking to turn them again to Himself
in His great love, longing for their regeneration, that they
depart from their evil ways, and walk again in His path of
righteousness. And ever He is ready to hearken unto the
sinner's prayer for forgiveness and help. Again, in the
Psalmist's words:

> The Lord is nigh unto all them that call upon Him,
> To all that call upon Him in truth.

To Jacob this truth came like the dawn of hope; he was
not alone in the world. Though no human being might accompany him, yet God was with him, and would be ever
with him, whithersoever he might go, and would at last
bring him back to this land, and fulfil through him His
promise to Abraham. Yes, it was God's very promise to
Abraham, that through him and his descendants all mankind
should be blessed, which had been renewed to Jacob. God
had confirmed the birthright to him. But now, purified and
with vision made clear by this long day and night of suffering and fear and sorrow, he had come to perceive what this
birthright really was. In this vision by night the gate of
heaven had opened for Jacob, through which he might once
more rise up to God. The way of repentance, atonement,
and pardon had been shown him, whereby true peace and
blessing might once more become his. It was not to be an
easy way nor short. It must be long and hard, must take
many years and bring much additional suffering and bitter
trial. True repentance can not come speedily, in a single
night, nor can perfect righteousness be attained in a passing
moment. As the sage of old said, "For gold is tried by
fire, and acceptable man in the furnace of adversity". All
this Jacob now realized fully. But with this realization came
the comforting and inspiring thought that God had not for-

saken him. It was the beginning of Jacob's regeneration. He had lain down a trembling, fearful sinner. He arose, a brave, strong man, firm in his faith in God's love, and strong in his determination to walk henceforth in God's path, that through him and his descendants God's promise might be fulfilled, and all mankind be blessed.

And as he rose from his hard bed, the very first sign of true repentance was manifested in him. Once more, with unutterable longing, his thoughts reverted to those dear ones at home whom he had wronged, his mother, upon whom he had been willing to let the evil curse come, his brother, whom he had cheated and robbed, and above all, his old, blind father, whom he had so basely deceived. Almost unconsciously the prayer welled forth from his heart that God might not only be with him upon this journey, and provide for his needs, and bring him back to this land, but, above all, that He might at last bring him again even to his father's house, no more in discord and deceit, but in peace with all the loved ones whom he had wronged, that he might labor to right the wrong, and return unto them love in fullest measure. That is always the first step toward true repentance. The rabbis taught that, despite His great love, God does not forgive the sins we commit against others, until we have ourselves first made every effort to right the wrong and obtain the wronged one's pardon.

We have heard very much thus far of God's unfailing love, and of how He bears constantly with men, seeking ever that they may return to Him and live. We remember the beautiful story of Abraham, who could not bear with the poor, ignorant, old fire-worshiper for a single night, though God had borne with him for a hundred years. We think, too, of the beautiful allegory, that God has given to every man two angels, who accompany him, one at his right shoulder and one at his left, wherever he goes. Whenever he does a good deed, the angel on the right smiles, and writes it in his book, and seals the record for all time. But whenever he does an evil deed, the angel on the left grows sad while he writes it in his book. But he does not seal his record until midnight. If during the rest of the day, the man repents, and bows his head and prays, "O God, I have sinned; forgive", the record is erased. But if he does not repent and acknowledge his sin, the evil record, too, is sealed forever. And both the angel on the right and the angel on the left weep sadly for the sin which had to be recorded.

We have heard much thus far of repentance, but now for the first time we have learned of one who repented. We shall see how he was purified, and how God pardoned him, and was with him upon all his journey. So God is with us and never forsakes us even if we sin. Ever He calls unto us to repent and return to Him. Ever He is with us and leads us on, and we need not fear. Ever He is our shepherd, and we do not want. Ever His great, eternal, wondrous love watches over us, both when we sleep and when we stir. And ever when we forget and turn from Him, and go astray from His path, still He is with us, and we can return to Him, as Father Jacob did, and be assured of His forgiveness and His help and His blessing.

NOTES

.V. 11.   Notice that Jacob came to this place by chance, and had known absolutely nothing of it previously. The use of the definite article in the Hebrew, reproduced in the English, *"the* place", instead of *"a* place", as we would expect, is difficult and mystifying.

Vv. 13-15 renew to Jacob God's promise to Abraham; cf. XII, 3, 7; XIII, 14-17; XXII, 18; XXIV, 7.

V. 17.   According to the ancient Semitic conception, there was a gate to heaven, through which the gods passed when they visited the earth; cf. the note to XI, 9. Occasionally heaven was conceived as having two gates, one in the extreme east, through which the sun emerged in the morning, and one in the extreme west, into which the sun entered in the evening.

V. 18.   The verse implies that the stone was consecrated by Jacob as a sacred object. Pouring oil upon a person or object was the usual method of consecration; cf. XXXV, 14; Exodus XXIX, 21; XXX, 25-33; XL, 9. In ancient Semitic religion sacred stones were commonly used. It was thought, in the earliest stages of religious belief that a god actually dwelt within such a sacred stone, which was therefore called a *beth-el*, i. e. a "house of god". In time Judaism outgrew this ancient belief, and the use of sacred stones was forbidden (Deuteronomy XVI, 22). But this belief is still reflected in v. 22 of this chapter.

V. 19. As has been said, *beth-el* means "house of god". Bethel was originally an important Canaanite city and shrine. Luz seems to have been its Canaanite name. The account of the capture of Bethel by the Israelites is contained in Judges I, 22-25. After the division of the kingdom Bethel became one of the national shrines of the northern kingdom (I Kings XII, 28-33). At Bethel the prophet Amos uttered his prophecies (Amos VII, 10). XII, 8 ascribes the founding of the sanctuary at Bethel, not to Jacob, but to Abraham. Cf. *Jewish Encyclopedia* III, 119b.

V. 22. The practice of giving tithes to the deity of the sanctuary was well established in ancient Israel; cf. Deuteronomy XIV, 22-29.

XIX

JACOB AND LABAN

(Genesis XXIX-XXXII, 2)

Return unto the land of thy fathers, and to thy kindred; and I will be with thee. (Genesis XXXI, 3.)

Create for me a clean heart, O God;
And renew a steadfast spirit within me. (Psalm LI, 12.)

Read Proverbs III, 1-7.

At dawn Jacob rose, a new man. Once more he set out upon his long, solitary journey. Yet how different was this from that awful yesterday. Then he felt alone and terror-stricken, forsaken both of men and God; today God was with him. Bravely, cheerfully, even happily he journeyed on, and at last he came to Haran, his beloved mother's birth-place, where his uncle Laban was dwelling. It seemed to him, so the wise rabbis told, that he had journeyed but a single day. So it is always when we know that God is with us. Then true happiness fills our souls; then days seem moments, and no worthy task is too hard, no obstacle too great. In the inspiring words of Mattathia to his brave son Judah Maccabee, "With God everything is possible".

The change which had come over Jacob, the rabbis taught, was manifest in his words to the very first persons he met upon his journey, the shepherds of Haran. For he greeted them by the significant title, "My brethren". The consciousness that all men are brothers, they taught, is the beginning of unselfishness. So it was with Jacob. He had deceived and defrauded his own brother, nor felt himself in any way his brother's keeper, nor responsible for his welfare and happiness. Now he was a different man, and so he hailed the shepherds, "My brethren, whence are ye?" And when the flocks had gathered, his cousin Rachel's among them, Jacob showed himself eager to help in the only way he could. Unaided, he rolled the great stone from the mouth of the well, that the shepherds might water their flocks. It was a little thing, but it showed the change in Jacob.

The rabbis told that when God saw this evidence of the change in Jacob, He was so pleased, that a miracle happened. For previously the well had been very deep, and its water had to be drawn up laboriously in buckets. Now, of its own accord, the water rose to the surface, so that the flocks could drink thereof themselves. There it remained during the entire twenty years of Jacob's sojourn in Haran. And the people knew that this had happened only because of Jacob, that he had brought blessing unto them, and therefore they loved him and were eager to keep him always with them. They felt him to be their brother, even as he had addressed them at first. One of the wise, old rabbis used to say, "One good deed causes another". So it was now with Jacob. But to him this wonder meant even more than to the people of Haran; he knew that God had done this, and that it was a sign that God would fulfil His promise, and would be with him, even here in this distant country.

The rabbis taught also that not only were Jacob's first words to the shepherds indicative of the change which had come over him, but also his second words, "Lo, it is yet high day, neither is it time that the cattle should be gathered together; water ye the sheep, and go and feed them". He had merely expressed his surprise at their procedure; yet it was also a partial rebuke of their laziness and indifference to their masters' interests. It indicated, too, that in his own labors for his uncle Laban, his conduct would be above reproach. He would not shirk a single task, no matter how hard; day and night he would guard the flock, and willingly sacrifice his own comfort and desires for his master's welfare. That is the true spirit of service, and Jacob had already begun to learn his lesson well. For his twenty years' service of his uncle Laban, bitter and hard and exacting, was to be but the training and preparation for a lifelong service of the supreme Master, in which there is no room for laziness, selfishness and self-indulgence, a service which would also prove hard and exacting, but never bitter, when performed in the right spirit of unselfishness, brotherhood, and love.

And there at the well Jacob met Rachel, his beloved. It must have seemed to him almost as if God had sent her, another proof that God was with him. The story of the love of Jacob and Rachel is one of the most romantic and beautiful in the entire Bible. The simple statement that the many years of hard labor which he served for her seemed but a few days, so great was his love for her, shows the human side of the authors, and makes us realize that Jacob is not altogether an imaginary, allegorical figure, but is depicted as a real man of flesh and blood, of love and selfishness, of strength and weakness, like ourselves, and that his struggles to conquer his evil inclinations differ not one whit from our own. We are indeed grateful for this delicate and delightful, human touch.

At last the seven years of service for Rachel were completed. Joyously Jacob prepared to receive his beloved reward. We can picture the expectant rapture with which he approaches the loved one and draws back the veil from her face, and the surprise, disappointment, and grief, when he finds that it is not Rachel at all, but Leah, the unbeloved. Bitterly he reproached her and her father for deceiving him. He had labored faithfully, and had fulfilled his part of the compact honorably and well. Had he deserved this treatment from either Laban or Leah? Why had Leah answered to the name of Rachel when he called unto her during the marriage? But Leah's answer, as related by the rabbis, silenced him forever. "Is there a teacher without a pupil?" she asked. "I merely profited by thy instruction. When thy father called thee Esau, didst thou not answer, 'Here am I'?" Then Jacob understood that he had been dealt with but in the same manner as he had dealt with his own blind father and his own brother; he could not complain. As the sage of old said, "The deceiver will himself be deceived". Sadly, but with the consciousness that it was deserved, Jacob accepted Leah as his wife, and then entered upon another period of seven years' hard service for Rachel.

The wise rabbi of old had said not merely that "One good deed causes another good deed", but also "And one evil deed causes another evil deed". So it was with Jacob, in the evil deed as well as in the good. For the deception which he had practiced upon Isaac and Esau had been only paralleled by, and had in a way justified the deception put upon him by Laban and Leah. Nevertheless God, in His justice, lets no evil deed go unpunished. We can easily see that Jacob's dislike of Leah, even though she was his wife, and all the unhappiness this brought her, were but the just punishment for her part in deceiving her husband. That which is gotten through deceit can never bring happiness. The end can never justify the means. We have seen this in the case of Jacob's getting the birthright and the blessing. We see it again here in the story of Leah.

We may be sure, however, that God had allowed Jacob to be deceived in this cruel manner, not merely as a punishment for the deceit he had himself practiced, but still more, as a test of his real worth, and to measure the change which had come over him during these seven years. On the whole it would seem that Jacob had stood this test well. He had realized that this was but a fit return for his own deception, and had accepted Leah as his wife, if not lovingly, at least loyally. Apparently he was well on his way toward complete purification and regeneration. And with this peace and happiness and quiet contentment were his during the first fourteen years of his service for Leah and Rachel. He discharged his obligations to Laban faithfully and loyally; and always there is the peace and joy of a satisfied and approving conscience in the knowledge that a task is well done. During these years, too, children were born to him, and all in all he had ample proof that God was with him, as He had promised, and was watching over him and providing for his needs, was indeed giving him "food to eat, and raiment to put on", even as Jacob had prayed.

But with the end of these fourteen years of faithful service, and the beginning of the third period of his sojourn with Laban, a change took place in Jacob. Continued success had tended to make him self-centered once more. Gradually the consciousness of God's blessing, and reliance upon God's help and providence gave way to reliance upon self and desire for material gain. As his family increased, the necessity of making proper provision for them pressed upon him. "When shall I provide for mine own house?" became his cry toward Laban. More and more his thoughts dealt with material things, and sought material rewards. And more and more he came to resent Laban's deceit and treachery, and to seek revenge in kind.

When the fourteen years of service for his two wives had passed, and it became necessary for Laban to negotiate other terms for Jacob's services, Jacob's opportunity had come. He knew that Laban realized that only through Jacob had he prospered so exceedingly, and therefore could not dispense with his services. He would make a cunning bargain with his uncle, and would show himself the shrewder of the two. He would offer terms which would seem to Laban's advantage, and which his grasping uncle would accept eagerly. But he knew many shepherd's tricks, by which he could turn the bargain to his advantage, and thereby he would provide for himself and his family, and would also have his revenge. The old, deceitful Jacob was not dead: he had merely lain dormant during all these years. Now he was again awake and active. Apparently these fourteen years of trial and suffering and seeming purification had availed naught. Only the outer surface of his nature had been altered; but the depths of his soul had not yet been reached.

So these six years passed and Jacob prospered materially. And whenever his perplexed and enraged uncle deceived him again, and changed his wages, as he did repeatedly, Jacob knew how to profit thereby. And he accounted for his success to his uncle, and possibly also to himself, by the old, oft-repeated claim that God was with him. Truly God was still with him, despite his deceit. But Jacob had now come to understand and interpret it, that God was with him only to protect and prosper him in his cunning. He had almost forgotten during these six years of prosperity through deceit, what the real purpose of God's being with him was.

Not improbably, too, during these six years his thoughts of home and his longing for the dear ones there had grown weaker and weaker. His desires and ambitions were centered upon something else. In all likelihood he had ceased to condemn himself for his treatment of his brother. After all it differed but little from his conduct toward his uncle Laban, and of this his present course of life approved. What mattered it that Laban's sons were beginning to eye him askance, and to mutter suspicions that they were being defrauded? It was clear that sooner or later they must separate; under present conditions they could not abide together long; and the parting must be in enmity and hatred. But meanwhile Jacob would push his advantage to the utmost. And if his conscience at times reproved him, or his better nature sought to reassert itself, he knew how to silence them, and to justify himself with the thought that Laban had first deceived him, and so merited this treatment, and he was only protecting himself. "Deceit can be met only by deceit". It is a common adage even today. But the story of Jacob proves its falsity. The sole truth in it is that in practice deceit is but too often countered by deceit; even as the wise rabbi of old said, "One evil deed causes another evil deed". Two wrongs can never make one right, but remain always two wrongs, and pave the way for further evil and unhappiness.

At last, after twenty years, when Jacob could abide with Laban and his sons no longer, God's command came, "Return unto the land of thy fathers, and to thy kindred; and I will be with thee". It was the answer to his prayer, spoken twenty years before. Had the word come six years sooner, at the end of his first fourteen years of service, how gladly would he have availed himself of it. Even though he was then poor in worldly goods, still he was rich in a clear conscience, in the satisfaction of faithful and loyal service, and in the love of wives and children. And during all those years thoughts of the dear ones at home and of reunion and reconciliation had been uppermost in his mind.

But now it was different. Now he was rich and prosperous. But was he truly happy? He must send for his wives to come to him to the field, where no one might hear him reveal his plans to them. And he must lie to them in order to justify his conduct, and claim that he had served their father faithfully, and that he had prospered only though God's blessing, and not through his own deceit. And he must steal away stealthily and in fear, lest his father-in-law prevent his departure, or at least keep back his daughters and their children and the flocks, and send him away empty-handed, as he had come twenty years before. His was indeed a guilty conscience. And with a guilty conscience there can be no true happiness.

At this moment his conduct must have begun to appear to him in a new light. And if he did not, as yet, condemn himself unqualifiedly, at least he must have had the feeling that even though he had prospered materially, none the less he had missed the real purpose of his sojourn in this foreign land, and was returning home but little better than when he had set out. Now he understood that it was not so much that God had prospered him, as his own deceit which had made him rich during the last six years. Nevertheless he could not but realize that even despite his deceit God had been with him, as He had promised.

And this realization was confirmed when Laban finally overtook him, and was prevented from wreaking his wrath upon him only by the vision of God which had come to him the previous night, and had bidden him refrain from violence in his dealings with Jacob. This, together with Laban's failure to find his stolen gods, had proved the superior power of Jacob's God over the gods of Laban, and that He was, at the end of these twenty years, still true to His word that He would be with Jacob and would protect him, and would bring him back to his father's house. The covenant was made with Laban, and they parted in peace and amity, instead of in hatred and strife. Jacob's eyes were opened somewhat and his spirit was chastened. He realized that without God's intervention his own strength would have availed little, and he must surely have perished. It was a humble and thoughtful man who journeyed onward, thankful that he had escaped this danger from Laban, and had parted from him in friendship, and wondering how he should meet the even greater danger, which, he now perceived, must confront him from Esau. Once more he must have prayed in the deep recesses of his heart, as he had prayed twenty years before, "If God will be with me, and will keep me in this way that I go". Truly he had need of God's protection now. And with this prayer something of the spirit of humility and repentance of those first fourteen years must have returned to him. And there must have welled forth the additional prayer, the longing of those first years, couched in the Psalmist's beautiful words:

> Create me a clean heart, O God;
> And renew a steadfast spirit within me.

So Jacob journeyed on to meet Esau.

NOTES

XXIX, 1. "The children of the east", i. e. nomads or semi-nomads, dwelling in northern Mesopotamia. Laban's tribe is evidently regarded as belonging to this group.

V. 2. In the Orient, particularly in the desert itself, and the country bordering on the desert, water is scarce, and consequently very precious. Therefore it is not uncommon that wells should be covered, as this one was, by a great stone, which frequently requires the combined efforts of many men to move, in order to prevent the water from being used by strangers or those not entitled to it, and also to keep out the sand and other things, which might otherwise choke the well. Whether this was the same well as that from which Rebekah had drawn the water for the camels of Abraham's servant, is not stated. Apparently, however, it was not, since that well seems to have been approached by a flight of steps (cf. note to XXIV, 16), while the water of this well was drawn up by buckets in the hands of the shepherds who stood at the mouth of the well.

V. 5. XXII, 3 and XXIV, 24 call Rebekah the daughter of Bethuel and the granddaughter of Nahor. Therefore by "son of Nahor" is meant presumably only "descendant".

V. 7. Sheep were usually watered toward evening, preparatory to being penned up for the night.

V. 8. Watering many flocks of sheep from one well is a slow task. Therefore the verse pictures the custom of these shepherds to assemble still early in the afternoon. It is also customary that the first shepherds to arrive at a well, water their flocks first, while the late-comers must wait. This was an additional reason for these shepherds coming early to the well.

V. 9. Among the nomad Semites girls are very frequently employed as shepherdesses, particularly of the flocks of their own families.

V. 10. Jacob, by his great strength, alone rolls away the huge stone. This usually required the combined efforts of all the shepherds.

V. 11. Among the Orientals weeping because of joy, even on the part of men, is a common practice. There is nothing of the occidental conception of tears as unmanly.

V. 12. For the meaning of "brother" here and in v. 15, cf. the note to XXVII, 29.

V. 13. It must be understood that this was the first word which Laban had heard of his sister in all these years since she had departed with the servant of Abraham. Furthermore, in the Orient blood kinship establishes an undeniable bond between men. Hence Laban's joy at beholding his sister's son. It is a common practice in the Orient, and in many other parts of the world, for relatives who have not seen each other for a long time, regardless of sex, to kiss each other upon meeting.

V. 17. In selecting a wife in the Orient especial attention is paid to beauty of the eyes.

V. 18. Among the ancient Semites, as among so many other peoples, girls are regarded as the property of their fathers, and must therefore be purchased from him by their future husbands. Where the latter is unable to pay the bride-price demanded, it is not uncommon for him, as here, to pledge his services to his father-in-law for a fixed period of years, usually five to seven .

As a rule the bride-price, or at least a considerable portion thereof, is given by the father to his daughter, and becomes her inalienable property. But if the father be avaricious, he frequently retains the entire bride-price for himself. XXXI, 15f. states that Laban was guilty of this departure from common and approved practice; this enabled Leah and Rachel to justify Jacob's possession of a large part of their father's flocks, by the implication that this portion of the return for Jacob's services should have been given to them.

V. 19. For the practice of marriage between cousins cf. the final note to XXV.

V. 26. Among many peoples in various parts of the world, the younger daughter may not be given in marriage before her older sister. This was probably an actual practice in Laban's tribe, and not merely a plausible excuse invented by him for the occasion, and in order to dispose of both his daughters for a good price and at one stroke.

V. 27. In the Orient marriage festivities, as in this instance, generally continue for an entire week. Jacob is not to repudiate Leah, but is to complete the marriage festivities with her during this week. Then next week Rachel shall be given to him, and in return for her he shall serve a further term of seven years. Leah was given to him at the end of the first period of seven years, and Rachel one week later, at the beginning of the second period. According to XXX, 25, Joseph was born to Rachel at the end of the second period of seven years; in other words she had been barren for six years.

V. 31. Children are considered in the Orient as a gift of the Deity; cf. XXX, 2. Numerous offspring therefore imply particular divine favor; cf. I Samuel I and II, 21 and Psalm CXXVII, 3-5.

V. 32. In ancient Israel it was the mother's privilege to name her children; cf. IV, 1 and 25; I Samuel I, 20. Later this privilege passed to the father; cf. V, 3; XVI, 15. Names given to children were generally descriptive of some thought or incident attendant upon their birth; cf. I Samuel IV, 19-22.

Sons are more desired than daughters, and a woman who has borne a son can reasonably expect better treatment and greater affection on the part of her husband.

XXX, 1. With Rachel's desire for offspring may be compared that of Hannah (I Samuel I, 1-20). In the Orient a childless wife is liable to be treated in time with little regard, and may even be divorced. The desire, therefore, to safeguard her position in the home, as well as the Oriental woman's natural and unrepressed longing for offspring, make her eagerly desirous of a large family.

V. 3. Cf. the note to XVI. The child born to a handmaid, when laid upon her mistress' knees, was regarded as formally adopted by the latter, and as actually her child.

Vv. 14ff. It is a common superstition in many parts of the earth that mandrakes possess magical properties, conducive to the promotion of childbirth; cf. Hartland, *Primitive Paternity,* I, 44-47.

V. 27. "I have observed the signs", Hebrew, *niḥashti,* i. e. "I have ascertained by the practice of ceremonies of divination".

Vv. 32ff. The customary wage of a shepherd in the Orient is a certain percentage of the newborn lambs or kids. Generally this is ten percent, half male and half female; cf. Musil, *Arabia Petraea,* III, 284, and Dalman, *Palaestinischer Diwan,* 33f. In this case Jacob asked for what would prove under normal conditions less than the customary wage, and Laban, suspecting nothing, was only too pleased to accept the proferred terms. As XXX, 38f. implies, the shepherd was expected to feed himself from his own share of the flock, and to restore all losses incurred by theft or wild beasts.

Vv. 35-42. The account of Jacob's trick seems to us obscure. But we must remember that a considerable portion of the people of ancient Israel, particularly in the southern kingdom, were shepherds, who would both understand and appreciate the cleverness of this trick. Apparently something of homeopathic magic, based upon the idea that like invariably causes like, lies at the bottom of this practice.

XXXI, 7 implies that during these last six years Laban, seeing Jacob growing wealthy by the terms of their bargain, had deliberately and faithlessly repudiated these terms and offered others, seemingly more advantageous to himself, which, however, Jacob knew how to turn to his own benefit. He represents this, half-deceitfully at least, as being the result of God's favor.

Vv. 10-12. These verses are apparently based upon a slightly varying version of Jacob's trick, which must have been current in ancient Israel along with the version recorded in XXX, 35-42.

V. 15. Cf. note to XXIX, 18.

V. 19. The *teraphim* were the family or household gods represented in the form of idols. They varied considerably in size. These of Laban were small enough to be put in the pack-saddle of a camel, upon which Rachel sat, while I Samuel XIX, 13 speaks of such an image in the house of David, which was approximately of human size and shape. In ancient Israel the use of these *teraphim* seems to have been common, and not at all inconsistent with the pure worship of Israel's God; cf. Judges XVII; XVIII, 14, 17, 18, 20; I Samuel XIX, 13; Hosea III, 4. The *teraphim* were apparently employed particularly in the practice of divination; cf. Ezekiel XXI, 26; Zechariah X, 2. Accordingly the rabbis sought to excuse Rachel's theft, by saying that she took the *teraphim* because she feared that they might disclose Jacob's whereabouts to Laban. Actually the story gives no motive for Rachel's theft, unless it be that suggested in the lesson, to prove the superiority of Jacob's God over the gods of Laban. For this reason probably the story told with considerable gusto not only that Rachel stole these gods, which were powerless to defend themselves, but also that she even subjected them to the greatest possible indignity by sitting upon them. In time the use of *teraphim* came to be regarded as inconsistent with the pure worship of God, and was prohibited (II Kings XXIII, 24; cf. I Samuel XV, 23). Cf. *Jewish Encyclopedia*, XII, 108f.

V. 21. "The River", i. e. the Euphrates.

V. 23. "The mountain of Gilead". Gilead was the common name for that portion of Palestine lying east of the Jordan and north of the Jabbok. Its actual boundaries seem to have been rather uncertain, and to have varied at different times. It is a rough, mountainous country. Vv. 47f. seem to offer a popular tradition, ascribing the origin of the name Gilead to Jacob, who called the heap of stones, which he erected on the boundary line between Syria and Gilead, *gal-ed* literally "the heap of the witness".

V. 24. The Aramaeans were an important branch of the Semitic race, and closely akin to the Israelites. The kingdom of Damascus, or Syria, during the 9th and 8th centuries B. C. the most powerful and dangerous rival of the northern kingdom of Israel, was the leading Aramaean state. The language of the Aramaean tribes and states consisted of a great many closely related dialects. After the Babylonian exile Aramaic gradually superseded Hebrew as the vernacular of the Jewish people. Certain portions of the Bible, viz. Jeremiah X, 11, Daniel II, 4b-VII, 28, and Ezra IV, 8-VI, 18 and VII, 12-26, are written in Aramaic, as are likewise considerable portions of rabbinic literature.

V. 33. Each of Jacob's wives had her own tent, in which she lived with her children. Jacob, of course, had no tent of his own, but abode with whichever wife he chose. As XXX, 16 implies, this was usually Rachel, his favorite.

Vv. 38f. Cf. note to XXX, 32ff.

V. 40. In certain parts of the Orient during considerable portions of the year, even though the days may be quite hot, the nights are frequently cold, and frost is not uncommon.

Vv. 45ff. The custom of setting up a memorial stone or heap of stones as the permanent reminder of a covenant or of some memorable event, was common in Semitic practice .

V. 46. "And they did eat there by the heap"; this was the ritual meal by which the covenant was ratified; cf. note to XXVI, 30.

V. 47 *Yegar-sahadutha* is the Aramaic equivalent of the Hebrew *gal-ed*.

V. 48. *Mizpeh* is apparently represented here as a secondary name of this heap of stones. It means "watchpost", or "place of lookout". Actually the district was called Gilead, while Mizpeh was probably the name of the particular spot in Gilead where this covenant between Jacob and Laban, was thought to have been made. It probably lay close to the boundary line between Syria and Gilead. As was suggested in the introductory chapter to the Jacob story, this incident of the covenant made between Laban the Aramaean and Jacob the Israelite, by which the boundary line between the territories of the two peoples was fixed, may very well be based upon some historical compact of similar nature, entered into between Syria and Israel, most probably during the reign of Ahab (875-854 B. C.). During the greater part of Ahab's reign the hegemony of Israel in the affairs of the numerous little states of western Asia seems to have been nominally acknowledged by Syria; cf. I Kings XX.

V. 53. "And Jacob swore by the Fear of his father Isaac"; this is an obscure and difficult expression. The compilers probably meant to designate the God of Israel by this term. Not improbably, however, in the oldest version of this story the actual name of a (or the) Deity stood here, and the compilers substituted the present non-committal expression in order to avoid the appearance of polytheism.

V. 54. This is probably a repetition, or a second version, of the incident of the covenant meal, already referred to in v. 46. Certain forms of sacrifice were accompanied by a ritual meal participated in by the sacrificer and his guests.

XX

JACOB AND ESAU

(Genesis XXXII, 4—XXXIII, 17; XXXV, 16-20, 27-29)

Thy name shall be called no more Jacob, but Israel; for thou hast striven with God and with men, and hast prevailed. (Genesis XXXII, 29.)

The sacrifices of God are a broken spirit;
A broken and a contrite heart, O God, Thou wilt not despise.
(Psalm LI, 19.)

Read Psalm XLVI, 2, 3, 4, 12.

Laban had departed. He had kissed his daughters and his grand-children farewell, and had set out upon his return to Haran. Now, at last Jacob could breathe freely. The danger from Laban was past; they had parted in peace, as alone befitted close relatives. Had it been otherwise, had Jacob been compelled to leave his uncle Laban, just as he had left his brother Esau twenty years before, with anger and enmity between them as the result of his deception, he might well have felt that these twenty years of trial and suffering in a foreign land had been all in vain, and that he was returning home but little changed from what he had been on setting out. His prayer then had been to return in peace to his father's house. He realized now that although Laban had deceived him, he, too, had not been altogether blameless in his dealings with Laban during these last six years. But their differences had been smoothed away, their quarrels settled, their misunderstandings adjusted; now there was peace between them, the peace which Jacob had learned to regard as life's greatest blessing. Now he stood upon the border of his native land, prepared to enter and to come to his father's house. It was the moment for which he had prayed and longed. Surely Jacob should have been happy.

But Jacob was far from happy. The quarrel with Laban, so narrowly averted, had opened his eyes. If Laban had been so enraged at having been deceived, even though he had himself first and repeatedly deceived Jacob, then how much more reason had Esau, so cruelly betrayed and defrauded of life's dearest blessings by his own brother, to still cherish his anger and to seek revenge! Now that he had escaped Laban's wrath, and the inevitable meeting with Esau drew closer, Jacob realized more clearly than at any time previously the full measure and import of the wrong which he had done to his brother. He had hoped that these twenty years might have allowed Esau's anger to cool; or if not, that he might appease Esau with a rich present of flocks and herds, such as he could easily spare out of his great abundance. Now he suddenly remembered that Esau was not of a forgiving nature, and, above all, that he had ample reason for hatred and revenge. And as he stood upon the border of the home land fear seized him, fear of his brother and his anger, but even more, fear of himself and his sin. In this connection the wise rabbis sagely asked, why should Jacob have feared so greatly before Esau, when he did not fear at all to fight the angel, or whatever it was, throughout the entire night? And they answered that he feared Esau because he knew how greatly he had wronged him. So we always fear before those whom we have wronged. And the rabbis also taught that before a man sins everyone fears him; after he sins he fears everyone. Thus, as the great poet said, "Conscience doth make cowards of us all".

But this very fear showed Jacob's real nature and character at this moment. For he was judging Esau entirely by himself. He, too, had been deceived by Laban. And how had he requited him? Only with counter-deceit. And how much worse was his conduct than Laban's! For he knew by bitter experience what deceit meant. Yet if, knowing all this, he had still met deceit with deceit, why expect Esau to act at all differently? Surely he dared hope for naught but hatred and revenge from Esau, and surely, too, he deserved no more. Now, too, he realized how he had fallen short in his dealings with Laban, and that two wrongs never make one right; that Laban's deceit had probably been the last trial sent by God to determine his real worth and the extent of his self-purification. Now he knew that he had fallen short. And if he, then why not Esau too? What reason had he to expect better treatment from Esau than he had accorded to Laban? He was judging Esau only by himself; and the evil light in which he now saw Esau, was but the reflection of the light in which he saw himself. So it is constantly with us; we judge our neighbors largely by ourselves. Often the faults we see in them are but the reflection of greater faults in ourselves. And often our condemnation of our neighbor should be a condemnation of ourselves.

So Jacob feared; and he took what precautions he could, the poor precautions which his fear suggested. He sent messengers to Esau to announce his coming, and, if possible, to sound Esau and bring back word of his probable reception of Jacob. In all likelihood had the report been unfavorable, Jacob would still have turned aside, even despite God's command to return, and His promise that He would still be with him. But all this Esau frustrated by coming himself with all dispatch, and attended by four hundred men, to meet Jacob. There could be no mistaking his evil intentions. The messengers reported all this but little before Esau himself arrived. It was too late for Jacob to turn aside. He must meet Esau, and that on the very next day.

Now even more did Jacob fear, for there seemed little chance of escape. But he would take what chance there was. Better to sacrifice half his possessions, than that everything be lost. So he divided his camp, the people who were with him and the flocks, the herds, and the camels, into two camps, so that, if Esau should attack the one camp, the other might still escape. It was a cunning plan, although even it seemed to offer little promise. Nor did it serve to restore Jacob's confidence or lessen his fear.

And then, suddenly, he bethought himself of the one source of protection and help, which had never failed him in all these years of trial, God. During the last six years of his sojourn with Laban he had come to rely more and more upon himself and his own strength and cunning, and less and less upon God's promise to be with him. But his narrow escape from Laban's wrath had made him realize once again what he had almost forgotten, that without God human strength and earthly devices avail little. Now, in this moment of greatest peril, when it seemed that his clever plans had come to naught, he turned to God with a prayer of humility and supplication, acknowledging his unworthiness of all God's guidance and bounty, and imploring His help and protection against Esau.

How typical is Jacob's conduct! We are all too prone to commit the very error against which the Bible warns, and to say in prosperity, "My power and the might of my hand have gotten me this wealth" (Deuteronomy VIII, 17f.). But when distress and danger confront us, and all earthly help seems weak and futile, then we, too, become mindful of God, and we turn to Him, as Jacob did, with prayers of humility and supplication. It is not too late; it is never too late for prayer, for we may be sure that God hears all prayers, when offered in sincerity of heart and purity of motive. As the Psalmist says,

God is our refuge and strength,
A very present help in trouble.
Therefore will we not fear, though the earth do change,
And though the mountains be moved into the heart of the seas.

And as the rabbis told, the gates of heaven are constantly opened wide, that the prayers of those who seek Him truly may come unto God.

The pity of it is that many pray so little, and that most of us turn to God only in moments of need, peril and distress. We have so much for which to thank God and to utter His praise. Day by day and hour by hour our lives are enriched with His bounties. And surely it were not too much if every day we would turn to God to thank Him for all His boundless love, and, even as Jacob did, to acknowledge our littleness and unworthiness, and to pray to Him for help and strength and wisdom, that we may use all His precious gifts aright, for the purpose for which He gives them. So our fathers prayed in ages past. Thrice daily they acknowledged God's greatness and besought the continuance of His favor. And their prayers and their faith in God kept them and kept Judaism alive. Verily their example should inspire us, their children, to like faith and devotion.

So Jacob prayed. But even prayer alone is not enough. Prayer must lead to renewed faith and nobility of action. Some prayer is actuated chiefly by selfish fear, or equally selfish desire, and springs from the lips rather than from the heart. But the true prayer, which is most pleasing to God, is that prayer which wells forth from the depths of a trusting, God-seeking soul, and brings with it that strength of faith and exaltation of purpose, which find their only expression in right and noble living. Was Jacob's an altogether true prayer? He had uttered beautiful words and noble sentiments, and had properly acknowledged God's greatness and goodness and his own unworthiness. But

instead of the absolute trust in God, which should have
followed upon this prayer, and unshaken reliance upon God's
promise to be with him and bring him back to his kindred
and his father's house, Jacob now resumed his cunning
plans for his own defense. It would seem that beautiful
though this prayer was, and true in every word, it was
still of the lips rather than of the heart, and was born more
of fear of Esau than of love of God and firm faith in Him.
It would almost seem as if Jacob had thought, "If God can
and will save me from this dire peril, well and good; but
if not, then all the more must I spare no effort to save
myself".

Then followed an anxious night. Redoubled preparations
were made to meet Esau the next morning. A rich present
was sent on in advance, with the hope that Esau's anger
might possibly be appeased with this. Then Jacob's wives
and children were set across the stream, that they might
be the first to meet Esau in the morning, and that the sight
of these weak and suppliant beings, his own flesh and blood,
might help to still Esau's anger. Jacob himself remained on
this side of the stream. He would cross only at the very
last moment; possibly he might still turn back and flee;
without sheep and cattle, wives and children to hinder him,
he might still escape. True, it would mean setting out on
his lonesome journey anew, just as twenty years before.
Even worse, now he would have no place whither he might
turn; and surely God would no longer be with him. But
at least he would be safe from Esau's wrath. Such must
have been the thoughts which thronged Jacob's guilt-laden
mind throughout this long night. For the moment he was
completely the old, crafty, self-centered Jacob once more.
He had expected that on this one last night at least, he
would be safe, and would find rest and comfort. But there
were no rest and comfort for him. As the Bible says, all
through that night there wrestled with him, someone or

something. The Bible calls it a man; but this may be for
want of a better term. Tradition has come to call it an
angel (cf. Hosea XII, 5), and perhaps it was that. But
if so, the story in Genesis gives no hint thereof. We know
only that it was something powerful and eager to conquer.
Yet it could be conquered, too; by morning dawn it could
be overcome. And if once overcome, it could be made to
bestow blessing. What could it have been?

May we not say that it was Jacob's other self, his wicked,
selfish, earthly nature, with which he strove during the
entire night? We have learned that man is the child of
two worlds, of earth and heaven. His body is of the dust,
but his spirit is inbreathed by God Himself. Ever these
two natures strive within him for the mastery, until at last
one is completely conquered. All through Jacob's life they
had striven. At first, in his early years, the earthly nature,
which seeks for selfish pleasure and gain had had the upper
hand, and it seemed as if the godlike spirit within were completely crushed. But we know that it was not dead, but
was only sleeping. Then throughout these twenty long years
the two natures had striven earnestly. At first it had seemed
as if the divine element would triumph. But in these last
six years once more the earthly nature had gained the upper
hand. Now had come the moment of the last and most
bitter struggle, when complete and final victory or defeat
must come for one or the other. All through the night the
earthly, selfish nature kept whispering, "Flee now; leave
the sheep and cattle to Esau; leave the wives and children
to their fate; better that they alone perish, than that thou
perish with them. Perhaps thou canst still find rest and
peace in some other land. And perhaps thou wilt in time
be able to avenge thyself upon Esau. He is a villain, and
thou canst expect no good at his hands". But to all this
the divine voice within kept answering in ever stronger
accents, "They are thy wives and thy children, and they look

to thee for help and protection, and thou mayest not desert them. And after all, without them what would life be worth? Hast thou not already betrayed and sacrificed thy family enough, and only suffered thereby? Remember, Esau is thy brother, and even as thou dost still love him, and seek peace with him, so he, too, may still love thee and long to forgive thee. Remember, too, that it was thou who didst wrong him, and therefore it must be thou who dost ask pardon; without pardon there can be no peace. And consider that thou hast come hither at God's command, and that He has promised to be with thee still, as He was with thee during these twenty years past. And thou mayest not disobey. And above all, think that thine is the birthright of Abraham and of Isaac, thy father; thou art charged to become a blessing unto mankind. This birthright thou didst eagerly desire for thyself, and win at great cost. But never canst thou be worthy of it, never canst thou become a blessing, if thou dost flee as a coward and shirk thy responsibilities. At the most, thou canst but die, but never canst thou escape or flee from God's commands".

All through the night the battle raged. Time and again the tempter seemed almost to conquer; ever and again Jacob was on the point of fleeing. But always something held him back; now it was the memory of father and mother, now of wives and children, now of God's promise, and the realization that God had truly been with him these twenty years, and had suffered no word of His to go unfulfilled. All through the long, dark night the battle raged. But with the morning dawn came victory, victory and blessing. "Thy name shall be called no more Jacob, but Israel; for thou hast striven with God and with men, and hast prevailed". With this earthly nature, to the voice of which men so often hearken, Jacob had striven during these twenty years, and particularly during this last night, and it had not prevailed; he had conquered it. With the divine voice within, the voice of God, Jacob had striven, too, and at last, after a bitter struggle, it had prevailed. He had entered upon the struggle twenty years before, a selfish, deceitful, young man. Now he emerged from it, purified, noble, victorious, but also old, wearied and limping; yet erect and happy withal. He was a different, a new, a better man; and as symbol thereof came the new name; no longer Jacob, "the Deceiver", but Israel, "the Champion of God", who was henceforth to fight the battles of the Lord, and become a blessing unto all mankind.

Jacob's struggle, too, is typical. Almost from the very moment of birth the two natures within us strive for the mastery. In youth especially we are apt to lend a willing ear to the seductive whisperings of our earthly nature, and allow it to prevail. But to most of us maturity, experience, and wisdom bring the awakening, when we become conscious of the deeper meaning and possibilities of life, when we come to understand that God has put us here on earth, not for the satisfaction of our appetites and pursuit after the will-o'-the-wisps of pleasure, but that we may live among our fellowmen, and by the right use of the powers and gifts which God bestows upon us in such boundless measure, help the world to grow better and mankind to live wiser, nobler, and happier lives.

Some awaken only to slumber again, and to let the world take its course, so long as it does not interfere with their own selfish desires. For them there is no struggle. They are conquered even before the combat can begin; and they must remain ever creatures of the dust, over whom the earthly nature has triumphed, and within whom the spirit of God is dead.

But others awake, and remain awake, throughout the long, dark night, while the battle rages, the battle with the other self. At first one combatant seems about to prevail, and then the other. The better nature may gain the upper hand for awhile, even as with Jacob during the first fourteen years, only to succumb in the end. There is no assurance that good will triumph of itself. It must be backed by unfailing trust in God, and strength of will and determination for the right, which endure for all time and under all circumstances, which can withstand the allurements of fortune and prosperity and smug self-complacency, as well as the discouragements of adversity and failure and self-condemnation. But when the faith be firm, the courage dauntless and the will steadfast, then victory is assured in the end. And with the first ray of the dawn, which heralds our new day, we step forth from the combat, changed mèn, blessed by the very evil powers with which we have striven, no longer the old Jacob, but now the new Israel, God's champion.

Yet we never emerge unscathed. The battle is too long and hard and exacting. Some of our strength is sapped, some of our vigor is abated, some of our youth is fled; it is the inevitable price of experience and wisdom; and we limp upon the thigh as we go; for this battle, too, must leave its wounds and scars. And if thereafter we go forward more slowly upon the course. of life, which leads toward the goal of existence which God has appointed for each of us, and if we limp, and at times even halt and falter, still it is all in accordance with God's plan, and we can only continue to push on as best we may. After all, as the Bible so wisely says, "the race is not always to the swift" (Ecclesiastes IX, 11); and he who limps in God's service will attain the goal of life more surely and speedily than he who runs after evil. True living consists in striving rather than in attaining, in fighting bravely and manfully throughout the long, dark hours of the night against the powers of evil which seek to conquer and submerge mankind, and in conquering just as the dawn breaks. Victory over evil can not be gained in the darkness of the night. Evil is the child of night, and lives and grows ever stronger in the black shad-

ows. It is only the radiant, illuminating, searching light of
day which it can not withstand, before which it must flee and
vanish. The battle must endure through all the long night.
Victory is but the crowning triumph of a single, final moment. True existence means to strive steadfastly with God
and with men for the right, and with the morning dawn,
which marks the close of life's struggle, even while it ushers
in the new day of radiant, eternal light, to step forth vic-
toriously as Israel, "the Champion of God", to receive God's
blessing, and to return in peace to the Father's house. This
is the true life of struggle and of service, which God, in His
wisdom and love, has bidden each one of His children to live.

So with the dawn Jacob became a new man. Jacob, "the
Deceiver", was gone forever; Israel, "the Champion of God",
had taken his place. And he crossed the river to rejoin his
family and to meet his brother, however he might receive
him. There would be no more fear nor deceit, nor unworthy
attempts to appease his brother's just anger. He would submit himself to Esau and accept whatever punishment the
latter might inflict. So he went to meet his brother, no
longer fearful, but humble and repentant. And imagine his
surprise when Esau, in turn, ran to meet him and threw his
arms around his neck and kissed him. It was so much
more than he dared expect that he could not but see God's
hand in it. And we may be sure that God's hand was in
it. But we may be sure, too, that it was Jacob himself,
above all else, who had brought about the change in Esau.
In all likelihod Esau had come with his four hundred men
to seek revenge. He, too, could picture Jacob only as the
deceiver of twenty years before. But when Jacob approached
humbly and submissively, his anger was disarmed; he forgot
all, save that this was his brother, with whom he had grown
up as a child, and whom, he now acknowledged, he had
missed during these twenty years, and whom deep down in
his heart he still loved. Anger and revenge were forgotten

in a moment, and peace and happiness were restored between them.

So at last Jacob's sin was forgiven, not only by Esau, but also by God, just because, as the wise rabbis taught, Jacob had done all he could to right his wrong, and had at last obtained Esau's pardon. Then God, too, was free to forgive. The hardest thing in the world is to acknowledge that we have done wrong and to ask pardon. Yet, strangely enough, it is the one thing which shows a truly great nature, and which is certain to abate anger and bring peace. If only people were quicker to acknowledge their sins and seek forgiveness, surely men would be nobler, and this world would be a better and happier place to live in.

Thus Jacob became a true man at last, worthy of the birthright and of God's love and blessing. And at last, as he had prayed, he returned in peace to his father's house. It must have been a joyful as well as a sad home coming; sad because of the absence of the beloved mother, who had made such a great sacrifice for him, as he now realized, and whom he could never repay; but happy to find his old father still alive, and to be able to recompense him somewhat for the great wrong done to him. We can picture Jacob now a loving, dutiful son, seeking only to bring happiness to his old father. And Isaac must have been truly happy in his last years. At last Isaac was gathered to his fathers in a ripe old age, and was laid to rest by his two sons, Jacob and Esau, in the Cave of Machpelah, at the side of the companion of his life and his love, Rebekah.

But Jacob lived on for many years, purified and ennobled, doing the will of God, working blessing in every way he could, and living worthy of the birthright of his fathers. We have heard much in these lessons of repentance, and of people who did not repent, and therefore had to suffer the inevitable consequences of their sins. Now we have come to know one who truly repented; and we realize all that repentance means, and that, even though it be difficult and exacting, it is not beyond human strength. And we understand fully the words of the Psalmist,

The sacrifices of God are a broken spirit;
A broken and a contrite heart, O God, thou wilt not despise.

Such a spirit and such a heart were Jacob's, and we know that his sacrifice was acceptable to the Lord, and that his repentance was true and lasting. And we understand, too, the words of the wise, old rabbi, "Who is a hero? He who conquereth his own evil inclinations".

In thinking of Jacob's entire life, and of repentance and all that it means, and how alone God's forgiveness can be attained, we are reminded of a beautiful story, which used to be told by the rabbis. A certain man, Eliezer ben Dordeja by name, had sinned greatly. Throughout his life he had committed sins without number, nor even once had felt the slightest compunction or fear before God. But one day an old woman said to him, "Eliezer ben Dordeja, thy wickedness is great, and thy sins are without number; never canst thou find pardon or work atonement; thou art hopelessly lost, and condemned by God to eternal punishment". With that terror seized upon Eliezer ben Dordeja. Suddenly he realized the magnitude of his offense and his utter hopelessness. Immediately the desire to sin left him completely; and only the desire to atone remained. But how might he atone; he understood nothing about this. In despair he fled out into the wilderness. There he beheld the mountains towering above him until their tops seemed to penetrate into God's very heaven. He sank down at their feet and prayed, "Ye mountains and hills, forgive my transgressions and seek pardon for me from God". But the mountains sadly answered, "Rather than seek pardon for thee must we implore mercy for ourselves from the Creator". Then Eliezer wrung his hands, and in despair he raised his eyes aloft to heaven.

"O ye heavens so high, the dwelling-place of God", he whispered, "do you implore pardon for me". But the heavens, too, answered, "Nay, for thee may we not implore pardon; for ourselves must we seek God's favor". Then Eliezer turned to the sun and moon. "Ye orbs of heaven, which give light and blessing to men", he prayed, "seek pardon for me of the Lord". But they, too, answered, "Nay, only for ourselves alone may we seek pardon". Then Eliezer understood, and to himself he said, "I know that each must seek pardon for himself of God, the Creator of all. Perhaps He, in His love, will still hearken to my prayer, sinner though I am". So he sat down upon the ground, with head bowed between his knees, and humbly he prayed to God. Long he sat, with broken and contrite heart, never moving nor stirring, but with thoughts turned ever to God and with unutterable longing filling his heart. At last his soul passed from his body. But even in that moment a voice was heard from heaven above, resounding throughout the world, "Eliezer ben Dordeja is reconciled to his God; his sins are forgiven, and he is called to eternal life with his Father in heaven". Such is true repentance, and only so may God's pardon be at last attained.

NOTES

XXXII, 4. This verse makes Esau dwell far to the south in the land of Edom, the land of his traditional descendants, the Edomites. The story would have been more dramatically complete and perfect, had it told that Esau and Jacob dwelt together at home with their father. But as was stated in the introductory chapter, actual historical conditions forbade this.

V. 23. The Jabbok is a small stream which rises in the mountains of Gilead, east of the Jordan, flows westward, and empties into the Jordan. Its current is very swift. During the greater part of its course it flows through a deep and narrow valley, with steep, precipitous sides. It is therefore quite an undertaking to cross this stream at any time. In this case this was all the more difficult, because Jacob had to transport his entire camp over the river, and that at night. Peniel was apparently situated at or near this stream. The exact site, however, is not known.

Vv. 31f. are not an integral part of the story, but rather an editorial note explaining the name of the place where the struggle is supposed to have taken place. *Peniel*, "face of God". According to the common belief in ancient Israel, no mortal could behold God's face and live; cf. Exodus XXXIII, 20. Peniel (also called Penuel), was one of the two towns east of the Jordan which was destroyed by Gideon because it had refused to aid him in his pursuit of the Midianites (Judges VIII, 8f. and 17).

V. 33. For the origin and meaning of this strange rite, cf. above, p. 201.

XXXIII, 3. Bowing to the ground seven times shows the degree of Jacob's humility before Esau.

V. 10. Ordinarily mortals might not look upon the face of a deity (cf. XXXII, 31; Exodus XXXIII, 20). To be permitted to do so was a mark of divine favor (cf. Exodus XXIV, 9-11); hence the comparison here.

V. 17 is also an editorial note, inserted to account for the traditional origin of the name *Succoth*, "booths", the other town east of the Jordan destroyed by Gideon (Judges VIII, 5-7, 14-16).

XXXIII, 18-XXXV, 5. As was stated in the introductory chapter, this whole episode of Jacob at Shechem is hardly an integral part of the Jacob story as prepared by the compilers. The tradition may have some historical basis in an actual attack upon the important and powerful Canaanite city of Shechem by the tribes of Simeon and Levi, acting conjointly, in early prehistoric days. An echo of this may be found in XLIX, 5-8. In its present form the whole story is obscure and difficult.

XXXV, 4. This incident of the burial of the foreign idols is likewise obscure. Tradition maintains that these idols were the *teraphim* of Laban, which Rachel had stolen and kept until now. This is, however, only a conjecture. Probably the verse means to imply that the servants of Jacob had brought with them from their home land their own household gods. Jacob now compels them to give these up and accept the worship of the God of Israel.

Earrings were, and still are, worn in the Orient as amulets or charms against evil. In ancient times they had ritual significance; cf. Judges VIII, 24-27.

V. 8. The mention here of Deborah, Rebekah's nurse, is a notable anachronism. For she could have been with Jacob's camp only if she had set out with him from his father's house twenty years before (cf. XXIV, 59). But according to XXVIII, 10ff. Jacob was entirely alone upon this journey. There is undoubtedly confusion between this tradition of the great tree near Bethel, sacred, or at least renowned, because of its association with a certain Deborah, and the tradition recorded in Judges IV, 5 of the sacred "palm-tree of Deborah", also located near Bethel, so-called because Deborah, the prophetess, was supposed to have sat beneath it, while revealing the oracle to Israel. It is clear that, as was stated in the introduction, this chapter, as well as the two preceding chapters, contains a brief summary of various Jacob traditions, not a part of the main Jacob story.

Vv. 9-15. These verses contain a late, artificial version of the two incidents of Jacob at Bethel (XXVIII, 10-22) and of the change of his name to Israel (XXXIII, 23-33).

V. 19. There is considerable confusion as to the exact location of Rachel's tomb. Bethel is situated north of Jerusalem upon the border line between Ephraim and Benjamin. Ephrath must be near by. This is borne out by I Samuel I, 1, which calls Elkanah, who came from Ramah, upon the western border of Ephraim, an Ephrathite. Likewise Jeremiah XXXI, 15 locates the grave of Rachel at Ramah as does also I Samuel X, 2. This, however, accords but ill with the statement of v. 19, that Ephrath was merely another name for Bethlehem, an important city six miles south of Jerusalem, and which would accordingly locate the burial-place of Rachel in the vicinity of this town. The solution of this difficulty is that there were probably in ancient Israel two places called Ephrath, one between Bethel and Ramah, and the other Bethlehem itself. The real burial-place of Rachel was near the former place. V 19 therefore records a mistaken tradition, due to confusing Bethlehem-Ephrath (cf. Micah V, 1) with the more northern Ephrath.

V. 27. Mamre was the name of the grove near Hebron where Abraham had dwelt (XIII, 18). This verse does not agree altogether with previous passages, which represent Isaac as dwelling, not at Mamre, but at Beer-sheba (XXVI, 23-33; XXVIII, 10).

XXXVI contains the genealogical table of the Edomites the traditional descendants of Esau, their various tribes and clans, and tribal leaders. The chapter is probably inserted here because of the natural interest of ancient Israel in Esau, the brother of Jacob, and in the Edomites their remote kinsmen.

V. 31 is of particular historical and literary significance because of its obvious reference to Saul, the first king of Israel. This reference proves absolutely that this chapter at least could not have been written by Moses, as tradition tells, but must have been composed, at the very earliest, some time after the reign of Saul.

XXI

JOSEPH THE DREAMER

(Genesis XXXVII)

I seek my brethren. (Genesis XXXVII, 16.)

Death and life are in the power of the tongue. (Proverbs XVIII, 21.)

Read Proverbs III, 1-7.

"Death and life are in the power of the tongue", the wise Book of Proverbs says. It is told that Rabban Simon ben Gamaliel once ordered his servant to bring from the market the best thing to be found there. To the good rabbi's surprise he brought a tongue. At another time the rabbi commanded him to bring the worst thing the market could offer. To his still greater surprise the servant again brought a tongue. "How is this", the master asked; "when I bade thee bring the best thing the market provided, thou didst bring a tongue. And now that I have ordered the worst thing, thou dost still bring a tongue?" "Good master", answered the wise servant, "dost thou not know that a tongue may be either the best or the worst thing in this world accordingly as its owner uses it?"

How true this is! Our tongues are gifts from God, given for blessing, to be used to further God's wise and good purpose, for which, we believe, He has placed us all here on earth. How much good can the tongue do, how much happiness can it bring, when it speaks words of kindness, love and truth! And how much evil can it work, and how much unhappiness can it cause, if it speaks words of falsehood, anger, or envy! Therefore the Bible says, "Death and life are in the power of the tongue". And the rabbis taught that though the tongue speaks in Rome, it can kill in Syria, and the slanderous words it utters are like a coal which can never be completely extinguished. And the Bible also says, "Thou shalt not go up and down as a tale-bearer among thy people" (Leviticus XIX, 16).

Yet just this is what Joseph did. Even against his own brothers he brought evil tales unto his father. Possibly they were true, and possibly they were exaggerated, for that is generally the way with evil reports. Had Joseph been inspired by sincere love for his brothers, and by the desire to help them correct their faults, his motives might have been commendable. But he seems merely to have delighted in telling all the evil things about his brothers he could, and in representing himself thereby as better than they. His dreams, too, seem to have suggested the same idea to his father and brothers, and most of all to himself, and for this reason especially he seems to have taken delight in recounting them. As yet none of them could have the least intimation of all that the dreams really meant. His father chided him for the assumption of authority implied in the dreams, and his brothers hated him, and little wonder. For there is no being more contemptible than a tale-bearer of this kind. Joseph was far from a lovely character when we first make his acquaintance. But we shall see how he, too, like his father, Jacob, was chastened and purified by the sufferings which his own misdeeds brought upon him, until at last he became a noble man and a worthy servant of the Lord, through whom God did a wonderful work. It has been said, that the worth of a man depends upon his two smallest organs, his heart and his tongue. The truth of this adage is well exemplified in the story of Joseph.

Probably Joseph was not altogether to blame, or rather he was not the only one to blame. In the first place, Jacob himself was at fault for manifesting greater love for Joseph than for his other sons, and for spoiling him as he did. Partiality is always a form of injustice, and injustice is always wrong and causes evil. We have seen this already in Isaac's greater love for Esau and Rebekah's greater love for Jacob.

And then, too, Joseph's brothers, it is clear, envied him his father's greater love and his ease and comfort at home, even though he was younger than they. Envy is always wicked, and it, too, always brings evil and sorrow, no matter what its cause. The rabbis told the following wise fable to account for the awkward hop in the gait of the raven. Originally he walked much more gracefully, yet not as much so as he wished. He observed the graceful step of the dove, and enviously tried to imitate it. But all in vain. He succeeded only in toppling over repeatedly and almost breaking his bones. And in consequence he made himself ridiculous in the eyes of the other birds. Then, realizing that all his efforts were useless, he decided to resume his former gait. But to his surprise and distress, he found that in his envious efforts to be something else, he had unlearned even how to walk. And ever since then he has had to hop along in his own awkward, graceless manner, despised and ridiculed by birds and men. Such is the evil and folly of envy and covetousness. Therefore our Bible says, as the last of the great Ten Commandments, "Thou shalt not covet". The truly great are those who can overcome envy and covetousness, and rejoice in the success and happiness of others.

The rabbis used likewise to tell this story. When the word of the Lord came to Moses, "Get thee up unto the mountain, for there thou must die; henceforth Joshua shall lead My people", Moses prayed, "O let me live and be the servant of Joshua, even as he was my servant; only let me cross the river with him and come to the Promised Land".

And God answered, "So be it as thou hast asked". Then the two men went to the tabernacle, and the cloud of God descended and separated them. When it rose again, Moses said, "Joshua, my master, what word did the Lord reveal to thee?" But Joshua answered, "Didst thou not hear it thyself? How strange; for whenever the Lord spoke to thee, I, too, heard His word and understood His bidding". Then Moses bowed his head, and his face reddened with shame, as envy whispered thoughts of evil. But only for a moment. Quickly he fell upon his face and cried, "O Lord, rather a hundred deaths than one thought of envy". Then Moses ascended the mountain and entered a cave and lay down upon the rocky floor. And the Lord came, and with a gentle kiss freed Moses' soul from his body and took it once more unto Himself, the true Promised Land, the goal of all life. Thus did Moses overcome envy.

We may be sure that Jacob suffered greatly in thus being compelled to witness the lack of love and brotherly feeling among his children. Perhaps he was reminded thereby of his own early treatment of his brother, Esau, and perhaps, too, he may have felt that he deserved this unhappiness as a further punishment for his youthful sin. We feel deeply for the old man in his sorrow. The picture of Jacob's grief, when his sons bring him Joseph's blood-stained coat, is pathetic indeed In fact, the entire story of Joseph is another masterpiece of the story-teller's art.

It begins with a rather foreboding picture, a father, old, doting, and partial, deceived in heartless manner by his own sons, and subjected to the deepest sorrow; the sons envious, deceitful and cruel beyond measure; and the one lad a tale-bearer, and supercilious and arrogant toward his older brothers. But it is only the beginning of the story, and serves but to whet the interest. Already this opening chapter hints that things will gradually, under God's wise and loving guidance, right themselves. Joseph's dreams point to a satisfactory outcome to the story. Above all, the words of Joseph to the stranger, "I seek my brethren", contain a world of meaning. For, as we shall see, they foreshadow his entire future life; his brothers will he indeed seek in the land of his bondage and glory, and their salvation will he work after he shall have himself become purified. And not this alone, but they also, will seek him, after their natures, too, shall have been purified and ennobled. Best of all, once more the aged father will be reunited with his darling son, and supreme joy will succeed to deepest sorrow. And throughout the story we shall see God's providence and divine purpose running, like a thread of gold through a web of silver, and God somehow, in a way which we can not fully comprehend, but still can realize and believe in, out of all the evil of Joseph and his brothers, at last bringing greater good for them and all about them, keeping alive many people, and enabling Joseph to fulfill the birthright of Israel, to be a blessing unto mankind.

We have already seen that the Jacob story is a unit of thought and narration, cast in dramatic form, and animated by one single, central theme. To a much more pronounced and perceptible degree is this the case with the Joseph story. When we omit such extraneous passages as the genealogical table in XLVI, 8-27, which, a moment's consideration will show, could not have been a part of the original narrative, but which was clearly inserted by some late writer or editor, the dramatic unity becomes immediately apparent. Like the Jacob story, the Joseph story, too, could very easily be cast into perfect dramatic form. It might be arranged thus:

Act I —Joseph the boy and his relations with his brothers.

Act II —Joseph in Potiphar's house.

Act III—Joseph in prison.

Act IV —Joseph the viceroy, and his first meeting with his brothers.

Act V —Joseph's second meeting with his brothers and
　　　　the reunion of the family.

Not only may the story be easily cast into dramatic form,
but the dramatic note pervades the entire narrative. The
dreams of Joseph's boyhood but foreshadow the actual relations which are later to obtain between him and his brothers.
Similarly the casting of Joseph into the pit by his brothers
is dramatically reversed when Joseph puts one of his brothers
into prison as hostage for the return of the other brothers,
including the youngest. Likewise there is dramatic paral-
lelism, vaguely felt by the old, grief-stricken father, but
more clearly perceived by the remorseful brothers, who
knew somewhat of Joseph's fate, between Joseph's going
down to Egypt as a slave, doomed apparently to a life of
hopeless toil and suffering, and Benjamin's coming to the
same country, and, because of the pitcher being found in his
sack, being doomed seemingly to the same fate. They had
deliberately sold Joseph as a slave; and now when they
would save Benjamin from this very fate, they are powerless. Dramatically, too, is their consciousness of guilt depicted, when Simeon is cast into prison, and they feel it to
be but the just punishment for the wrong they had done to
Joseph (XLII, 19-24). And equally dramatic is the scene
where the brothers converse openly before Joseph, and
reveal their innermost thoughts, and acknowledge their guilt
and express their remorse for their crime, unaware that
Joseph understands their every word.

Above all, the tragic pathos of the scene where Judah
steps forth before the mighty, and seemingly implacable
Egyptian lord, and offers himself for the lad Benjamin, in
order that the latter might be saved from slavery, and their
father might be spared the killing grief of the additional
loss of his youngest son, is unsurpassed, not only in the
Bible, but in all literature. It, too, constitutes a dramatic
reversal of an earlier situation. The brothers had sold

Joseph as a slave almost without hesitation, and with only two of them willing to speak a mild word on his behalf, and with no thought of the grief they must thereby cause their aged father. Now one of them is ready to yield himself to the awful lot of Egyptian slavery, in order that the other brother might be saved from the very fate of Joseph, and that their father might be spared the renewal of his grief.

It were futile to attempt to record all the points of artistic excellence of the Joseph story. Suffice it to say as a piece of narrative and dramatic art it stands in the forefront of the world's literature. It is not without significance that whenever one of the stories of the Bible is selected for narration, it is almost invariably this story of Joseph. This is due entirely to the realization, largely unconscious, of its surpassing merit as a piece of narrative literature.

But this very fact raises the question of the historical truth of the story. And the answer, established by science, is that the story is a noble and beautiful romance through and through, with very little historical basis. We know from Egyptian monuments that there dwelt in ancient Palestine, before the entrance of the tribes of Israel into the land, a small clan or tribe, which was called *Joseph-el*. *Joseph* may very well be a contraction of this name. This tribe may have continued to dwell in Palestine until the advent of the great body of the tribes of Israel, and may have become incorporated with them, and thus the name Joseph may have become current in Israel. But there is not the least corroborative evidence that there was ever an actual man Joseph, who played the role of the hero of the story.

On the other hand, documents found in Egypt tell of a certain man named Yanhamu, who held a position in Egyptian political life under Amenophis IV (1375-1358, B. C.), somewhat similar to that which Joseph holds in the story.

He was governor of Yarimuta, presumably a grain-producing district in the eastern part of the Nile Delta, and he probably supervised the gathering of the grain for the national food supply. The name is Semitic, and probably indicates that the man was a Semite, although not necessarily, nor even probably, an Israelite. He differed from Joseph in that he seems to have employed the powers of his office and his great influence with the king unjustly, oppressively, and for his own advantage. It is not at all improbable, however, that the position which this man held suggested a portion of the plot to the authors of the Joseph story. They seem to have been well acquainted with Egyptian life and manners (cf. XLIII, 32, and the pure Egyptian names, *Potiphar, Zaphenath-paneah, Asenath* and *Poti-phera*) and literature, and may therefore have drawn upon Egyptian history for the original of the figure of their hero.

Certainly the episode of Potiphar's wife is borrowed directly from Egyptian literature. There is a well-known Egyptian tale, found upon an ancient papyrus, which tells of two brothers who dwelt together, the older married and the younger single. One day the older brother sent the younger brother from the field where they were plowing, to bring some seed. When the younger brother came to the house, he found his brother's wife combing her hair. He took two large measures of seed and prepared to depart. However, when the woman beheld his beauty and strength, her heart became inflamed with love for him. But he rejected her advances indignantly and bitterly rebuked her. But he said nothing to his brother of what had happened. The woman, however, feared exceedingly. Therefore she anointed herself with fat, and made herself like one to whom an evildoer had offered violence. When the older brother returned home in the evening, his wife did not receive him as usual. Instead she lay stretched out upon the bed, as if injured. When he asked her the cause, she answered, "No one has had to do with me except thy little brother, since when he came to take the seed corn for thee, he found me sitting alone, and said to me, 'Come, let us make merry an hour and repose! Let down thy hair!' Thus he spake to me, but I did not listen to him (but said), 'See, am I not thy mother, and is not thy elder brother like a father to thee?' Thus I spoke to him, but he did not hearken to my speech, and used force with me, that I might not tell thee. Now if thou allowest him to live, I will kill myself". (Translation of Brugsch, *The True Story of the Exodus,* 134-136). At these words the younger brother fled, pursued by the older brother. His subsequent fortunes do not concern us. The resemblance of this story to the episode of Potiphar's wife is so striking, that the conclusion is unavoidable that the latter is borrowed from the former. And if so, then there can be no further doubt that the entire Joseph story has little basis in historical fact, or is aught else than a pure romance, a beautiful and artistic piece of dramatic literature.

But again we must come to the same conclusion, to which we came with regard to the creation and flood stories, which, as we learned, were borrowed from Babylonian myths. The authors did not borrow idly, nor merely to give dramatic expression to some idea or plot in their minds. The Joseph story, too, is but the means by which they gave concrete expression to a fundamental teaching of Judaism. This is summed up in the significant words of Joseph to his brothers, when, after their father's death they fear that he will avenge himself upon them, "Ye meant evil against me, but God meant it for good, to bring to pass, as it is this day, to save much people alive" (L, 20). Joseph's brothers had wronged him and had sold him into slavery. Yet through God's providence he arose to an exalted station, and became the sole means whereby both Egypt and Israel were kept alive. Thus, out of the brothers' evil, under God's providence, great good resulted.

So it is, these authors would tell us, in all life. God has endowed man with freewill, with the power to choose between good and evil. But the evil which men do is not eternal. Somehow, in ways which we can not comprehend, but the evidences of which we can see in all life and history, and particularly in Israel's history, God changes the evil which men and nations do into good. Even as the beautiful rose blossoms forth from out the dirt and dung, in accordance with God's law, so, likewise in accordance with God's law, out of men's evil deeds greater good and blessing must in time spring forth for later generations. Men may mean it for evil, but God means it for good. God has not merely created the world and set it going, and since then sits back in passive idleness; God is still in the world, guiding the destinies of men and nations aright in accordance with His wise and beneficent laws, changing evil to good, and bringing mankind steadily forward upon the path of truth and progress, which leads to the goal of human existence which He has appointed.

This is the teaching of Judaism, and this is the message of the Joseph story, the central theme which animates it and gives it unity and purpose, and of which it is the concrete and convincing illustration. It gives the answer to the question which the analysis of the opening chapters of Genesis must have raised in thinking minds. If God has created everything for good, and if He has endowed man with freewill, whereby man can work good or evil as he chooses, what becomes of the evil which man may do, and how does it accord with God's purpose of good? The Joseph story gives the answer; men may do evil if they choose; but somehow, out of this very evil God in His own time brings greater good for all mankind. Thus the Joseph story rounds out, as it were, the thought of the Book of Genesis, and constitutes a most fitting conclusion for this introductory book of the Pentateuch and of the Bible.

NOTES

V. 2. It is not clear why Leah's name is omitted here.

V. 3. What is generally translated "a coat of many colors", was really a coat with long, hanging sleeves, such as is commonly worn by persons of importance in the Orient. It prevents its wearer from hard, manual labor, and is therefore indicative of rank. That Joseph should wear such a coat implies that he was free of the hard labors of his brothers, and also that he was of higher rank than they. Therefore this coat was their chief source of vexation.

V. 10. The mention here of Joseph's mother is strange indeed. Possibly it may refer to Leah as Jacob's chief wife, now that Rachel was dead. However, there is an additional difficulty in this connection. XXX, 25 implies that Rachel gave birth to Joseph at the end of the first fourteen years of Jacob's sojourn with Laban. According to XXXV, 18, Benjamin was born on the return to Canaan, six years later. But in the Joseph story proper, although Joseph is a full-grown man, and has been viceroy of Egypt already during the seven years of plenty and the first two years of famine, and had also been in prison for over two years, and had been a slave in Potiphar's house for some time before that, in other words, had been in Egypt for at least eleven or twelve years, Benjamin is still a mere lad when he comes down to Egypt with his brothers. (According to XXXVII, 2 and XLI, 46 twenty-two years must have elapsed between the sale of Joseph as a slave and Benjamin's coming to Egypt; for if Joseph was thirty years old at the beginning of the seven years of plenty, he must have been thirty-eight or thirty-nine when Benjamin stood before him. In all likelihood, however, these verses, too, are not a part of the original narrative.) This would imply that, since Benjamin is still a lad when he comes to Egypt, he was not yet born when Joseph was sold as a slave, and therefore that his mother was still alive at this time, just as the language of the verse indicates. It would seem, therefore, that there were two traditions in ancient Israel in regard to the birth of Benjamin. The one told that he was born on the homeward journey to Canaan, and that his mother died at the birth and was buried on the way. And the other told that he was born some time after they had returned and settled in Canaan, and even after Joseph had been sold as a slave. According to this second tradition he was indeed a "son of Jacob's old age" (XLIV, 20).

V. 14. The mention of Hebron here is disturbing. Hebron lies on a straight line fully forty-five to fifty miles from Shechem. The intervening country is mountainous, and travel, even under the most favorable conditions is difficult. It is impossible therefore, on the one hand, that the sons of Jacob should have driven their flocks from Hebron to Shechem, and then on to Dothan, some fifteen miles further, and on the other hand, that Jacob should have sent Joseph, while still a lad, all this distance to ascertain his brothers' welfare. It is clear that the words, "out of the vale of Hebron", in their Hebrew equivalent, were not a part of the original narrative, but were inserted to harmonize this story with XXXV, 27, which tells that Jacob came finally to his father's house at Hebron. Omitting these words, we get the impression that this entire incident happened while Jacob still dwelt at Shechem (cf. XXXIII, 18-20). We can readily understand that the sons of Jacob might well pasture their flocks from Shechem as far as Dothan, and that Jacob might well send the young Joseph in search of them. This is borne out by the further fact that Joseph was finally buried at Shechem (Joshua XXIV, 32), for this implies that Shechem and not Hebron, was Joseph's original home.

Vv. 28a and 36, which call the merchants of the caravan Midianites instead of Ishmaelites, are a small fragment of a second version of the Joseph story, which was at one time current in ancient Israel. Notice that XXXIX, 1 repeats what has been already told in XXXVII, 36.

V. 34. Rending the garments and wearing sack-cloth were from the most ancient times the regular signs of mourning in the Orient.

XXXVIII. This story of Judah is not a part of the Joseph story at all, but is a fragment preserved from an older work, and was inserted in this place by some late writer or editor. XXXIX, 1 is the direct continuation of XXXVII, 35. According to XXXVIII Judah was dwelling apart from his brothers in the vicinity of Adullam in southern Palestine, while according to XLIII, 3ff. he seems to have been dwelling with his brothers. The chapter is of particular interest because of its account of the birth of Perez, according to Ruth IV, 12 and 18, one of the ancestors of King David.

XXII

JOSEPH IN EGYPT

(Genesis XXXIX-XLI)

The Lord was with Joseph, and he was a prosperous man. (Genesis XXXIX, 2.)

Trust in the Lord with all thy heart,
And lean not upon thine own understanding.
In all thy ways acknowledge Him,
And He will direct thy paths. (Proverbs III, 5-6).

Read Proverbs III, 1-8.

Thus Joseph came down to Egypt and was sold as a slave to Potiphar. His future seemed black indeed. Yet God had not forsaken him; and with God, as we have learned, everything is possible. As the Bible says, "The Lord was with Joseph, and he was a prosperous man". God was with Joseph, because He had in mind a great work to be done through him. Joseph was to be the agent through whom God worked His wise purpose; but like his father Jacob in his youth, he had first to be purified, to be made fit for God's service. His inclination toward selfishness had first to be purged from his soul. But Joseph seems to have been naturally of a kindly and lovable nature. As a child he had probably been spoiled by his indulgent father, while his brothers, too, had not exerted a helpful influence upon him. But at heart he was sound and good; hence the task of purification was easy for him, when compared with Jacob.

Joseph had yielded to the temptation of selfishness in his relations with his brothers, to the desire to have more of the love of his father and more of power and authority than were rightfully his. So now God tried him by a like temptation. In the house of his master, everything was entirely in his charge; he might do with everything what he wished, save one thing, which belonged to his master alone. It matters not what that one thing was. It suffices to know that, as the rabbis told, ofttimes Joseph was tempted to take it for his own. No one would have known the difference, not even his master. The battle was hard and long. As Joseph went about his tasks, the thing constantly enticed him, "Come and take me for your own; no one will be the wiser; why not be happy while you may?" Often Joseph stretched out his hand; but always something held him back. Now it was the image of his old father. And with it came the thought, "O my beloved father, should I do this wicked thing, how might I ever again look upon thy face? How wouldst thou be shamed, didst thou know that thy son had yielded to this temptation. Perhaps God may still, in His infinite love, bring me back to thee. But never will He do so, if I yield to this sin". Again it was the thought of the birthright of Abraham which had in some way descended from Jacob to him. "How can I become a blessing unto all the families of the earth", he thought, "if I begin by wronging one single man, and he my kind master? No; I can be worthy of this precious birthright only by remaining pure, and by doing good to my master, even as he has done good to me. He has trusted me, and put everything in my hands except this one thing, and I must be faithful". With thoughts like these Joseph resisted temptation. The more he resisted and the oftener he put temptation from him, the stronger he became, and the easier it was to conquer, until at last the desire to sin left him completely. Then his natural instincts of goodness and love began to assert themselves openly, and he became ready and fit to live in accordance with the birthright of Abraham.

Temptation comes to everyone, young and old. It comes in countless ways, for the allurements of sin are many. There may be some who are never tempted to do wrong. Outwardly they do seem good, and we have no right to say that they are not. Yet for all we know, when temptation does come, they may yield without a struggle. The truly good is he who has fought and conquered. He is tried and tested; no matter what comes, we know that, like Joseph, he will resist temptation and always do the right. Temptation is a trial which we must all undergo, to determine whether we are really pure at heart and strong and fit to do God's work. An automobile must be tested before it leaves the shop, a cannon before it is put to actual use, a battleship, before the government will accept it. But even more does God test His creature and His servant, man, to determine whether he is strong to do the great work of usefulness and blessing for which God has created him. So, as we have learned, God tested Abraham and Jacob; so now he tested Joseph; and so, in His own wise way, He tests all of us.

In this battle against temptation God has given us many powerful allies. There are our parents, who guide us while young, and help us to grow strong and to form right habits, which will enable us to conquer more easily. When temptation comes, the thought of them, and the shame and sorrow they must suffer, did we yield, and the poor return we thus make for all their care and love and faith in us, the thought, too, that we can never again look them squarely in the eye, nor meet their look of loving trust with answering look, may well restrain us, also, and strengthen us to resist.

Then, too, the thought of our glorious birthright, which we must forfeit if we yield to sin, should strengthen us, as it did Joseph. Surely we can never become blessings to mankind, if we sin against a single person. We can live true to our birthright only when we use every gift of God rightly.

Ofttimes we hear people say, "Why should not we Jews do what other people do? Why must we always strive to be better and hold ourselves aloof from pleasures which other people enjoy?" They do not understand, or are too weak to resist temptation. As we have learned, we Jews may not do all that others do; we must be better because of our birthright; because we can be a blessing only by being better, and resisting temptation more steadfastly, and, by our teaching, our example, and our help, bringing others to become like ourselves, pure, noble and good. We must strive to be better in every way, that thereby we may uphold the standard of truth and right which God has placed in our hands. The Jew who yields to temptation, or will not strive to live better than all around him, is unworthy the name Jew and the eternal birthright of Abraham, our father. Surely the realization of all this should help us to resist temptation and to fit ourselves to do God's work.

But though Joseph bravely resisted temptation, none the less he was falsely accused of having done the very thing he had not done. In consequence he was thrown into prison, where he remained for several years. But even here God did not forsake him. Probably this, too, was a part of his trial. And here, too, Joseph stood the test nobly. He was cheered by the thought that he had been innocent of the crime of which he had been charged, and was confident that in due time his innocence would become clear. Therefore, instead of complaining at his sad lot and despairing of God's help, he made the best of things. He endeavored to be useful even in prison. Thus he found favor with the governor of the prison and all who were there, even his fellow-prisoners. Day by day their trust in Joseph grew, and they found pleasure and comfort in his cheerful presence. Even in prison he was discharging his birthright and bringing blessing to those about him.

We need not wait to attain high position to begin our

task of diffusing blessing. The very humblest can work blessing of some kind, if only he have the will and the unselfish disposition. The rabbis used to tell of a wise man who one day met the prophet Elijah in the market place. Full of curiosity, he asked the prophet who of all the busy crowd would enjoy future life. "None", answered the prophet slowly. "What!" said the sage, "of all this crowd not one?" Just then two men entered the market place. They seemed poor, and no one noticed them or greeted them. "These two will enjoy future life", said the prophet. The wise man went to them and reverently asked, "Tell me what is your business, and what are your virtues, and what your deeds?" "Virtues? deeds?" they asked, perplexed. "We have none of these. We are poor men and live by our hands alone. Our only merit is that we have merry hearts. When we meet one who is sad, we strive to cheer him. And when we learn of two who are enemies, we seek to make peace between them. Thus we labor to do the will of our Father in heaven". In this way we may all work blessing.

So even in prison God was with Joseph and he prospered, and did his work, as always, as best he could. As a slave in Potiphar's house he had been faithful to his duties; now as a lowly prisoner he still did his work well. And all this fitted him for the far greater work which God meant him to do very soon. It reminds us of the wise saying of the Bible,

Whatsoever thy hand attaineth to do by thy strength, that do.
(Ecclesiastes IX, 10.)

and the modern proverb with much the same meaning, "Whatever is worth doing, is worth doing well". Whatever we do now is training for something bigger and better tomorrow. So it was with Joseph, and so it is with us.

Therefore all who came to know Joseph trusted him. It is a wonderful thing to win the trust and confidence of people. The man who can do this will surely attain success and honor. People may say of him, as the Bible says of Joseph, "God is with him". And God will be with him. As we have learned already,

> The Lord is nigh unto all them that call upon Him,
> To all that call upon Him in truth. (Psalm CXLV, 18.)

Such a person does by his actions call upon God to be with him. We can all win trust and confidence in a very simple way, merely by deserving it, by being truthful and upright, by keeping our word always, and never taking advantage of others. And then God will be with us. This was the real secret of Joseph's success.

Because they trusted in him both the butler and the baker told Joseph their dreams. In those days people thought, as some do still today, that dreams really foretell the future. Therefore there were professional interpreters of dreams. But because they trusted Joseph so completely, they asked him to interpret their dreams. But Joseph set them right with an answer full of wonderful meaning. "Do not interpretations belong to God?" "I can not interpret your dreams myself. Everything comes from God with some purpose of good". He felt all the truth of the wise saying of the Book of Proverbs:

> Trust in the Lord with all thy heart,
> And lean not upon thine own understanding.
> In all thy ways acknowledge Him,
> And He will direct thy paths.

And when he stood before the mighty king, on the very threshold of success and glory, still he answered, "Not I can interpret your dreams, but God alone. What God is about to do, He hath declared unto Pharaoh, in order to fulfil His divine purpose".

This thought of God's help and protection, and that everything comes from Him, reminds us of a charming story of the rabbis. Once there were in a city two blind men, who used to beg for bread. One had the habit of saying, "He is helped whom the king helps". But the other would gently correct him, "He is helped whom the Lord helpeth". One day the king himself passed by and heard the words of the two blind men. When he reached his palace he ordered that a loaf of bread be filled with gold pieces and be sent to the blind man who had said, "He is helped whom the king helps". Imagine the blind man's surprise when he found that help had indeed come from the king. But when the package was opened, surprise gave way to disappointment; the king's help was only a loaf of bread, and so heavy that it seemed hardly fit to eat. In his disappointment he sold it to the other blind man for a few pennies, and then continued his begging. The second blind man took the loaf home. Heavy as it was, his poor family would still be glad to eat it, and would be thankful for the help God had sent. But when the loaf was cut, out rolled so many pieces of gold, that the blind man became rich and needed no longer beg for bread. Thereafter the first blind man continued to beg alone. One day the king passed by again, and to his surprise found the beggar still there. "How is this?" he exclaimed. "Did I not send thee a loaf of bread some time ago?" "Yes, your majesty", answered the beggar, "but it was so heavy, I thought it unfit to eat, so I sold it to my companion for a few pennies". "Fool that thou art", said the king, "the loaf was filled with gold pieces, wherewith I thought to help thee, since thou didst say, 'He is helped whom the king helps'. Thy companion was wiser than either thou or I. Truly he alone is helped whom the Lord helpeth". Therefore,

> Trust in the Lord with all thy heart,
> And lean not upon thine own understanding.

One little thing in particular shows the change which had

come over Joseph. As a boy at home he had been quick to carry to his father tales of his brothers' evil conduct. But now when he tells his story to the chief butler, he merely protests that he is innocent of wrongdoing. There is not a word of condemnation of his brothers or of Potiphar's wife. He seeks now not to incriminate others, although he could do so truthfully, but merely to establish his own innocence. It would seem that misfortune and experience, cooperating with his naturally gentle disposition, had taught him to think as well and as kindly of others as possible, rather than to think ill, as he had done as a boy. Possibly, too, he realized how greatly his conduct must have irritated his brothers, and that, without this, they would not have treated him as they did.

This is indeed a lesson which we might all learn with great profit to ourselves, and for the blessing and happiness of our fellowmen. We are all too prone to think evil of others and to lay upon them as far as we can, the blame for our own misdeeds, sufferings, and failures. It is only the honest and strong man who is ever ready to examine his own actions carefully, and to acknowledge his shortcomings, assume his share of responsibility for wrongdoing, and forgive and forget wrongs which have been done to him. Yet if we would all do this, how much better and happier a place to live in would this world be; and how much happier and more beloved would we ourselves be, did we try to think good instead of evil of our neighbors, even though they may have wronged us somewhat.

So Joseph learned by bitter experience to think and to act. It shows more clearly than anything else, how completely he had changed, and how he had been purified of his sin, and strengthened and ennobled and made fit to do the great work, for which God had called him, and had brought him down to Egypt. In all his misfortunes we can readily see God's hand at work preparing Joseph for the great and useful task which awaited him. What that was, and how Joseph performed it, and the great blessing he wrought, and how he lived true to the birthright of Abraham, we shall now see.

NOTES

XL, 3. " Evidently this captain of the guard was not the same person as Potiphar, Joseph's former master, cf. XXXIX, 1.

V. 20. The birthday of the king was, and still is today, frequently celebrated as a national holiday, upon which the king manifests his pleasure and goodwill by bestowing rewards and honors upon deserving subjects.

XLI, 1. "The river" is, of course, the Nile, from which all Egypt still today as in ancient times, derives its chief sustenance.

V. 6. In Egypt the east wind, blowing in the summer from the burning Arabian Desert, becomes at times almost unbearable for men, while the crops are occasionally blasted by its awful heat.

V. 14. The Egyptians were accustomed to shave their heads completely. Joseph appears before them in the regular Egyptian garb.

Vv. 42f. With these insignia of the high office to which Joseph is raised cf. the similar scene in Esther VIII.

V. 43. *Abrech* is in all likelihood a Hebrew, or at least a Semitic word, which was taken over by, and became current in the Egyptian language. It possibly means literally, "bend the knee".

V. 45. As was said before, *Zaphenath-paneah, Asenath,* and *Poti-phera,* as well as *Potiphar,* are all good, and even common, Egyptian names. The meaning of *Zaphenath-paneah* is uncertain; various interpretations have been proposed by Egyptian scholars. *Asenath* probably means, "belonging to the goddess Neith"; *Poti-phera* means "he who belongs to the sun-god Ra"; *Potiphar* is probably an abbreviation of *Poti-phera.* According to the story Potiphar and Poti-phera were two different men, since they held different offices. However the similarity of their names led the rabbis to confuse them, and to tell that Asenath was the daughter of Potiphar and his wife, who tempted Joseph, and that she was given by God to Joseph as the reward for his virtue.

V. 46. This verse, coupled with XXXVII, 2, implies that by this time Joseph had been in Egypt for thirteen years.

XXIII

JOSEPH AND HIS BROTHERS

(Genesis XLII-XLV)

Let thy servant, I pray thee, abide instead of the lad a bondman to my lord, and let the lad go up with his brethren. (Genesis XLIV, 33.)

Hatred stirreth up strifes;
But love covereth all transgressions. (Proverbs X, 12.)

Read Psalm XXXIV, 12-15.

Thus Joseph became ruler of the great kingdom of Egypt, second only to the king himself. He was charged particularly with the task of safeguarding the food supply of the land for the seven years of famine, soon to come. Needless to say, he discharged this important task in the same conscientious and able manner, in which he had performed the many little tasks which had fallen to his lot as a slave. Those had been his trial and preparation for this great work, and he had completely proved his fitness and worth. Not only had he risen to high position, but he had also married the daughter of one of Egypt's greatest lords, and two sons had been born to them, Ephraim and Manasseh.

Yet despite all this honor and success and family blessing, Joseph was not perfectly happy. Always there was in his heart the longing for his dear ones at home. His thoughts constantly reverted to his aged father, and he wondered whether the old man were still alive, and how he had withstood the shock of the loss of his beloved son. Of his brothers, too, he thought now lovingly and with compassion. He realized that they had not been altogether to

blame. He understood the meanness of his former conduct,
and how greatly he must have irritated them, to make them
do what they had done. And his heart was filled with longing to see them once more. He was especially eager to see
his youngest brother, Benjamin, the child of his own dead
mother, who had been but a mere prattling babe when he
had been sold into slavery, and whom, it seemed to him, he
loved now like one of his own darling sons. If only God
would extend His favor, and bring them all together once
more in peace and love; that was his one prayer and hope,
the one thing necessary to make his happiness complete.

The rabbis tell that this was not a vain hope on the part
of Joseph. He knew that the famine had extended even to
Canaan, and that sooner or later, his brothers must come
down to Egypt to buy grain, just as other peoples were
doing. So Joseph stationed guards on all the roads leading
to Egypt, with instructions to report to him the names of
all travelers. At last, one day in the second year of the
famine, the word came; his brothers had come down to
Egypt. Immediately the longing for peace and family reunion seized upon him with redoubled force. But with it
came a thought of caution. Perhaps his brothers might not
wish to be reunited with him; perhaps they still cherished
their old hatred; and perhaps, too, they were not worthy of
forgiveness. So he commanded his servants to watch his
brothers and report their conduct, and at the proper moment bring them before him.

Now the brothers, too, had experienced a complete change
of heart. Even at the moment of their crime they had hesitated. Reuben had really wanted to rescue Joseph, and
Judah, too, had spoken a good word for him, and had induced the brothers to sell him as a slave rather than kill
him outright. And during all these years, they had observed
their old father's constant sorrow, and realized their in-
ability to comfort him. Now they were filled with remorse

for their sin, and were eager to do whatever they could to right the wrong. So, the rabbis told, when they came down to Egypt, their minds were busy, not so much with the thought of buying food, as of possibly finding Joseph and bringing him back with them, and thus restoring the happiness of their old father. Therefore, they did not immediately go to the place where grain was sold, but scattered about the country in search of Joseph. They had no idea that he had become anything but a slave, and so they searched for him wherever they imagined a slave would most likely be found. But to no avail. At last, in utter despair, and realizing that their dear ones at home were in dire need of food, and that they might tarry no longer, they repaired to the place where grain was sold. So, at last, they came before Joseph. And, as the Bible says, and there is a world of meaning in the words, "Joseph knew his brethren, but they knew not him".

All these days, according to rabbinical tradition, he had kept informed of their conduct. He had been at a loss to explain why they had wandered all over the country, instead of coming immediately to purchase grain. He could not be sure yet what kind of men his brothers really were; therefore he determined to try them thoroughly, before revealing himself to them. Besides he was disappointed when he saw that they were only ten, and that Benjamin was not among them. So he pretended to be, as he seemed to them, a high Egyptian officer, speaking only through an interpreter, and therefore apparently not understanding their language. And because they had first wandered all over Egypt, he spoke to them roughly and charged them with being spies. It was the beginning of their trial. We need not recount it here, for the Bible tells it graphically and convincingly and with touching pathos. We can not but feel all the regret of these sinning men, and the sincerity of their longing for the happiness of their old father during the few years remaining to

him. No sacrifice was too great to safeguard the old man,
and at least prevent increase of his sorrow. All this Joseph
realized fully, and his heart went out to his brothers. With
difficulty could he restrain himself, and often he was on the
point of revealing himself and terminating their trial and
punishment; for it was ·indeed a punishment for their sin,
and they fully recognized it as such, and that they had
merited it. But he held himself in check, until he could be
sure that they had truly repented and had departed completely from their evil ways. Besides he must see Benjamin
at all costs. So the trial went on.

The climax was reached when, in the moment of greatest
despair, when it seemed that Benjamin must remain behind,
also like his brother, a slave in Egypt, and their father must
thus be doubly bereaved of his two best-beloved, Judah
stepped forth from among his brothers and spoke these heroic
words, "Let thy servant, I pray thee, abide instead of the
lad a bondman to my lord, and let the lad go up with his
brethren". He realized full well all that this meant, that
never again would he behold his own children, and that the
lot of a slave in Egypt was hard indeed. But not a thought
did he give to all this. Simply and frankly he offered himself, in order that the old father might at least be spared the
sorrow of losing his beloved Benjamin. It is one of the
noblest acts in all literature and history, Judah thus offering
himself for the sake of his father and his brother. It was
just the reverse of the sentiment which had prompted the
brothers when, regardless of the old man's happiness, they
had ruthlessly sold Joseph as a slave into Egypt. It proved
how completely Judah and his brothers had changed.

Joseph needed no further proof. Weeping he threw himself into their arms, exclaiming, "I am Joseph; doth my
father yet live?" And when his startled brothers, still fearing Joseph's vengeance, hastened to confess their guilt, he
reassured them with the significant words, the thought run-

ning through the entire story, "It was not you that sent me
hither, but God; for God did send me before you to preserve life". God's hand was in the whole event, for a wonderful purpose of good. So Joseph forgave his brothers and
they were once more united in true, brotherly love. We are
reminded of the inspiring sentence from the wise Book of
Proverbs,

> Hatred stirreth up strifes;
> But love covereth all transgressions.

So it was throughout the entire story of Joseph. Hatred
and envy had stirred up much strife, and, as is always the
case, had brought sorrow and pain to all; but at last true
love had covered all transgressions, and had caused all
wrongs which Joseph had done to his brothers and they to
him, to be forgiven and forgotten. We understand now how
truly hatred, even when the wrong be real and great, is the
part of folly, and brings only strife and sorrow, and that
forgiveness is always the part of wisdom and love. And
though it be one of the hardest lessons in life, let us still
learn, like Joseph, to forgive and forget, that life may be
sweeter, happier, and richer for everybody.

So Joseph's brothers stood the hard and bitter test, even
as he had stood it, and proved fully that they had been
purified of all thoughts and desires of evil, and were fit for
great and noble things. So God tries us all to learn whether
we are worthy to do the great and good work He has in
mind for all creatures. Those whom He would use for the
greatest tasks He tries most severely. We have seen this
in the case of Abraham, Isaac, Jacob, and Joseph. And the
supreme test is always that, like Judah, we be willing to go
into slavery, or even to lay down our life for others. For
this is the truest test of unselfishness, and unselfishness is
the first requisite in the service of God, the willingness to
do for others, even the humblest of God's creatures, regardless of all that it may cost.

The rabbis used to tell a charming story of the way in which God tried Moses, to determine whether he was fit to become the deliverer and leader of Israel. One day, when Moses was herding the sheep of his father-in-law in the wilderness, he saw a little lamb leave the flock and hurry away. He followed eagerly, to bring it back, but the lamb ran on so rapidly that Moses had to go a long way before he could overtake it. He became foot-sore and weary, yet still the lamb hastened on, just beyond his reach, and still the faithful shepherd hastened after it. At last the lamb came to a spring, and drank eagerly of its cool waters. Then Moses understood. "Poor creature", he murmured, thou wast thirsty and so hurried ever on, away from my out-stretched hand, and I did not understand. Now thou art faint and worn, and canst not retrace thy steps". So, weary and spent though he was, Moses took the little lamb on his own shoulder, and brought it back in safety to the flock, and gently put it down beside its mother. Then he father's voice, "Thou hast a tender heart for all My crea-tures; thou art a gentle and faithful shepherd of the flocks of men; now thou art called to shepherd the flocks of God". So Moses was tried, and so are we all tried. May we all stand the test, as did he and Abraham and Isaac and Jacob and Joseph and his brothers, our fathers, and may we all be strong to do the will and the work of God, our Father in Heaven.

NOTES

XLII, 9. With this verse Joseph's dreams that his brothers would one day bow down to him, are dramatically fulfilled.

V. 13. The answer of Joseph's brothers to him, "We are twelve brethren, the sons of one man in the land of Canaan", is full of meaning and inspiration. As indicated in a previous lesson, they express most forcibly our fundamental idea of Jewish brotherhood and unity. Regardless of where Jews may dwell, what languages they may speak, how they may dress and worship, we are still and always, "brethren, the sons of one man in the land of Canaan". To this one man all our traditions go back, and from him we mark the beginning, in a way, of our Jewish consciousness.

V. 24. Reuben, the oldest brother, had by his words, spoken in Joseph's hearing, proved his innocence and his good intentions with regard to Joseph at the time when the latter was sold into Egypt. Therefore, it is implied, Joseph has Simeon, the next oldest, and the one therefore most responsible for the wrong done to him, cast into prison. This was the first instance of what must have seemed to the brothers a mysterious power possessed by this strange Egyptian to read their innermost thoughts and rate them all in their proper order and at their true value. Other instances follow, and contribute greatly to the dramatic effect of the story.

V. 25. Their money is put into their sacks, partly as a test of their honesty, and partly as an additional inducement for them to return.

V. 37, telling that Reuben offered his two sons as surety for the safe return of Benjamin, is a duplicate of XLIII, 9, which tells that Judah became surety therefor. The two verses are from two different versions of the Joseph story. The Judah version was the one current in the southern kingdom, of which Judah was the leading tribe. For this reason it ascribed to the traditional ancestor of the tribe of Judah the role of the noble and self-sacrificing leader and spokesman among the brothers, which the other version, composed in the northern kingdom, assigned to Reuben the oldest brother.

XLIII, 7 shows how greatly the brothers were impressed by the Egyptian's inexplicable and seemingly supernatural knowledge of their private family affairs, of which, so they believed, they had themselves disclosed not a thing to him. It is a most effective and artistic touch.

V. 32. Probably, as is usually explained, the Egyptians did not eat with the Israelites because the animals whose flesh was eaten by the latter, were sacred among the Egyptians; cf. Exodus VIII, 22.

V. 33. The rabbis interpreted this verse to mean that Joseph appointed his seat at the table to each in the order of their ages. The brothers, noticing this, and remembering also that Joseph had unerringly selected Simeon, the one among them most responsible for the wrong done to Joseph, to be cast into prison, were astounded, and regarded this as further proof that Joseph must be possessed of occult powers and knowledge. This impression was heightened by the reference to the pitcher with which Joseph practiced divination (XLIV, 2, 5, 15). All this adds greatly to the dramatic force of the story, and evidences further the supreme artistic powers of the authors. Divination by means of water poured into oil, or oil poured into water, while the diviner, usually a priest, notices the form which the globules assume, and their position at either the top or bottom of the pitcher, and from this prognosticates the future, was common in the ancient Orient, particularly in Babylonia. This seems to have been the form of divination implied in the use of the pitcher by Joseph.

XLV, 8. By "father" is probably meant counsellor, the one with whom Pharaoh regularly consulted before doing anything, and on whose bidding therefore he always acted; it implies therefore a person with authority even over Pharaoh; cf. Trumbull, *Studies in Oriental Social Life,* 237-254.

V. 10. The land of Goshen was presumably that portion of Egypt just adjacent to the Isthmus of Suez, a district hardly capable of agriculture, but suitable for sheep-herding, the evident occupation of Joseph's brothers. This district has always been a favorite resort of Semitic nomads from the Arabian Desert, who sought refuge in Egypt. We can readily understand that, if the Israelites thus dwelt upon the eastern border of Egypt, their eventual exodus was greatly facilitated.

XXIV

JOSEPH AND JACOB

(Genesis XLVI-XLVII, 12)

The days of the years of my sojourning are a hundred and thirty years; few and evil have been the days of the years of my life, and they have not attained unto the days of the years of the life of my fathers in the days of their sojournings. (Genesis XLVII, 9.)

Not by might, nor by power, but by My spirit, saith the Lord of hosts. (Zechariah IV, 6.)

Read Isaiah LVIII, 6-7.

The story of Joseph is drawing to its close. There is still to tell only how his father and brothers came down to Egypt, and how they were received by him and by his proud Egyptian associates.

From a number of references upon Egyptian monuments, as well as from the specific statement of XLIII, 32, we know that the Egyptians were none too kindly disposed to the Semitic shepherds of western Asia, who from time to time sought shelter and sustenance in Egypt. Sheep and cattle herding was regarded by the Egyptians as a menial occupation, fit only for people of the lowest class. Nevertheless Joseph had never concealed the fact that he was a Hebrew, whose people were shepherds, even though the duties and obligations of his office compelled him to live and dress as an Egyptian, and to conform to all the forms and practices of Egyptian culture. Even amid his Egyptian environment, of which he felt himself an integral part, and the development of the civilization which he sought to promote in every way possible, he knew how to remain loyal to the traditions of his past, and to safeguard and live by the spiritual truths and principles which he had brought with him as a precious heritage from his father's house.

Nor did he hesitate to declare before the assembled Egyptian court, his cultured friends and titled associates, that these Israelite shepherds, plain and unpolished, and possibly even uncouth though they must have seemed to the Egyptian lords and ladies, were his brothers. Nor did he shrink, cultured Egyptian though he was outwardly, from embracing and kissing them, and inquiring lovingly and anxiously after the welfare of his aged father. His sole concern was for their safety and happiness during these seven years of famine. He might easily have provided for them in their old home in Palestine, by sending supplies to them at regular intervals. He might thus have spared himself the constant reminder of his lowly, and from the cultured Egyptian standpoint, even base, shepherd, Israelite origin, which their presence must necessarily furnish. But no such thought entered his mind even for a moment. He was not ashamed of his origin, lowly and mean though it might seem to some, who were animated by false standards of cheap and superficial culture. On the contrary, he gloried in this origin, for he realized full well that to it he owed all the spiritual knowledge, insight and strength which he possessed, which had alone enabled him to endure all trials, and to rise to his exalted and honorable station, and which now prompted him to use all the powers and privileges of his high office, not for his own selfish advantage, but for the benefit and blessing of his fellowmen. In comparison with these spiritual treasures, Egyptian culture and refinement were as nothing, except in so far as they heightened the spiritual value of the former, and lent direction and force to their application.

Nor was he ashamed of his father and his brothers. Instead he proudly presented five of his brothers and also his aged father to the mighty Pharaoh himself. And instead of

regarding them with contempt, as some might have expected, Pharaoh accepted them as they were, appraised them
at their true worth, and appointed them overseers of his own
flocks and herds.

Loyalty has always been regarded by Judaism as a prime
virtue, loyalty to kindred, to home, to the past, loyalty to
religion, to country, to God. The prophet declared that
among the things more pleasing to God than even sacrifice,
fasting, and ritual worship, were,

> To deal thy bread to the hungry,
> And that thou bring the poor that are cast out to thy house;
> When thou seest the naked, that thou cover him,
> And that thou hide not thyself from thine own flesh.

There is a powerful temptation when success, prosperity,
and social advancement come, to leave poor or unprogressive
relatives and friends behind, to feel that we have outgrown
them, and that circumstances compel new associations. We
find it the easiest and most natural thing in the world to
excuse, or even to justify, such a course. But to everything
that expediency and selfish inclination may suggest, the word
of the prophet answers inexorably,

> Hide not thyself from thine own flesh.

Loyalty declares that we may not rise at the expense or to
the neglect of others. Love and friendship which have been
tried and tested, may not be cheaply cast aside. If we rise,
we must carry our loved ones with us, to whatever station
we may attain. It is told of both President Garfield and
President McKinley, two of our martyred presidents, that
when they were inaugurated into the highest office of the
land, each insisted that his aged mother come from her distant home, to be at his side on that great occasion. During
the entire ceremony, while her son was delivering his in-
augural speech, and outlining his policies of administration,

there sat each mother in her simple, black dress, amid all the magnificence and pomp of high officialdom. And the first act of each noble son, after he had taken the solemn oath of office, and the ceremony of inauguration was completed, was to turn to his aged mother, with the smile of love and loyalty on his lips, and to kiss her reverently and tenderly before all the assembled multitude. Thereby he proclaimed to the world that more than to anyone else he owed what he was, and what he might still become, to his mother. Neither president was permitted to complete his term of service. Garfield died a victim of the assassin's bullet after only a few months' of office, and McKinley suffered the same fate almost immediately after his second term had begun. But each has left an example of exalted manhood, nobility, and loyalty, which may well inspire the American people for generations to come. And the story of Joseph furnishes a like example and inspiration unto all the descendants of Jacob.

And when the old man, Jacob, stood before the mighty king, a singular thing happened. It was not the powerful king upon his throne, who proved superior, but the old man, in his simple shepherd garb, with long, flowing beard, with all the marks, not only of age, but also of dignity, of vast experience, and of actual striving and communing with God. To Pharaoh's question, "How many are the days of the years of thy life?" the old man answered simply, "The days of the years of my sojourning are a hundred and thirty years; few and evil have been the days of the years of my life, and they have not attained unto the days of the years of the life of my fathers in the days of their sojournings". In this answer there is an intimation of deep wisdom, of sad, yet invaluable experience, purchased at a great price, of inexpressible yearning to solve the riddle of all the true goodness of life, which divine wisdom keeps enshrouded in eternal mystery, and discloses only bit by bit to those chosen mortals who seek earnestly to know God's way. And then Jacob blessed Pharaoh; the simple, old shepherd blessed the mighty king; and the latter bowed his head upon his throne, beneath the old man's outstretched hands.

This little incident beautifully illustrates the old Jewish virtue of reverence for old age. The Bible has commanded, "Thou shalt rise up before the hoary head, and honor the face of the old man" (Leviticus XIX, 32). It has also said,

> The hoary head is a crown of glory,
> It is found in the way of righteousness. (Proverbs XVI, 31.)

and again,

> The glory of young men is their strength,
> And the beauty of old men is the hoary head. (Proverbs XX, 29.)

This virtue Israel has always cherished, and its young men and women have always accorded to their elders and superiors in wisdom, the respect and reverence to which their age, experience, and knowledge entitled them. In ancient Israel the elders, as they were officially called, were the leaders and counsellors of the people, to whom all hearkened readily and willingly. It is told of Abimi, the pious son of Abahu, a great and wise teacher of old, that once he brought his aged father a drink of water for which the old man had asked. But finding that his father had fallen asleep in the meantime, as very old men are liable to do, he waited patiently and reverently and without moving, in order not to disturb his father, until the latter awoke, so that he might quench his father's thirst at the earliest possible moment. Thus he literally fulfilled the Biblical command, "Thou shalt rise up before the hoary head, and honor the face of the old man".

But even more, this incident symbolizes again the triumph of the spiritual over the temporal and the material, of eternal truth over evanescent might and power. Before the dignity of old age, knowledge and experience, and the wisdom which comes from God alone, even the king upon his throne must bow. The prophets of Israel have exemplified this truth time and again. Here, more than ever, Jacob is typical of Israel, the exponent of spiritual truth and power, even as Pharaoh upon his throne is typical of all that is material. In Jacob's words, and in his acknowledged superiority and authority over Pharaoh, we feel the full truth of the prophet's inspired words,

"Not by might, nor by power, but by My spirit, saith the Lord of hosts."

The purpose of existence will be attained at last, and all life will become pure and holy and beautiful, not by might nor by power, but only by the spirit of the Lord of hosts. Jacob blessed Pharaoh; and so Israel, God's messenger, filled with His spirit, has blessed all the nations of the earth. And throughout the ages it has safeguarded and lived true to its God-given birthright, to be a blessing unto all the families of the earth.

For all Jews today, and particularly for us Jews in America, this story has a particularly pertinent message. We occupy a position strikingly similar to that of Joseph. We dwell in an environment and culture quite different from those in which our fathers dwelt. We, too, with comparatively few exceptions, occupy in this country positions of honor and esteem, and even of power and influence for good. We are loyal citizens of our nation, and gladly assume all the responsibilities and obligations of citizenship. We share in its culture; we dress like our fellow-citizens, and consort freely with them; and we speak the language of the country, of which we are an integral and recognized part. Yet this does not necessitate, nor even imply, that we become unmindful of the traditions of our past, or fail to cherish the precious heritage of the spirit, which has descended to us from our fathers, or that we need become ashamed of our

Israelite origin. Rather the example of Joseph should teach and inspire us to realize that only by living as Jews, in the midst of whatever environment we may come to live, by safeguarding our ancient virtues, and applying the knowledge of God and of the meaning and purpose of life which Judaism upholds, to the needs and problems of our nation and our fellowmen, can we realize our own destiny and mission, and bring blessing and life unto them in the midst of spiritual famine. It is our eternal obligation to hold fast to the knowledge of God which has been revealed to us, and to proclaim this knowledge and God's law of life unto all the world, that men may live thereby, and learn to walk in God's way, and realize the great truth which Israel has ever proclaimed, "Not by might, nor by power, but by My spirit, saith the Lord of hosts". Thus, and thus alone, can we bless the peoples among whom we come to dwell, even as Jacob blessed Pharaoh.

So Joseph's father and his brothers came down to him in Egypt, the land of his triumph and glory, and he provided lovingly and abundantly for their needs. So, under God's protection, they dwelt happily for many years, and the Egyptians were blessed by their presence in the land.

NOTES

V. 4. It was the pious duty of the favorite son to close the eyes of his father after death.

Vv. 8-27 were inserted into the main narrative by some late writer. Obviously they disturb the continuity of the story.

V. 21 makes Benjamin a grown man at this time, with ten children. It shows how little this inserted passage accords with the remainder of the story.

V. 28 is the direct continuation of v. 5 of the original narrative.

XLVII, 11. "The land of Rameses", i. e. the district bordering upon the Isthmus of Suez, in which the city of Rameses, built according to Biblical tradition by the Israelite slaves (Exodus III, 11), was situated.

XXV

JACOB'S BLESSING

(Genesis XLVI-L)

Ye meant evil against me; but God meant it for good, to bring to pass, as it is this day, to save much people alive. (Genesis L, 20.)

The law of the Lord is perfect, restoring the soul. (Psalm XIX, 8.)

Read Psalm XIX.

The wonderful romance of Joseph is finished. It remains merely to bring the story to a proper close by picturing the happiness of the father and brothers in Egypt, and to suitably reenforce the central theme. For, as we see now, all these narratives are merely successive chapters of this one, great Joseph story, and this is most effectively, dramatically and artistically told, and is therefore one of the very greatest, as it is one of the oldest, classics of the world's literature. Through it all there runs one central theme, which the story was intended by its author or authors to concretely illustrate. It is the thought of God's absolute providence, which guides the destinies of men and nations with fixed and wise purpose, and even out of all the evil which men do, somehow, in a way passing human understanding, brings greater good and blessing for all men. "Ye meant evil against me, but God meant it for good, to bring to pass, as it is this day, to save much people alive", Joseph answers his brothers, when, after his father's death, they fear that Joseph might now avenge himself upon them. "It was not you that sent me hither, but God", in order to fulfil His wondrous purpose of good, for Israel and all mankind. We can not fathom all God's purposes, nor measure all His wisdom and love. We can only say with the Psalmist:

> How weighty also are Thy thoughts unto me, O God!
> How great is the sum of them! (Psalm CXXXIX, 17.)

And with the great prophet of old, we must say again, as we have already said more than once:

> For My thoughts are not your thoughts,
> Neither are your ways My ways, saith the Lord.
> For as the heavens are higher than the earth,
> So are My ways higher than your ways,
> And My thoughts than your thoughts. (Isaiah LV, 8-9.)

We can not measure God's wisdom and goodness and love by our little, human standards. We can only trust in Him with perfect faith that, whatever happens to us and to all people, it will somehow surely be for the best in the end, that nothing in life merely happens, and above all, nothing happens for evil alone; but God's hand is in everything, and His love watches over all His children and protects them and leads them on, for He is our shepherd. And so, when grief and pain and trial come to us, as they must at some time come to all men, we need not despair nor complain, but remember that everything cometh from God for some deep purpose of goodness and love, even though we may not understand.

One story of the rabbis well illustrates this thought. There was once a slave upon whom his master had bestowed many gifts, and whom he had always treated with uniform kindness. And the slave loved his master in return and did his every bidding loyally and gladly. But one day the friends of the master said to him, "Thy slave loves thee only because of thy good gifts. Withhold these, or do evil unto him, and thou wilt see his love vanish". Thereupon the master summoned the slave, and silently gave to him some fruit which was exceedingly bitter. The slave took the fruit as he had taken all the master's gifts, and ate it without a word or a moment's hesitation. Nor did he offer the slightest objection or question, nor make the least sign that the fruit had a bitter and unpleasant taste. When he had finished, one of the master's friends asked, "How couldst thou eat so bitter a fruit without complaining or making some sign?" But the faithful slave answered, "My master has always treated me with utmost kindness and love. He has showered untold blessings upon me. And everything he has done, I have seen repeatedly, has behind it some wise purpose of goodness and love. Now that for the first time in all my life he gives me something bitter of which to taste, should I doubt, or complain, or refuse to do his bidding? Should I rather not take the occasional bitter which he gives to me, together with the abundant sweet, and trust that this, too, is for good, even though I do not understand?"

This is the true faith in God which Judaism has always taught, and in which its followers have always found strength and courage to bear the many hard and cruel blows which have befallen them. Israel's history has been bitter indeed, and full to overflowing with trial and suffering and sacrifice. But Israel's men and women have always trusted in God, the God of their fathers, of Abraham, Isaac, and Jacob, and have never hesitated nor doubted nor complained too much. Bravely and nobly they have made their sacrifices for God, and calmly they have repeated in absolute faith and trust the inspiring words of the great sufferer of old,

Though He slay me, yet will I trust in Him.   (Job XIII, 15.)

Though the way oft seemed too long and hard, and the goal was hidden in darkness, yet they knew with perfect faith that God was still leading them on in His pillar of cloud and fire unto His promised land of peace and happiness and love. And though men meant evil against them, still in His own wise way God meant it for good, that Israel might the better fulfil its mission of being a blessing unto mankind.

We can not help thinking of that other beautiful story from our Bible, of Moses asking that he might behold God's face, and of the answer which came to him, "Thou canst not see My face, for man shall not see Me and live" (Exodus XXXIII, 20). So it has ever been with man. Ever he has sought to see God's face, and to know all His ways and all His wise and loving purposes. But ever the answer has come back, "Thou canst not see My face, for man shall not see Me and live". To mortal man it is not given to see God face to face, nor to read aright all the wondrous mystery of His ways and His purposes. We can only, at the most, through God's favor, catch some fleeting glimpse of His back, and hear His true name whispered, as He passes before us in all His majesty and glory. Yet from all this we may form some dim, vague picture of His true greatness and goodness and love. In all the world round about us, in all the events of life and history, of Israel's history, and of our nation's history, and of the world's history, we see countless evidences of God's being and power, and of His wisdom and goodness and love, and of His divine, all-protecting providence. God is everywhere and His hand is in all things, for good and blessing and love. And so we declare with the Psalmist:

> O Lord, our Lord,
> How glorious is Thy name in all the earth!
> Whose majesty is rehearsed above the heavens.
> When I behold Thy heavens, the work of Thy fingers,
> The moon and the stars which Thou hast established;
> What is man that Thou art mindful of him?
> And the son of man, that Thou thinkest of him?
> Yet Thou hast made him but little lower than the angels,
> And hast crowned him with glory and honor.
> Thou hast made him to have dominion over the works of Thy
> 　　hands;
> Thou hast put all things under his feet. (Psalm VIII, 2-7.)

And we think of the words of that other inspiring Psalm:

> The heavens declare the glory of God,
> And the firmament showeth His Handiwork;
> Day unto day uttereth speech,
> And night unto night revealeth knowledge.

Yet, despite His grandeur and His power, He is mindful of His children, and in love has given them His law to guide them. And so the Psalm continues:

> The law of the Lord is perfect, restoring the soul;
> The testimony of the Lord is sure, making wise the simple.
> The precepts of the Lord are right, rejoicing the heart;
> The commandment of the Lord is pure, enlightening the eyes.
> The fear of the Lord is clean, enduring forever·
> The ordinances of the Lord are true, they are righteous altogether.

This is the real faith in the God of our fathers, which every true Jew must feel and understand and accept, that it become the guide and blessing of his entire life. This is the lesson taught impressively and convincingly by the story of Joseph. And if we but learn the lesson, and live in accord with it all our lives, then we shall be true Jews, worthy of the birthright of our fathers, which has, through God's providence, come down to us through all these generations. The dying Jacob blessed his two little grandchildren by declaring that in later years all Israel would bless its children in their names with the beautiful words, "God make thee as Ephraim and as Manasseh". Through all the centuries since then, when the Jewish father came home from the synagogue on Friday eve, he first kissed his beloved wife and blessed her; then he laid his hands upon the heads of his little children, with the words of father Jacob, "God make thee as Ephraim and as Manasseh". If we but live true to our sacred heritage, and strive to realize the purpose of our lives, and to become as God has commanded us through Abraham, a blessing unto all the families of the earth, then shall we, too, merit the beautiful and comforting blessing of our fathers of old, "God make thee as Ephraim and as Manasseh".

The rabbis also told that our father Jacob did not really die, that God merely kissed him, and thus released his soul from his body. His body was laid to rest in the sepulchre of his fathers. But his spirit hovers over and about us, his children, blessing us by his presence, and smiling the smile of love and happiness, when any of his descendants performs one single act which brings blessing unto others, and so helps to fulfil the birthright of Abraham and Israel.

One other thought, the rabbis remind us, these closing chapters of Genesis suggest. Abraham and Isaac had sought to bless but one son each, and thereby they caused enmity and strife between their children. But on his deathbed Jacob summoned his sons and blessed them all equally, and bade them stand together and become strong in each other's love and help. They had realized the evil of family strife and discord, and they had repented of their crime against their brother. Thereafter they remained united as their father had bidden them, and not they alone, but their descendants as well. Thus in time, the people of Israel came into existence, and we are here today. It is the best proof of the great truth, so well exemplified in the history of our own beloved American nation, that in union there is strength.

It reminds us of one other of the many beautiful stories which the rabbis used to tell. In the beginning, when the world lay newly created by the word of God, the waters rolled in great billows, and beat against the very throne of the Creator. Then God spoke His word, and the waves were gathered together into one great mass, the sea, and the earth rose trembling from amidst the waters. But the sea still poured its waves mercilessly into all the deep valleys, between the high mountains; and one wave called to another, "Come and let us batter down these lofty peaks.

We are the strongest force which God has created, and we will work our will". But God sternly rebuked them, "Why boast ye of your strength? I shall send the sand to bar your way". But the waves laughed and mocked when they saw the tiny grains of sand, and said, "What foes are you? One of us can destroy you all". But into the grains of sand God had put a bit of His divine wisdom. "Hearken to the boast of our enemies, the waves, they said. It is true that should one of us be separated from the rest, he could accomplish nothing, but must be blown away by the wind. Let us therefore hold close together and strengthen each other. Thereby shall we do the will of our Maker, and overcome our enemy". Ever since the tiny grains on the seashore have held together in close embrace. And though the waves beat upon them, all their beating merely binds the grains of sand closer together. Ever they bar the way of their enemy, the waves, as these roll in upon the land. And here and there the sand has even forced the proud waves back into narrower confines.

In peace and unity and brotherly love and cooperation lies true strength to do the will of God. So Jacob commanded his sons, and ever since all Israel has lived, with but occasional forgettings now and then, yet forgettings which have always brought misfortune and misery, as brothers, strengthening each other and helping each other. Still today our brothers call unto us for help and support. And never dare we forget the words which Joseph's brothers spoke to him, as true today as then, "We are twelve brethren, the sons of one man in the land of Canaan". All Israel are brothers, united by descent from father Jacob, and by common faith in the God of our fathers, the God of all mankind; and all Israel share in the glorious birthright of Abraham. In union and peace and love lies our strength. Laboring in this spirit of brotherhood, and with complete faith in God, we shall be strong to do His will and to fulfil the purpose for which He has created us, and has protected us through the centuries, to be a blessing unto all the families of the earth. And at last, through our faith and our labors and our sacrifices, our mission will be fulfilled; then the hope of the ages will be realized, the goal of existence will be attained. Then, not Israel alone, but all mankind will be united in eternal brotherhood and love; then hatred and strife will no more be known in all the earth, but all men will unite as brothers to do the will of God, the Father of all.

The Bible tells that when the dying Jacob gathered his sons about his bed for blessing, he addressed them with these words, "Hearken unto Israel, your father". It was a solemn word of admonition, spoken at a solemn moment. But by a slight change in the vocalization of one little word of two letters, the rabbis gave to it even deeper and richer meaning. By the omission of one little dot under a letter, the word which means "unto" came to mean "God". And so they interpreted the opening words of Jacob's blessing of his sons, "Hearken; the God of Israel is your Father". It was a declaration unto his sons and unto all Israel of the unity and the fatherhood of God, which Israel has ever proclaimed. And the rabbis told that Jacob continued to address his sons, "Perhaps there is doubt in your hearts about God". But as one man they answered him with the ringing words, *Sh'ma Yisrael, Adonai Elohenu, Adonai Eḥad,* "Hear, O Israel. the Lord our God, the Lord is One" (Deuteronomy VI, 4). Their words had a double meaning; for under the name Israel they were addressing both Israel their father, and Israel, their descendants to come. And when Jacob heard their declaration of faith and of self-consecration to the cause of the God whose unity they had proclaimed, he murmured the response, *Baruch shem k'vod malchutho l'olam va'ed,* "Praised be the name of his glorious kingdom forever and ever".

Since that time the children of Israel have repeated these

words every morning and every evening, "Hear, O Israel, the Lord our God, the Lord is One. Praised be the name of His glorious kingdom forever and ever". Even as spoken by the sons of Jacob, so also with us today they have a two-fold meaning. They are addressed to the fathers and the generations of the past, and still declare our faith, that their God, the God of Israel, is our Father today, even as He was of old, and that to His cause and His service we consecrate ourselves, even as did the patriarchs, Abraham, Isaac, and Jacob. They are addressed also to the future generations of Israel, our children who will come after us, bidding them realize that the God of Israel is one and eternal, and that He will be their Father, too, and they will be His children and His servants and witnesses, even as were their fathers. Still today the blessing of Jacob rests upon us, his children, and his words ring in our ears, "Hearken; the God of Israel is your Father". And there is no doubt in our hearts as we answer day by day with the declaration of Israel's faith and Israel's eternal consecration to its sacred mission, the precious birthright of service and blessing, "Hear, O Israel, the Lord our God, the Lord is One".

The Book of Genesis has told us of God's creation of the universe and of all mankind as His children, and of His selection of Israel to be His servant and the messenger of His law of life unto men; it has told of God's trial and purification and preparation of Israel for this mission of service and blessing, which has descended to it as a precious birthright; it has shown also that on this mission Israel walks not alone, that God is ever with it, and with all men, guiding and leading on, changing the evil which men do to good, and controlling the destinies of men and nations so that mankind must steadily draw nearer to Him and to the true knowledge of Him. And Israel goes upon its mission strong in its faith in God, upheld by His protection and His help, rejoicing in the glorious privilege which He has given unto it as His chosen people. And day by day we repeat the sacred words, and thereby reconsecrate ourselves ever anew to God's service, *Sh'ma Yisrael, Adonai Elohenu, Adonai Ehod,* "Hear, O Israel, the Lord our God, the Lord is One", *Baruch shem k'vod malchutho l'olam va'ed,* "Praised be the name of His glorious kingdom forever and ever".

NOTES

Vv. 13-27. These verses are hardly a part of the original narrative. They were introduced apparently to heighten the glory of Joseph by representing that the system of taxation and of royal possession, obtaining in ancient Egypt, was instituted by Joseph.

V. 22. The priests of Egypt enjoyed unusual powers and privileges.

XLVIII, 3-7. These verses too have been inserted into the original narrative, and disturb the continuity of the story. V. 8 is the direct continuation of v. 2. This episode of the adoption of Joseph's two sons by Jacob is somewhat obscure. Apparently it represents an attempt to account for the historical fact that two tribes by the names of Ephraim and Manasseh were included among the tribes of Israel, while there was no tribe of Joseph. Since all the other tribes were called by the names of the sons of Jacob, this tradition tells 'that Ephraim and Manasseh were adopted by Jacob as his sons, and thus also became qualified to have tribes named after them, and that they took the place of Joseph.

V. 19. After the settlement of the tribes of Israel in Palestine Ephraim became the most powerful and leading member of the northern group of tribes, to which Manasseh also belonged. This is the historical basis of this legend that Jacob blessed Ephraim as the firstborn instead of Manasseh.

V. 22. The Hebrew word for "portion" (literally "shoulder") here is *shechem*. There is a play upon the name of Shechem, the important Canaanite city, which later became the chief city of the tribe of Ephraim and the first capital of the northern kingdom (I Kings XII, 25). According to tradition Joseph was buried there (Joshua XXIV, 32). This verse implies that he was buried there because this place was given to him by Jacob as his individual possession; cf. XXXIII, 18ff. and XXXIV.

XLIX, 2-27. These verses are really an ancient Hebrew poem

which described certain historic or legendary conditions within the tribes of Israel, probably during the period just preceding the reign of David. The names here refer to the tribes rather than to the individual sons of Jacob. This ancient poem was embodied in the original narrative, even though a large portion of it has little of the nature of a blessing. The poem contains numerous references, more or less obscure, to historical conditions which obtained among the separate tribes in the days immediately preceding the establishment of the united kingdom by David. Deuteronomy XXXIII offers an interesting parallel to this passage.

L, 2f. In ancient Egypt people of the higher classes were usually embalmed. Embalming was a complicated process which required from thirty to seventy days. It was performed by a special class of physicians.

V. 3. The usual period of mourning was seven days. The verse states therefore that the mourning for Jacob was protracted far beyond the customary period.

V. 4. Joseph himself could not come before Pharaoh, since, owing to his mourning he had allowed his hair and beard to grow. To appear before the king unshaved and in the garments of mourning would have violated the fundamental principle of Egyptian court etiquette; cf. XLI, 14.

V. 11. *Abel-mizraim* really means "meadow of Egypt". However the verse confounds *abel* with the similar Hebrew word *ebel*, which means "mourning". This place lay east of the Jordan, and therefore far off the direct line of march from Egypt to Hebron. It is not clear how the funeral cortege could have come to this spot. Probably this tradition, and with it vv. 7-11, was not an integral part of the original narrative, but arose in time to account for this otherwise inexplicable place-name, and then was inserted into this place by some late writer.

V. 23. For the significance of the custom of laying a new-born child upon the knees of a foster-parent cf. the note to XXX, 3.

V. 24. By "brethren" is meant here the descendants of his brothers, the early children of Israel.

V. 26. By coffin a sarcophagus was probably meant. Only tne very greatest were so buried. An interesting rabbinic legend about the coffin of Joseph is recorded in Ginsburg, *Legends of the Jews*, II, 181ff.

SCHOCKEN PAPERBACKS

JEWISH LIFE AND THOUGHT

Cecil Roth History of the Jews   SB9

Widely recognized as the best one-volume history of the Jews
in English. Combining the highest standards of scholarship
with the human touch, it describes the social, religious, and
cultural development of the Jewish people from Biblical times
to the present.   *paper $1.95*
Outline and Discussion Guide available, 35c per copy

Elias Bickerman   SB36
From Ezra to the Last of the Maccabees
GREEK FOUNDATIONS OF POST-BIBLICAL JUDAISM

In this basic introduction to post-Biblical Jewish history, a
great scholar examines, in the light of the contacts between
Greek and Jewish culture, the elements that shaped the Jewish
people after their return from the Babylonian Exile.
     cloth $3.50   paper $1.65

Emil Schürer   SB8
A History of the Jewish People in the Time of Jesus
Edited by Nahum N. Glatzer

This new, abridged edition of the First Division of Schürer's
monumental work presents the political history of Palestine
from the Maccabean revolt to the fall of Jerusalem. It gives
a panoramic view of the ancient world against which we can
see the variety of Jewish life, the Dead Sea sects, and early
Christianity. New bibliography.   *cloth $4.50   paper $2.45*

Jacob Katz Exclusiveness and Tolerance   SB40
JEWISH-GENTILE RELATIONS IN MEDIEVAL AND MODERN TIMES

A fresh interpretation of the ideas which influenced Jewish-
Christian relations from medieval times to the 18th century.
Katz shows how the dialogue between Christian and Jew continued unimpaired despite social pressures and religious zeal
on both sides.   *paper $1.75*

S. D. Goitein Jews and Arabs   SB83

Explores fully the cultural, social, and intellectual relations between Jews and Arabs during three thousand years of contact. "This historical survey merits the attention of anyone seeking deeper insight into the long and colorful history of Arab-Jewish relations. . . ."—*The Christian Century*

cloth $5.00   paper $1.95

Solomon Schechter   SB15
Aspects of Rabbinic Theology
MAJOR CONCEPTS OF THE TALMUD
Introduction by Louis Finkelstein

The classic statement of those ideas which form the religious consciousness of the Jewish people regardless of sect or denomination. Schechter's scholarship, compelling style, and warmth have exercised a lasting influence on Jew and Gentile alike.

paper $1.95

Gershom G. Scholem   SB5
Major Trends in Jewish Mysticism

This is the established work on the history of Jewish mysticism from its beginnings in antiquity to its latest phase in Hasidism. Bold, profound ideas and symbols are analyzed and evaluated, revolutionizing our entire outlook on Judaism and the role of mysticism in Western thought.   *cloth $6.00   paper $2.25*

Samuel Hugo Bergman Faith and Reason   SB56
AN INTRODUCTION TO MODERN JEWISH THOUGHT

Here are the intellectual biographies of six major representatives of diverse strands of modern Jewish thought: Hermann Cohen, Franz Rosenzweig, Martin Buber, A. D. Gordon, Rav Kook, and Judah Magnes. Dissimilar thinkers, they converge in their concern with the issue of reason and faith.

paper $1.45

Nahum N. Glatzer   SB21
Franz Rosenzweig—His Life and Thought

Rosenzweig's unwavering Judaism was free of apologetics, provincialism, dogma. This selection from his diaries, letters, pamphlets, and books presents a personal biography and a masterly view of his intellectual and religious journey.

cloth $6.00   paper $2.25

Martin Buber Israel and the World   SB66

ESSAYS IN A TIME OF CRISIS

Buber clarifies the relation of Jewish thinking to contemporary movements, and analyzes critically those trends in Jewish life which weaken the teachings of Israel. "One of the most meaningful interpretations of Judaism to appear in modern times."—*Journal of Religion*

cloth $3.75   paper $1.95

Nahum N. Glatzer, *editor* A Jewish Reader SB16

A revised edition of IN TIME AND ETERNITY

Eighteen centuries of Jewish life and thought are reflected in this famous anthology: formal theology and simple faith, philosophy and folklore, practical law and mystical contemplation. Each selection is fully documented.

cloth $3.00   paper $1.75

R. Travers Herford The Ethics of the Talmud SB23

SAYINGS OF THE FATHERS

The most comprehensive guide in English to the essential source book of Rabbinic thought on mastery of the moral life. Travers Herford's introduction and commentary are an authoritative supplement to the text which is printed here in Hebrew and English.   *cloth $3.50   paper $1.75*

Nahum N. Glatzer, *editor*   SB32

Hammer on the Rock

A MIDRASH READER

The wisdom and poetry of the Talmud and Midrash, in a selection of over 200 representative passages — an introduction to the dynamic, yet often misinterpreted world of Talmudic thought. "A masterpiece of editorial discrimination. . ."
—*Jewish Spectator*   *cloth $3.00   paper $.95*

Judah Halevi The Kuzari   SB75

AN ARGUMENT FOR THE FAITH OF ISRAEL

Introduction by Henry Slonimsky

A basic text of Jewish literature. The foremost poet and thinker of the Jewish Middle Ages explores in the easy style of Platonic dialogue, the nature of Israel's religious faculty, revelation, prophecy, the Holy Land, and the special role of the Jewish people.   *paper $1.95*

SCHOCKEN PAPERBACKS

Gershom G. Scholem, *editor* SB45
Zohar—The Book of Splendor

The Zohar is the basic work of Jewish mysticism, the pro-
foundest achievement of the Kabbalah. In introducing his
selection, the greatest living authority on Jewish mysticism
examines the Zohar's origins and literary character.
cloth $3.00 paper $1.25

Leo Schwarz, *editor* Memoirs of My People SB51
JEWISH SELF-PORTRAITS FROM THE 11TH
TO THE 20TH CENTURIES

A lively thousand-year record of the personal experience of
Jewish men and women — mystics, troubadours, false mes-
siahs, and common folk. Each document mirrors the spirit
of an epoch. ". . . a most wonderful collection."—*Saturday
Review.* *paper $1.95*

Martin Buber Tales of the Hasidim SB1/SB2
VOL. I EARLY MASTERS / VOL. II LATER MASTERS

These delightful stories — concise, vigorous, often cryptic —
are tales of the Zaddikim, the masters or leaders of the impas-
sioned religious movement which swept Eastern European
Jewry in the 18th century and which still has many followers.
Each tale is a legendary anecdote expressing the moral intens-
ity and holy joy whereby God becomes visible in all things.
cloth, each $4.50 paper, each $1.75

Martin Buber Ten Rungs—Hasidic Sayings SB18

These penetrating, often haunting, tales and aphorisms are
unified by a recurrent image: life as a spiritual ladder on each
rung of which man "finds the holiness of God everywhere
and at all times." Buber, whose philosophy owes much to
Hasidism, is the ideal editor of these Hasidic sayings.
paper $.95

Louis I. Newman The Hasidic Anthology SB46
TALES AND TEACHINGS OF THE HASIDIM

A lexicon of Hasidic teachings on every conceivable topic. It
contains the tales, proverbs and paradoxes — by turn wry and
gentle, pungent and profound — through which the Hasidic
Masters conveyed their wisdom to their disciples.
paper $2.45

SCHOCKEN PAPERBACKS

Bella and Marc Chagall Burning Lights   SB35
36 drawings
A charming double portrait of childhood in the Russian mar-
ket-town in which Marc and Bella grew up. Bella Chagall's
warm, humorous stories of her pious Jewish family are illustrated by 36 of her husband's incomparable drawings. "Pure
pleasure to read, evocative, wistful . . ."—*N.Y. Herald Tribune*
cloth $4.50   paper $1.95

Hanan J. Ayalti, *editor*   Yiddish Proverbs   SB50
"Truth never dies — but leads a wretched life." The short say-
ings in this book offer the essence of Jewish wit and wisdom.
They have the power of the proverb, but the wry quality of
Jewish humor. The English is printed side by side with a
Yiddish transliteration. Woodcuts by Bernard Reder.
cloth $3.00   paper $1.25

Zborowski and Herzog Life Is With People SB20
THE CULTURE OF THE SHTETL
Introduction by Margaret Mead
Through hundreds of years the *Shtetl*, the small-town Jewish
community of Eastern Europe, developed a way of life
uniquely its own. This is a definitive study, by a team of Col-
umbia sociologists and anthropologists, of a great culture.
It is a moving and universal human document.   *paper $2.45*

Melford E. Spiro Kibbutz—Venture in Utopia SB63
The established and standard work on the collective settlement in Israel. Spiro shows us the daily life, attitudes, and
problems of a fellowship of people wholly committed to the
practice of socialist and Zionist ideals. His new preface surveys recent developments.   *cloth $5.00   paper $1.95*

Bernard J. Bamberger The Story of Judaism SB77
A comprehensive, readable history of Judaism — the inner
content of Jewish life, religious ideas, observances, and institutions. "Over 3000 years of Jewish existence have been dis-
tilled into a single volume . . . a formidable task for any
scholar . . . admirably accomplished by Dr. Bamberger."
—*Library Journal*   *paper $2.45*

Hayyim Schauss Guide to Jewish Holy Days SB26
HISTORY AND OBSERVANCE
The rich symbolism, ritual practices and prayers, special foods, customs and folkways are all traced to their historical roots. "Presents a panoramic view . . . Highly recommended as a text for class study and home reading."—Azriel Eisenberg, Director, Jewish Education Committee *paper $1.75*

Levi and Kaplan SB87
Guide for the Jewish Homemaker
Contemporary, creative homemaking as it derives from the Jewish tradition. Detailed practical counsel in such matters as developing menus, planning a wedding, finding books and records for cultural enrichment. "Fascinating to Christians as well as Jews . . . not only for its housewifely advice but for its explanation of traditions."—*N.Y. Times* *paper $1.95*

Bernard J. Bamberger SB62
The Bible—A Modern Jewish Approach
A concise introduction to the Hebrew Scriptures, their literary structure, and chief concepts of God, man, and society. Analyzes the role of prophecy, the idea of the Chosen People, and other key aspects, providing both factual information and a basis for intelligent discussion. *paper $1.25*

Morris Adler The World of the Talmud SB58
A guide to the Talmud and its historic background, and an introduction to the life and thought of the Talmudic sages. By his perceptive choice of examples, Morris Adler conveys to the uninitiated reader the flavor of the Talmud and much of its substance. *paper $1.45*

Ludwig Lewisohn SB71
What is This Jewish Heritage?
Introduction by Milton Hindus
A clear and persuasive answer to the questions troubling American Jews who find themselves in the middle region between orthodoxy and assimilation. Lewisohn writes eloquently of the ties of society, of the classic religious heritage of Israel, its literature, and its way of life. *paper $1.25*

Leo Baeck The Essence of Judaism   SB6

This classic of Jewish religious thought, first published in 1922 and now completely revised in this new edition, is both a comprehensive examination of Judaism and an invaluable key to understanding the background of Christianity and Islam.   *cloth $4.00   paper $1.65*

Samuel S. Cohon Judaism—A Way of Life SB38

INTRODUCTION TO THE BASIC IDEAS OF JUDAISM

An informative guide both for Jews and non-Jews. The author, a liberal Jewish theologian, traces Jewish ideas and practices back to their sources in the past. He appraises them in the light of contemporary experience, and suggests their relevance to the modern world.   *paper $1.95*

Ruth Rubin A Treasury of Jewish Folksong   SF1

A Treasury of Jewish Folksong invites one to sing the music of the Jewish people at home. It is a rich store of Yiddish and Hebrew songs which express the lives of every age and sort of Jew, from the solicitous East European mother to the modern Israeli pioneer. It includes lullabies, children's songs, love songs, holiday songs, songs of life and work, and much else. The lyrics are given in English transliterations of the original, so that if Yiddish and Hebrew are unfamiliar to the singer, he can still truly enjoy the original atmosphere of these songs. Singable English versions are also provided. Simple, authentic piano settings bring this book right to the piano, where it belongs. With drawings by T. Herzl Rome.
                    cloth $6.00   paper $2.95

Daniel M. Friedenberg, *editor*   SF2
Great Jewish Portraits in Metal
Introduction by Cecil Roth

This is a superbly produced, large-format, encyclopedia of nearly two hundred outstanding personalities depicted on medals and plaques in the Friedenberg Collection of the Jewish Museum. Each is accompanied by a concise biography. The Introduction by Cecil Roth surveys the history of Jewish coins and medals; a special section of the book is devoted to examples of historical and commemorative medals. This handsome volume is both a survey of the art of the medal from antiquity to our time, and a graphic view of Jewish history. In his Introduction, Cecil Roth calls it "a monument to Jewish genius."
                    cloth $6.50   paper $2.25